Following the Paths

A Companion to
Paths to Understanding

General Editor Warren Laxton
County Adviser David Naylor

MACMILLAN
EDUCATION

Hampshire Education Authority

First published 1986
Reprinted 1987

Published by
MACMILLAN EDUCATION LTD
Houndmills, Basingstoke, Hampshire RG21 2XS
and London
Companies and representatives
throughout the world

Printed in Great Britain by
Vine & Gorfin Ltd
Exmouth

Printed in Hong Kong

British Library Cataloguing in Publication Data
Following the paths: a companion to Paths
to understanding.
1. Religious education—England—
Hampshire
I. Laxton, Warren
200′7′104227   LC410.G7
ISBN 0-333-42884-6

Contents

Acknowledgements

The author and publishers wish to thank the following who have kindly given permission for the use of copyright material:

Collins Publishers for extract from *Miracle on the River Kwai* by E. Gordon, Fontana (1963)

Durham Music Ltd for the song *Black and White* by David Arkin, music by Earl Robinson © 1956, 1970 and 1971

David Higham Associates Ltd on behalf of the estate of Dylan Thomas for 'The Hunchback in the Park' from *Collected Poems*, J. M. Dent & Sons Ltd

International Commission on English in the Liturgy, Inc for excerpts from the English translation of *The Roman Missal* © 1973

John Murray Ltd for extract from *Get Ready for Battle* by Ruth Prawer Jhabvala (1978)

Every effort has been made to trace all the copyright holders but if any have been inadvertently overlooked the publishers will be pleased to make the necessary arrangements at the first opportunity.

Cover photographs have been kindly provided by Judy Harrison and Nora Horrigan

General Editor

Warren Laxton

Contributors

Elaine Bellchambers
Alan Brine
Beti Fleming
Warwick Griffin
Nora Horrigan
David Naylor
Pru Phipps
Basil Savage
Sue Sayers
Janet Trotter

Editorial Panel

Alan Brine
Warwick Griffin
David Naylor
Patrick Souper
Janet Trotter

Resource Research

Dawn Thompson

Foreword

This volume represents another important phase in the Authority's development of Religious Education within its schools. The attractiveness of its format and the stimulating nature of its content are fitting ways of expressing the importance that the Education Committee places on this vital area of the curriculum.

The various contributions, edited with great care and skill by Warren Laxton, are the work of a group of dedicated Hampshire teachers. Our thanks are due to them for the response they have made to the initiatives of the County Adviser for Religious Education, David Naylor.

I am sure the book will be a help and inspiration to teachers in Hampshire and throughout the country.

P. D. MERRIDALE
Chairman
Hampshire Education Committee

Preface

In approaching Religious Education the teacher has to answer three main questions:

Why teach this subject at all, and this aspect of it in particular?

What content is both relevant to the subject and appropriate to the pupils?

How is an understanding of religion to be made accessible to these particular pupils?

Religious Education in Hampshire Schools (1978), Hampshire L.E.A.'s Agreed Syllabus, and *Paths to Understanding* (1980) effectively respond to the first two questions. The former provides a framework of objectives for the subject, whilst the latter, with its various schemes of work, both indicates the wide range of content offered by the subject and shows how a balanced programme of R.E. could be planned on the basis of the principles embodied in the Agreed Syllabus.

The chief purpose of the collection of material in this book is to share ideas on the third question. Its central concern is not so much with the *programme* of Religious Education as with the variety of teaching and learning *processes* involved. The schemes of work are not intended as blueprints. They present imaginative ways in which teachers have conducted work in their classrooms; some are amplified by additional observations, proposals or possibilities. The hope is that after reflecting on the ideas set out in this book teachers will be encouraged and assisted in their own efforts, and that they will continue to explore ways of making Religious Education an interesting, significant and valued part of school experience.

DAVID NAYLOR
County Adviser for Religious Education

General Introduction

This book is a companion, not a successor, to *Paths to Understanding*. In no matter of substance does it supersede its precursor. Both books hold that the proper aim of Religious Education is *understanding*, an appreciative understanding of religion as a significant factor in human life, culture and history; and both illustrate the conviction that the proper approach to the subject is one of unprejudiced, but not uncritical, openness. The specific objectives are those set out in *Religious Education in Hampshire Schools* (Hampshire Education Authority 1978) and reproduced, for the three age-ranges 4–8, 8–12 and 12–16, in *Paths to Understanding*. These objectives are not reproduced again here: the material is classified less precisely, as suitable for the age-range 5–13 (Primary) or 11–16 (Secondary). A set of objectives for R.E. with students aged 16–19 (not catered for in the 1978 document) is added.

Where this book differs from *Paths to Understanding* is in its more intense focus on what happens in the classroom. It offers many examples of the kind of detailed development which all teachers have to plan, whatever the topic under investigation, if they are to succeed in taking their pupils towards the defined objectives. Often these examples include statements of principles which inform the work. There are also, however, several articles devoted to the underlying principles and to general considerations of practice, viz.: "Planning Integrated Topic Work" (Primary); "Introduction" and "Classroom Practice in R.E." (Secondary); "Moral, Social and Religious Education with Older Pupils" (Secondary); and "Visitors as Contributors to R.E. and Assembly", which is relevant to all age-groups. The Secondary-level examples deal with religion quite explicitly; the Primary-level schemes incorporate much explicitly religious material in a wider context, in which it is a natural element, while the context itself provides other material and skills relevant to growth in religious understanding. At many points suggestions are made about relating classroom work to the school Assembly.

As with *Paths to Understanding*, most of the material has been contributed by serving teachers. A small Editorial Panel has worked on the drafts submitted, and is responsible for their final form—abbreviated, amended or expanded, and rewritten perhaps several times. The Panel has not, however, seen fit to render every contribution into an identical style or lay-out: although the various items remain anonymous, personal characteristics of their authors are still evident, and help to breathe life into the written text. Examples of pupils' work are a refreshing, and encouraging, feature. At several points (indicated by superscript numbers) some qualification, comment, cross-reference or further suggestion has seemed desirable, and a footnote appears.

The organisation of the book into Primary and Secondary sections, and the specifying of age-ranges alongside each scheme, is convenient and necessary, but should not limit teachers' reading and vision. A teacher may well feel that content (and perhaps methods) employed in a particular scheme would be suitable for the different age-range which is his/her concern. For this reason "all teachers are strongly recommended to read the entire contents, adapting for their own use material which may appear in [either] section". Not only is a "careful reading" required of the teacher, but a "sympathetic, imaginative and constructive response"; for the schemes are not "definitive models laid down by authority", but material for teachers to *use* selectively, having in mind three questions:

(a) "Will any of them, in whole or in part, help me to achieve the objectives?
(b) Which specific content, methods and ideas will be most appropriate (with reference to one particular objective or to several) for my school, class and pupils?
(c) Will it also be appropriate for me, in the sense that it engages my interest, enthusiasm and skills?"

(The quotations are from the General Introduction to *Paths to Understanding*.)

Details of recommended resources and of books etc. mentioned are given with each scheme, either within the text or in a list at the beginning or (more commonly) at the end of the scheme: any books currently out of print may be available from a library or Resource Centre. A number of useful addresses, including Information Centres of various religions, are listed on p. 122–4. A Glossary, giving brief explanations and pronunciations of unfamiliar words (mostly terms with religious connotations), and a selective Index, including both content and classroom procedures, are appended.

PRIMARY AGE-RANGE
Planning Integrated Topic Work

The task of planning a worthwhile curriculum is complex. If the programme is to be coherent, and a serious attempt made to develop both general basic competencies and those more specific to the disciplines contributing to an integrated topic, detailed planning is essential. During planning the following principles and stages should be kept in mind.

1 Establishing the Policy

This task should involve the whole staff. Reference should be made to the appropriate curriculum guidelines and, in the case of Religious Education, to the relevant Agreed Syllabus. It is useful to compile a grid for topic work, in order to avoid repetition of material and to promote pupil progression within the disciplines involved. At this stage, a grid for a Junior school might look like the one shown below.

2 The Choice of Topics

It is advisable to select topics which give wide scope for a variety of learning experiences and for the development of particular competencies. As a general rule the topics chosen need to be "large" concepts or ideas; for example, the topics of "Communication", "Communities", and "Memories and Remembering" all have clear potential for developing linguistic, historical and geographical skills as well as those associated with Religious Education.

3 Exploring the Scope and Potential of the Topic

Once the topic has been chosen it is useful (and creative!) if a group of teachers can freely offer, in a "brainstorming" session, a wide variety of ideas drawn from their experience.

4 Identifying the Contributory Disciplines and Shaping the Topic

Having identified a number of directions in which the topic might be developed, and which areas of experience (social-political, ethical, linguistic, mathematical, physical, aesthetic, religious, scientific) might be incorporated, teachers will be in a position to determine what contributions to the topic could be made by the several disciplines. The topic on "Difference" (see p. 48f.) provides an example of the sort of chart which can usefully be made at this stage. (See overleaf.)

Finally, the topic has to be given a shape and an inner dynamic. A proposed sequence of work should be mapped out, in full awareness that it will almost certainly need some amendment as the work proceeds.

	AUTUMN	SPRING	SUMMER
Year 1	Belonging* Possessions	Light and Colour India*	Water The Neighbourhood
Year 2	Sounds Memories and Remembering*	Communication Shelter	Treasure Weather
Year 3	Fire Difference*	Food Celebration	The Sea Places
Year 4	Imagination Worship	Community Patterns	Exploration Myself

*Topics developed in this volume

N.B. Festivals and the stories associated with them will punctuate the work on topics.

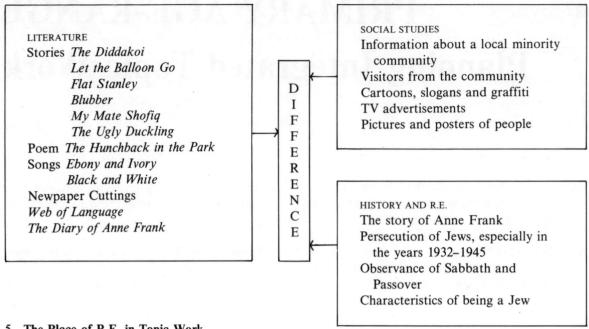

5 The Place of R.E. in Topic Work
In R.E. the choice of topics will be guided by the objectives of the relevant Agreed Syllabus. Generally topics in the Primary/Middle school will fall into three main categories in relation to R.E.:

- topics in which *R.E. objectives have a central place*
  e.g. Festivals, Worship, Jesus
- topics in which *R.E. is one of a number of disciplines* employed to illuminate the topic
  e.g. Water, Buildings, Communication
- Topics in which *no specific contribution to explicit R.E. objectives* is envisaged and where efforts to incorporate it would force the logic of the topic. Any topic, however, which develops children's ability to reflect on experience has relevance for religious understanding.

**6 Teaching and Learning Activities
(the development of competencies)**
It is important that these should be mapped out. The following learning experiences might usefully be considered, particularly in connection with R.E.:

(i) story telling
(ii) writing—both personal and descriptive
(iii) handling evidence and texts
(iv) talking and discussing
(v) visits
(vi) inviting visitors into the classroom
(vii) visual material—slides, videos, posters, film-strips
(viii) engaging in art work, both group and individual
(ix) exploring themes through drama, mime and movement
(x) reading novels, stories and poems, or parts of them.

The particular competencies to be developed via these activities can be tabulated, as in the example shown opposite taken from the topic on "Difference" (see p. 49):

7 Questions of Time
Topics of the type advocated will often have a life-span of approximately half a term, although in many schools variations to the half-termly block pattern will almost certainly be desirable and necessary. A topic on the local community may require a full term. On the other hand, mini-topics of 2–3 weeks may be necessary so that balance is preserved: the programme could, for example, be punctuated by annual festivals. The basic grid should be seen as flexible, and open to negotiation and development so that a balance between planning and spontaneity may be maintained.

8 Checking the Diet
If each topic is structured as in (4) above it should be possible to extract particular skills and content (for example, historical or geographical) and to check these against the objectives. In the case of R.E. the checklist provided is in the Agreed Syllabus. Questions which should be asked include:
(a) Are the topics appropriate for the age-group for which they have been chosen?
(b) Do the topics provide sufficient scope for sequencing and development in each curriculum area?
(c) Does the grid made adequate provision for achieving the objectives set out in the Agreed Syllabus? For example, an objective which refers to "the impact of Jesus" might well require specific mini-topics, additional to the more general topics contained in the grid.

9 Resourcing the Topic
Effective topic work demands a wide variety of resource materials, and important decisions need to be made about their storage and retrieval.

ANALYTIC	REFLECTIVE	EXPRESSIVE
Examining evidence	Observing and listening carefully	Linguistic Engaging in discussion
Following arguments	Interpreting personal observations and experiences	Responding orally to questions Summarising discussions etc.
Examining relevance of material to issues being explored	Assessing and interpreting evidence	Compiling lists Descriptive writing Personal writing
Discriminating between types of language	Considering causes and consequences of actions	Dramatic Mime, role-play, drama on, for example:
Discerning significant features in stories, events, symbols and people	Determining orders of importance and value	Aspects of Difference; Aggression and Prejudice; Respect and Acceptance
	Forming reasoned judgements	
	Making decisions	Constructive Making pictures and patterns in various media
Discerning significant points made in discussion	Forming concepts	
	Detecting stereotypes, bias and prejudice	Making bar-graphs Making models in clay, plasticine, paper and scrap material
	Self-understanding	Making props and scenery for drama work (e.g. hide-outs)
	Understanding other people's beliefs, attitudes and behaviour	
	Assessing personality and character	
	Considering appropriateness of different types of language for different purposes and situations	
	Discovering forms in which to express the ideals and feelings of individuals and groups	

10 Evaluating the Work

A topic should be evaluated while it is in progress. At its conclusion, however, it is also useful to evaluate more formally and to ask (and answer!) such questions as:

(i) What have the pupils learned and what instruments are used for assessing this?

(ii) Has the topic maintained the pupils' interest? What particularly motivated them?

(iii) What range of learning activities have the pupils experienced?

(iv) What contact have the pupils had with the eight areas of experience listed in (4) above?

(v) What has the teacher learned about sequencing the topic? How might he/she modify it if teaching it again?

(vi) What foundations have been laid for the next topic the pupils will be undertaking?

Change

INTRODUCTION

This First school topic aims to put flesh on the objectives set out in the Hampshire Agreed Syllabus (1978), viz.:

to enable children:

(a) *to grow in awareness of themselves, and to develop a positive attitude to their own emotions, life and learning;*

(b) *to grow in awareness of others, and to develop relationships in a secure and tolerant setting;*

(c) *to develop their interest in, and their ability to reflect upon, the world around them;*

(d) *to clarify and enlarge their ideas about religion.*

The topic, with its sub-themes, is of particular value to young children because it explores the experience of change in themselves, other people, and the world around them, and should reveal that such change is not necessarily a cause for fear but can herald opportunities for growth, development and celebration.[1]

Spring being a time of renewal, and Easter a festival which is essentially about transformation, the topic is appropriately located in the Spring term. It capitalises on the changes and community celebrations related to the season.

The topic is covered in six sub-themes, as shown below.

Two books of general usefulness for the teacher are:

Gregory R.	*Thirty Books for Infant R.E.*	Teaching Media Resource Service, Russell House, 14 Dunstable Street, Ampthill, Bedford MK45 2JT (1984)
Barratt S.	*Tinder-Box Assembly Book*	A. & C. Black (1982)

SUB-THEME	CHILDREN'S LEARNING ACTIVITIES	RESOURCES
1 Changes in Technology	Look at a range of old and new things in the children's environment: cars, clothes, irons, machinery, telephones, video-recorders, etc. Discuss feelings about old and new things. Tomorrow's World: children imagine or invent some equipment which they would like to have around when they are older (e.g. when they themselves are mums and dads).	A variety of old and new objects
2 Changes in Locality and Community	Walk around the locality, identifying old and new buildings and changing use of land. Interview individuals about their memories of changes within the community. Investigate changes that have taken place within the school, examining school log-books, pictures, textbooks, exercise books, equipment (e.g. slates), etc.	

[1]*At some point it would be worth considering with the children some things which do not, or cannot, or should not, change: it would be unfortunate if the notion were conveyed that change for its own sake is desirable—there may be good reasons for resisting it.*

SUB-THEME	CHILDREN'S LEARNING ACTIVITIES	RESOURCES
3 Changes in Nature	Look for early signs of Spring in the area round the school. Observe, list and illustrate contrasts between what appears to be dead (e.g. twigs) and the new life about to unfold. use a magnifying glass to examine buds etc. in detail.	
	Observe and chart the time taken for buds to open in the classroom, as compared with those outside. Consider the reasons for the difference.	Poem: "Bare Twigs", in Farncombe A. *Moments*: N.C.E.C./Denholm House 1982
	Trace the various stages in the growth of a daffodil.	Poem: "Daffodil Gold", in Woodland E.J.M. ed. *Poems for Movement*: Bell & Hyman 1984
	Study the life-cycle of a caterpillar. Hand round a tray containing chrysalises among dead leaves and twigs, for the children to identify its contents. Examine the chrysalises and discuss the main stages in their life-cycle.	Carle E. *Very Hungry Caterpillar*: Puffin 1974 "Small Creatures" Slides: Philip Green Educational, Redditch, Worcs. Back C. *Tadpole and Frog*: A. & C. Black 1985
	Other changes in Nature may also be observed, e.g. birds nesting, hatching chicks, animals being born, rearing a lamb.	Poem "Bird's Nest", in Farrimond R. ed. *Seeing and Doing: A New Anthology of Songs and Poems*: Thames/Methuen 1983
	Drama and music-making can be linked with seed-growing, buds opening, harvest, and the caterpillar's life-cycle.	Grieg: "Morning", from Peer Gynt suite
4 Changes in Self	Collect photographs of the children and their families at various stages of their development: these act as foci for talking about the ways in which the children have changed physically.	
	Some might visit playgroups or nursery schools attended, to remind them of their earlier years.	
	Portray different moods in mime and drama, and discuss such questions as: What makes us happy, sad, excited or angry? What has caused the changes? Make collages of these moods.	
	Consider what changes the children are likely to encounter in the future. Invite visitors from the Junior/Middle school to which the	Hans Christian Andersen's stories 'The Ugly Duckling' and 'The Snow Queen'

SUB-THEME	CHILDREN'S LEARNING ACTIVITIES	RESOURCES
	children will probably move. Talk about changes in ourselves and others, considering such questions as: What are the signs that we have changed? (appearance, likes and dislikes, degrees of freedom, birthdays, etc.) What are the signs that other people have changed? How and why do our relationships with other people change? How do we react to changes?	Issue No. 8 of the twice-termly magazine *Hands Together*: Scholastic Publications Ltd., Westfield Road, Southam, Leamington Spa, Warwickshire CV33 0BR
5 Stories about Change	Almost every story, of course, includes characters who change, incidents which cause such changes, and moods which change as the story progresses. Those mentioned below have been found especially useful with young children.	
	John Brown, Rose and the Midnight Cat, Rose and her Old English Sheepdog, John Brown, live happily together. When the stray cat first appears John Brown resents its intrusion into their special relationship. Only when Rose falls ill does he realise that he has been selfish and that all three of them can live happily together.	Wagner J. *John Brown, Rose and the Midnight Cat*: Kestrel Books 1977
	The Two Giants. Sam and Boris live in idyllic surroundings but spoil their happiness by quarrelling over a pink shell. A mix-up over a pair of socks reminds them how sadly their relationship has changed and they become friends again.	Foreman M. *The Two Giants*: Hodder and Stoughton 1983
	Joachim the Policeman. Joachim is authoritarian and efficient, but one morning finds that a small boys' football match is fun to watch in spite of the noise. Thenceforward his attitude to his job changes so drastically that he is dismissed from the force. He joins a travelling show and pulls the strings of a puppet policeman.	K. Baumann & D. McKee *Joachim the Policeman*: A. & C. Black 1974
6 Celebration of change	The aim in this sub-theme is to introduce the children to the events and ideas associated with the festival of Easter, and the period leading up to it, by means of an exploration of signs, symbols and related activities.	Wetz P. & P. *Easter and the Spring Festivals in the Primary and Middle School*. Available from the authors, The Wheatsheaf, 56 Park Street, Kings Cliffe, Peterborough, PE8 6XN

SUB-THEME	CHILDREN'S LEARNING ACTIVITIES	RESOURCES
	(a) <u>Signs and Symbols</u>[2] . Children go out in groups to look for signs and symbols in the environment—signs of Spring, road signs, signs on buildings, advertisements, etc. They record, report on, and perhaps make a display of, their discoveries. (This work could be linked with basic map work, or with the collecting of badges and flags.) Discuss the meanings of the various signs and symbols observed. Talk about the ways in which the children try to convey ideas and feelings by non-verbal means. Collect and study a number of Easter Cards. What signs and symbols are used to represent this festival? Why are they used? (b) <u>Shrove Tuesday</u> Tell the story of the origin of Shrove Tuesday ceremonies, which signify people's preparation for the period of Lent (a time of self-denial for many Christians, in memory of Jesus' experience in the Judaean wilderness). Each child makes a pancake after a class discussion about ingredients and processes. Children work in groups to design a Pancake-making Machine (cf. Ed. de Bono's challenges to children to design Dog-walking machines.) The "Pancake Plipper-Plopper" was designed by a 6-year-old child.	Bennett O. *Festivals*, in Exploring Religion series: Bell & Hyman 1984 Harrowven J. *Origins of Festivals and Feasts*: Kaye & Ward 1980.

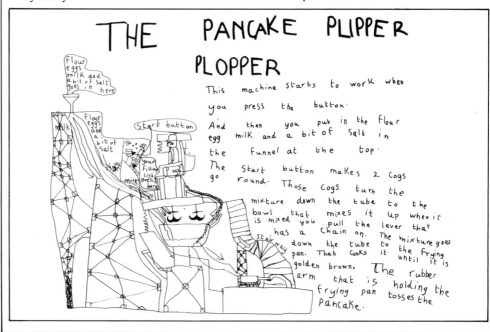

[2]*A tricky area, in which it is difficult to be either precise or consistent. A sign may develop (at least for certain people) into a symbol; a symbol may lose its power and decline into a mere sign. Fundamentally, a sign is arbitrarily chosen, has a single unmistakable meaning, and denotes something specific; while a symbol "grows" out of a community's life, has wide connotations, and possesses the potential to evoke profound personal responses. (e.g. a cross: this may act as a sign, meaning "this building is a church"; or it may act as a symbol, which for the Christian believer expresses a story and a theology about Jesus, and motivates the response which faith in Jesus demands.) The teacher should try to keep the basic distinction in mind.*

SUB-THEME	CHILDREN'S LEARNING ACTIVITIES	RESOURCES
	Consider with the children occasions where some kind of "change" is required as a preparation for a different or special activity (e.g. changing clothes before P.E., or before a party; changes in a family's normal routine before going on holiday; a change in thinking or in attitude before receiving a visitor or visiting someone in hospital.) Look at Shrove Tuesday and Lent as occasions, for Christians, for change, in anticipation of the sadness and joy of the Easter season.	
	(c) <u>Easter</u> Talk about the signs and symbols of Easter. Engage in activities associated with Hot Cross Buns, Easter Eggs and Easter Bonnets.	Poster "Easter". C.E.M., Lancaster House, Borough Road, Isleworth, Middlesex TW7 5DU
	Hot Cross Buns	Fairbairn N. & Priestley J. *Holy Week*, in Living Festivals series: R.M.E.P.
	Make some buns.	Shannon T. *Christmas and Easter*: Lutterworth 1984
	Discuss the symbol of the cross on the bun—a reminder of the death of Jesus. Tell briefly the story which gives rise to the symbol.[3]	
	Eggs	
	Paint Eggs.	
	Investigate different ways of cooking eggs: changes during the cooking process.	
	Have (hard-boiled!) egg races.	
	Discuss the symbolism of the egg—a reminder of the resurrection of Jesus.	
	Tell the story of Mary's visit to the tomb and her report to the disciples.	
	Easter Bonnets	
	Each child designs and makes an Easter Bonnet.	
	Display the bonnets, and parade wearing them.	
	Tell the story of the origins of wearing Easter Bonnets, and discuss the significance of the custom.	

[3]*"Tell . . . the story".* It should be told as a story, a word which neither implies nor rejects its factual accuracy; and it should be told in a way which will engage the hearers, so that they become listeners—"briefly" does not imply an unimaginative summary. The story should go beyond the sadness and despair of the crucifixion, to include at least the prospect of a happier ending, which may be spelled out "next time" in the story of Mary's transformation when she visits the tomb.

SUB-THEME	CHILDREN'S LEARNING ACTIVITIES	RESOURCES
7 Summing-up the Topic	Children make a collage based on ideas explored in 1–6 above. Present slides of death and rebirth and of things which change, for discussion in small groups. Hold an Assembly based on O. Wilde's story *The Selfish Giant*: Puffin 1982 Hold a final Assembly in which children tell other classes about their collage and read some of their written work.	

Food

INTRODUCTION

People have been described as celebrating animals, and celebration often takes the form of holding parties, eating, making speeches, singing, dancing, and playing games. Religious groups, naturally enough, celebrate in these ways.

This topic seeks to interest children in the processes relating to the food they eat, and introduces them to some special, often symbolic, uses of food. It aims to develop within the children:

(a) a recognition of networks of relationships and of interdependence, within both human societies and the natural world;

(b) a delight in the variety which is present in the natural world;

(c) a sensitivity to the ways in which human groups often use food when celebrating events which are important to them;

(d) an ability to reflect upon the world and, in particular, upon the fact that while they have adequate food, many children live in hunger.

Since Harvest-time figures largely in this scheme, it would most appropriately be located in the first half of the Autumn term.

The topic is covered in four sub-themes, as shown below.

SUB-THEME	CHILDREN'S LEARNING ACTIVITIES	RESOURCES

1 The Food we Eat: Sources, Preservation and Preparation.	(a) <u>A visit to a fresh-fish shop</u>
	Identify the different sorts of fish on sale, noting their characteristic shapes and sizes. Buy a selection of fish.
	
	Back in the classroom:
	
	  Talk about the sights and smells of the fish shop. Draw and identify some of the fish bought during the visit.
	
	  Cook fish in a variety of ways. Compare their appearance before and after cooking.
	
	  Sample together some of the cooked fish. Are there preferences as regards methods of cooking?
	
	  Tell the story of a fish finger.
	
	(b) <u>Activities with fresh vegetables</u>
	Bring a number of fresh vegetables into the classroom. Name them. Sort and classify them on various criteria such as: colour; those which grow above/below ground; those which are peeled/scraped in their preparation; those which are eaten raw/cooked.
	
	Observe and chart the deterioration of the vegetables over a week. How could they be preserved?
		Wall Chart "Identifying Fish" from Sea Fish Industry Authority, 24 Bedford Square, London WC1B 3HH

SUB-THEME	CHILDREN'S LEARNING ACTIVITIES	RESOURCES
	Look at and talk about methods of preservation, viz. canning, freezing, bottling, salting. Taste foods preserved by each of these processes, and discuss preferences. Consider the importance of these processes for the home, for shops, and for transportation of food (lorries, ships, etc.).	
	Contrast the limited methods of preservation (and thus the limited possibilities of importing food) available in the past. The local harvest was all-important; therefore the productivity of crops was a subject for prayers, and the in-gathering of the harvest an occasion for thanksgiving and celebration. Draw on the children's experience of Harvest Festivals.	Harvest Posters from Pictorial Charts Educational Trust, 27 Kirchen Road, London, W13 0UD; also from Athena International, PO Box 13 Bishops Stortford, Herts.
	(c) An investigation into the sources of our food Make a collection in the classroom of tins and packets of food. As a class or group activity, discover the country of origin of each food, and mount a display linking tins and packets to places on a large map.	
	Outline the stages by which items from other countries (e.g. oranges from Spain) reach the local shop.	
	Tell the tale of a tea-leaf.	Slide Set "Our Cup of Tea": C.W.D.E., 128 Buckingham Palace Road, SW1W 9SH
	Arrange for the milkman to visit the school (with his float) and to describe his job.	
	Tell the story of a bottle of milk.	
2 A Basic Food: Bread	(a) A visit to a farm at harvest time[1]	
	(b) A study of an ear of wheat Take apart an ear of wheat.	
	Count the number of wheat grains.	
	Make detailed drawings from observation.	
	Do simple experiments in germination, recording the results. Contrast the apparent lifelessness of a grain with its capacity to germinate, given the appropriate conditions. Discuss the conditions necessary for a good crop.	Filmstrip "Wheat": St. Paul Book Centre, 199 Kensington High Street, London W8 6BA

[1]*The class which was engaged on this topic made two other visits at this time. One was to the Museum of English Rural Life at the University of Reading, where there are excellent displays of old farming equipment wagons, corn dollies, and so on; the other (on the same day) was to the Shire Horse Centre at Maidenhead. A Visit to the Hampshire Farm Museum, Manor Farm, Upper Hamble, Botley (Botley 6302) would be worthwhile.*

SUB-THEME	CHILDREN'S LEARNING ACTIVITIES	RESOURCES
	Express in music and movement the life-cycle of a grain of wheat.	
	(c) <u>Group activities</u> Make bread, butter and jam.	
	Share, in a celebration meal, the things that have been made.	Peet V. *Bakery*: A. & C. Black 1979
3 The Balanced Diet	Distinguish different categories of foods, in relation to bodily needs; construct sets which include a wide range of normally available foods, representing these in pictures and words.	Whitlock, R. *Thinking about Food*: Lutterworth 1980 (for the teacher)
	Explore what a child needs—both the kind of food and its quantity—in a week in order to maintain good physical health. Make charts or lists of these requirements. Groups could discuss how they would break the total into daily consumption, or even into individual meals.	Bennett O. *Food for Life:* Save the Children Fund/ Macmillan Education 1982
	Present and discuss the fact that many children do not have a balanced or adequate diet.[2] This may best be tackled by means of a case study of a child living in a Third World country. Set out on a table a typical day's food of a British child, alongside a typical week's food of many a Third World child. Children could write on "A day in the life of a Third World child", or on their suggestions for helping to alleviate hunger and misery. (Refer back to 1(b) above, on preserving food stuffs; to 2(b), on the conditions for good crops and harvests; perhaps to 1(c), on the exporting of home-grown crops).	Peterson P. *Boy in Bangladesh*: A. & C. Black 1981 Scarsbrook A. & A. *Pakistani Village*: A. & C. Black 1979 Sample Diet Sheets: African Caribbean, S. E. Asian and British Children, from C.W.D.E. (as above) Fact Sheet "Food in Calcutta" from Christian Aid, PO Box No. 1, London SW9 8BH *Food*, in Round the World series: Save the Children Fund/Macmillan 1981
4 Favourite and Forbidden Foods, and Foods for Special Occasions	(a) <u>Favourite, and not-so-favourite, foods</u> Children collect information from each other about their likes and dislikes; perhaps also about foods which they do not eat, and about others which they would not want to eat if offered to them (e.g. seaweed, snails, blackbird pie). Record the information in graphs, charts, etc.	Burningham J. *Would you rather . . .* : Armada Books 1984
	(b) <u>Foods not eaten by some individuals</u> Children may contribute information, perhaps from their own experience, about people who abstain from certain foods for reasons other than personal	

[2]*Awareness of facts, some understanding of causes, and a degree of empathy, are the concerns here; avoid creating in the children any sense of personal responsibility or guilt. If, however, children express the wish to give help, this should be taken seriously and some way of giving practical effect to their wish should be devised.*

SUB-THEME	CHILDREN'S LEARNING ACTIVITIES	RESOURCES
	preference. These may include: the demands of training for some sport; the wish not to get too fat; doctor's orders; objection to eating meat. (c) <u>Foods not eaten by certain religious groups</u> Children might be encouraged to find out about these by talking with friends and neighbours. Many religious people observe regulations about prohibited foods, among them: Jews (prohibitions against pork, various seafoods, and products from animals not killed in the approved manner); Muslims (prohibition against alcoholic drinks); Hindus (prohibition against the flesh of cows).[3] (d) <u>Foods not eaten, or restricted, at certain times</u> Examples include the Christian season of Lent (see section 6(b) of the topic on "Change"), the Muslim Fast of Ramadan, and Oxfam-style Hunger Lunches in aid of Third World famine-stricken areas. Presented simply with the facts, children might come up with suggestions as to the reasons for such restrictions, of which two are obvious, viz. self-discipline or "training", and developing the ability to stand in another person's shoes. (e) <u>Foods with which communities celebrate particular events and memories</u> Explore with the children the actual use of certain foods within religious rituals, and the stories which underline the rituals; helping them to appreciate something of the symbolic significance of the food—of what the eating and sharing of it means to the participants.[4]	"The Jewish Home" and "The Hindu Home", booklets in Ask about Religion series: C.E.M., Lancaster House, Borough Road, Isleworth, Middlesex TW7 5DU Farncombe A.: titles in Our Friends series: N.C.E.C./ Denholm House Press "Exploring a theme: Food" (booklet): C.E.M. (1985) (as above) Filmstrip "Celebration Meals": BBC Radiovision 1979

[3]*How such prohibitions originated is uncertain, and opinions differ as to their value for the religious community and its members. Children may have their own suggestions about the reasons for certain prohibitions, and about their possible consequences.*

[4]*Only a very limited treatment will be appropriate, a "starter" towards understanding a feature central to many religions. The main points are that the food focuses the participants on a particular event or person, and that it unites them with one another.*

SUB-THEME	CHILDREN'S LEARNING ACTIVITIES	RESOURCES
	Examples are: Bread and Wine (Eucharist/Mass/ Lord's Supper), and the story of the Last Supper; Unleavened Bread (Passover), and the story of Exodus; Prasada—food brought by Hindus to the temple as an offering and, after prayers, shared by all those present.	Issue no. 12 of the twice-termly magazine *Hands Together*: Scholastic Publications Ltd., Westfield Road, Southam, Leamington Spa, Warwickshire, CV33 0BR
5 A Celebration	Children plan a meal to celebrate some special event or occasion such as the anniversary of the opening of the school, the arrival of a group of visitors from another country, the departure of a member of the staff. Children discuss the meanings symbolised by the foods they have chosen.	

An Approach to India

INTRODUCTION

Context

This topic was designed for children aged 7+ attending a Junior school on a modern estate on the fringe of a town which has experienced considerable development and expansion over the last twenty years. The children were of mixed abilities and responded readily to a wide range of activities. They had little experience of children from another culture.

The class had previously worked at topics which were mainly science and history based. The school topic grid offered a selection of general themes for each age-group and in the lower school provided scope for the exploration of "Lifestyles".

Objectives

Indian culture is full of colour and for the children has the added fascination of the unusual: they will enjoy exploring this theme. They will be enriched by a whole range of new experiences and by the stimulus of varied points of view and newly gained knowlege. Ideally, they will be interested enough to find out all kinds of facts about India for themselves. They will talk to their parents about it, and become alert to information related to the theme appearing in television programmes, newspapers, magazines and books.

Much of the work will be concerned with experiences, knowledge, attitudes, sensitivities and skills which are basic to an understanding of religion and to progress in the religious quest; it thus serves as an introduction to the investigation, at a later stage, of more explicitly religious material. It should, however, in its own right achieve the objectives of helping children:

> to think about their own lives and about the advantages and disadvantages of being a child;
> to think about the quality and significance of family life, home and possessions, and to compare their own experience with that of children in India;
> to learn how children in India live and how they express their experiences, feelings and ideas;
> to understand through stories some of the beliefs and values characteristic of Indian culture.

Principles and Methods of Work

Within a flexible timetable the India topic is organised in a framework which includes such activities as group and school Assemblies, basic skill work in language and mathematics, games and physical education. The topic is planned to last for just over half a term, and an average of approximately two hours a day is set aside for it. Special enthusiasms, visitors and practical sessions may well require some adjustment in the plan.

In each week a variety of activities is included. Stories and discussion, drama, slide sequences, cooking, writing and art work all find a place. A balance is also achieved between class activities, group discussion and activity, and individual work on assignments. Throughout, an attempt is made to give preference to firsthand experience and to ensure that, wherever possible, the Indian experience is related to the children's own lives.

A typical day could be planned as follows:

9.00– 9.30	Individual work on writing and illustrating personal booklets.
9.30–10.30	Class newstime. Showing and talking about objects of interest. Listening to the story "The Banyan Deer", followed by discussion.
10.50–12.00	Slide sequence—scenes of an Indian bazaar. Group drama—bargaining.
12.00–12.15	Individual work in basic mathematics.
1.25– 2.30	Discussion, using large photographs showing groups of people. Personal writing based on the photographs: "What is about to happen?"
2.50– 3.25	Explanation and demonstration of weekly assignments. Groups cooking chapattis.
3-25– 3.40	School Assembly.

If all goes well by the end of the project the children will have produced:

> Pieces of tie dyeing and squeeze dyeing
> A clay puja lamp or a model of an Indian god or doll
> A hand puppet
> A piece of weaving
> An Indian face mask
> Writing based on workcards on Indian animals and general culture
> A class dramatisation of "At the Bazaar"
> Group drama on the theme of good and evil.

They will also have experienced:
> Cooking and eating chapattis, curry and rice
> Indian words and customs

15

Making music and experimenting with sounds

Listening to a wide range of stories, studying particularly the story of Rama and Sita

The cumulative effect of visual material, tape-recordings of Indian music, and short stories and poems from or about India, all offered by the teacher as a background to the topic, either as introduction to various stages of the work or as interludes in it.

Main Resources Needed

On page 25 a detailed list of resources and useful addresses is given. Before this topic is started the following items need to be prepared:

1 A plentiful supply of pictures, posters, photographs and slides showing important aspects of Indian life, viz: occupations, domestic activities, possessions, buildings, temples, gods and goddesses, water, transport, animals, food and cooking, clothes, buying and selling, music, plants and crops, climate, customs, writing, language.

2 A range of Indian stories and poems both for the children to read and for the teacher to read and re-tell.

3 A basic stock of art paper, crayons, paint and brushes, card and paste.

4 A varied range of workcards based upon the aspects of Indian life listed in 1 above.

5 At least one tape-recorder and several blank cassette tapes, plus tapes of Indian music.

6 A portable cooker, and a prepared list of British and Indian foods required (arrangements having been made for purchase and storage). Cooking utensils, plates and bowls.

7 A slide projector and screen.

8 Old sheets or lining material and the equipment needed for tie and squeeze dyeing.

9 Modelling clay for making items for sale in the bazaar, and other models.

10 Incense sticks.

11 Small and large boxes for collecting typical British and Indian possessions.

12 A collection of tools and equipment typical of various occupations.

13 A set of slates and chalks.

CONTENTS

Introductory Unit (Based on the children's experience)

A The family community
B Family tasks and routines
C Family mealtimes and cooking
D School routines

Linking Unit

Indians in Britain

Life in India

A   Clothes
B1

B2   Indian food, and associated customs
B3
C   Contrasts
D   Stories of India
E   Setting up a shrine
F   The possessions of Indian people
G   An India Day

Review by the Class Teacher

Lists of Resources and Addresses

INTRODUCTORY UNIT

A   The Family Community

1   *Teacher's Introduction*

The teacher begins by giving the children a review of the topic and what they can expect in the weeks ahead. Although brief this explanation can refer to:

The use of the children's own experience in creating and exploring the activities of an imaginary British family.

The work to be done in discovering how Indian families live.

Things which can be brought to school to help in the work.

Things which the children can be alert to, in their surroundings and in school, which refer to India.

2   *Discussion*

Pictures and posters showing various aspects of family life are displayed. The discussion can be guided to cover such points as:

The names of people who make up a family.

The various activities shown.

The emotions evident in the pictures (love, care, acceptance, friendship, contentment, peace; also anger, jealousy, indifference, aggression, frustration).

3   *Group Work*

The children can then be divided into small groups. Each group is asked to create its own imaginary family. Guidance as to what should be discussed may include:

Members of the family: their number, names, ages, occupations.

Their main physical and emotional characteristics; their interests and talents.

How they get on as a family, including both good and bad aspects.

Any especially interesting things about the family which may make it distinctive.

4   *Expressive Work*

The children can express the ideas which arise in their group discussions in several ways:

A written list of the main facts about the family.

A dramatisation of an incident which the group thinks is characteristic of its family.

Paintings of the family or of its individual members.

Personal writing, expressing their own feelings about the family which the group has created.

B Family Tasks and Routines
1 *Discussion*
Using plenty of pictures, posters and slides showing family activities, ask the children to identify and define all the tasks undertaken by the people shown. A list of these can be compiled on the blackboard or the overhead projector.

2 *Group Activity*
With their imaginary British family in mind the children are asked to produce a list dividing the tasks into three categories:

Tasks for which the children are responsible
e.g. tidying their belongings
feeding their pets
cleaning bicycles
Tasks the adults undertake
e.g. paying bills
feeding and clothing the family
cleaning and decorating the house
Tasks shared by the whole family
e.g. washing up
cleaning the car
walking the dog

3 *Discussion followed by group activity*
Discuss with the children some of the routines occurring within their imaginary families, using questions such as:

What happens when you get up or at bedtime?
Is there a routine on bath nights?
Do you have a different routine on Saturday or Sunday?
Are there routines for special occasions?

4 *Expressive activities*
Each group of children can make:

A permanent record of the different categories of tasks they have decided upon.
A written and illustrated plan of the chosen routine for their family, to include a careful list of the sound effects they want and their positions in the plan.
A tape-recording of their special routine or a dramatisation of it.

This last activity, to be done in groups, requires a quiet room or area for success, and probably some adult help. Time for thought and opportunity to experiment with sound effects are essential. When completed, the tapes or dramatisations may be presented for the rest of the class to enjoy.

C Family Mealtimes and Cooking
A good example of routine and responsibility is that of a mother feeding a family.

1 *Introductory visit and discussion*
Invite a mother, or several mothers, to come into school to talk to the children about the procedures involved in feeding a family. Before the mothers meet the children, ensure that all parties know what is expected of them.

The mothers to be ready to talk about planning, shopping, storing, preparing, serving; and to bring with them such things as a shopping list, a basket with some typical favourite foods, a purse and housekeeping money, a selection of storage tins and kitchen utensils.

The children to know the main aspects of the subject to be dealt with by their visitors, and to be helped to frame some prepared questions. They can be prompted to observe particularly the methods and routines the mothers use in preparing, cooking and serving food to their families.

N.B. Use the visit to help the children to gain social experience in conversation and courtesy. Guide the discussion to maintain relevance and confidence, but be ready to allow fully spontaneous dialogue as appropriate.

2 *Expressive activities*
Follow up the visit by:

Cooking a simple meal of sausages, peas and potatoes, inviting the mothers back to help.
Discussing with the class their reactions to the visit and such things as companionship, the pleasures of sharing, the customs associated with meal times, the practice of "saying grace".
Practising in small groups the setting out of a place at table.
Writing up and illustrating mealtime routine and menu for the imaginary family.

D School Routines
1 *Class discussion*
Refresh the children's minds about routines and with their help go through the routine of a morning in school, building up a plan of it on the blackboard.

2 *Group activity*
Refer to some of the routines in school, such as: registration, lining up for Assembly, a P.E. lesson, dinner time, end of the day.

Get each group to map out the precise steps by which these routines are effected. Ask them to describe the details verbally or with blackboard drawings so that the rest of the class may appraise their accuracy.

3 *Expressive activities*
Ask each group now to choose a member of their imaginary family and to compile a chart to show their routine activities either before or after school hours, with an illustration of each activity. If the group chooses one of the children in the family, the

chart might include: getting out of bed; washing and dressing; eating breakfast; making the bed; leaving for school.

LINKING UNIT

Indians in Britain

Some of the routines in the lives of imaginary British families have been studied through the medium of the children's own experience. Now a start can be made on a comparison with an Indian family's life-style. The work is based upon a Hindu way of life but does not assume that there is such a thing as a typical Indian family. A constant alertness is necessary to avoid stereotyping.

1 *Introduction*

EITHER Give the children direct experience by inviting an Indian mother and father from the locality into school. Prepare the children so that they have a fund of appropriate and useful questions which will help to reveal the similarities and differences between British and Indian ways of life; prepare the Indian visitors to talk about their families, their homes and possessions, their customs, the games their children play, and the things which they find unusual, interesting or disturbing about their life in Britain.

OR Show the children a selection of slides from the set "Family in Vadala Village". Prepare them to watch out for aspects of life which they would want to ask about if someone from the village was with them in the classroom.

2 *Class discussion*

Remind the children of the words describing family relationships used in Introductory Unit A, viz; love, care, acceptance, friendship, contentment, peace, anger, jealousy, indifference, aggression, frustration. Do they apply to both cultures?

If Indian visitors talked to the children and agreed to being recorded on tape, play back selected sections to promote discussion and to ensure that the children hear and understand.

In either case (visitors or slide sequence), give the children an opportunity to review the information available thus far about houses, clothes, general environment, food and the things Indian children do. Also give them time to comment on things which they find interesting or puzzling, and invite them to make comparisons.

LIFE IN INDIA

A Clothes

1 *Visual presentation*

Invite the Indian visitors back if available. Discuss with them beforehand the slides to be shown. Ask them to come in Indian clothing.

Show again slides on an Indian way of life from "Family in Vadala Village". Perhaps the visitors would like to comment on these.

Direct the children to look closely at: the clothes people wear (the type of material and how the clothes are put on); the marks of caste and status; the personal ornaments.

2 *Class discussion*

Learn a few Indian words, e.g. ways of greeting and parting.

Show how the sari and dhoti are worn.

Discuss how the clothes are made and why the types of material used are chosen.

3 *Expressive activity*

Children make their own saris or dhotis out of old sheeting. Dye, using sheets or cheap lining material, and decorate with braid.

B1 Indian Food, and Associated Customs

1 *Introduction and discussion*

Display various Indian foods, including rice, red lentils, dried peas, almonds, coconut, figs, mangoes, pawpaws, a selection of spices, aubergines and peppers.

With the help (if available) of either an Indian visitor, or someone who has spent a considerable time in India:

Identify the items on display. Explain how meals are planned, and food bought, stored and cooked.

Use slides from "City and Village Trade in Western India", in amplification of, or as a substitute for, the information gained from the visitor.

Give the children opportunity for questioning and discussion.

2 *Group discussion and activity*

Now the children have some basic impressions of India they can create an imaginary family. Using pictures, posters and cut-outs from magazines they can make a visual representation of at least the children in their family. They can discuss and report to the class the details of this imaginary family.

In small groups the children can practise bargaining. They can discuss the implications of this system of trade, its advantages and disadvantages. Does it happen in British shops and markets?

In preparation for a dramatisation of a bazaar scene the groups can decide the parts which each member of their family will play: e.g. stall-holder, shopper, bystander, money-changer, musician.

3 *Expressive Activities*

Make and decorate clay models of fish, meats and

other perishables. Display them on the ground as in an Indian scene with other fruit, nuts and cereals. Dramatise the bazaar scene. Listen to "In the Bazaars of Hyderabad" and extracts from *Get Ready for Battle*. Paint pictures of impressions gained from the literature and the dramatisation.

Extracts from *Get Ready for Battle*

1 *Joginder Nath was sitting in one of his own chairs outside the shop, fanning himself with a bamboo fan to give some relief from heat and flies. The flies were attracted by all the food in the bazaar. Next to Joginder's shop was a sweetmeat-seller and opposite a meat shop with big chunks of raw meat hung from iron hooks. There were little barrows lined up all along the street, selling fruits that were bursting and oozing in the heat. Many people and crowds thronged the bazaar, they pushed against each other and trod discarded mango-peels into the dust.*

2 *Vishnu, Gautam and Sumi sat on a shaky little wooden bench outside a sweetmeat-seller's and drank buttermilk out of tall brass tumblers. It was evening and the bazaar was crowded, with everyone out to enjoy the cool air. The shops were lit up with electric bulbs and the barrows with flares of naphtha light, and there was music blaring out of various radios, sweet, sad music played at top volume.*

On the opposite side of the road there was a small patch of empty ground where a cloth merchant's stall had recently been gutted by fire. Here a hawker of medicines had taken up his stand and was extolling the virtues of his product. He had an assistant who squatted on the ground, beating a little barrel-shaped drum and singing a song.

In the Bazaars of Hyderabad

What do you sell, O ye merchants?
Richly your wares are displayed.
Turbans of crimson and silver,
Tunics of purple brocade,
Mirrors with panels of amber,
Daggers with handles of jade,

What do you weigh, O ye vendors?
Saffron and lentil and rice.
What do you grind, O ye maidens?
Sandalwood, henna and spice.
What do you call, O ye peddlers?
Chessmen and ivory dice.

What do you make, O ye goldsmiths?
Wristlet and anklet and ring,
Bells for the feet of blue pigeons,
Frail as a dragon-fly's wing.
Girdles of gold for the dancers,
Scabbards of gold for the king.

What do you cry, O ye fruitmen?
Citron, pomegranate, and plum.
What do you play, ye musicians?
Sitar, sarangi, and drum.
What do you chant, ye magicians?
Spells for the aeons to come.

B2 Indian Food, and Associated Customs

The food theme can be used to introduce some language work, i.e. exploring the use of adjectives. The link with India is maintained by using coconuts and mangoes.

N.B. It is helpful to have another adult in the room with you when opening the coconuts as they are tough nuts! It also helps when it comes to distribution.

1 *Class discussion*
Each of the children is given a piece of coconut and a sip of coconut milk. The basic parts of the fruit are named and a word list put on the blackboard. A brief discussion of some of the more obvious adjectives can confirm that the children understand what they have to do. Parts of the shell are passed round for them to touch and observe at close quarters. The children then write two or three adjectives to describe:

the look and feel of the outside of the coconut;
the smell, colour and texture of the inside;
the taste of the milk and flesh.

A similar process is used with the mangoes.

2 *Group activity*
The children split into groups and pool their words. Between them they come up with a description of either the coconut or mango.

Two typical impressions:

Mangoes
Our mangoes were tasty, the flavour
of pears, apricots and peaches.
The gold of oranges inside and soft and juicy.
The juice dripped down our chins, staining
our clothes and making us very sticky.

Coconut
The coconut is hard, hairy, round and prickly.
It feels heavy when held.
The inside is smooth white and waxy looking.
It is thick and crunchy to eat.
The coconut reminded us of the ivory of an elephant's tusk.
Sweet syrupy, clear like water, the coconut milk was liked by some and disliked by others.

3 *Conclusion*
Some of the group writing may be read to the class. The lesson ends with the children listening to the story "The Monkey and the Mango Tree."

B3 Indian Food, and Associated Customs

1 *Introduction*

In general discussion with the children revise the information given in Section B1 on how Indian people, living in India, store, prepare and cook their food.

2 *Prepare, cook and eat a meal*

Suggested and tested menu:

Either Chapattis, rice and dhal (lentil curry);

or Rice, meat curry (including tomato, onion, apple, sultanas and curry powder), popadoms.

Observe the Indian customs when eating the meal:
Sit on the floor. Little bowls of water for washing fingers. Picking up food with right hand only (if Hindu).

3 *Educational value and organisation*

Several of the activities in this lesson can be of considerable educational value:
A shopping expedition to buy the raw materials.
Careful use of implements and correct use of cooker—safety instructions to avoid danger of burning or spillage must be clear, and fully observed.
Observance of good hygiene: washing hands, cleanliness of utensils, care in serving.
Organisation and safety may be enhanced by enlisting the help of adults and older pupils, and by using several cookers.

4 *Expressive activities*

Suggested ways of following up the Indian meal are:

(a) Look again at selected slides from "Family in Vadala Village" and "Young in India". Discuss the customs associated with an Indian meal, raising such matters as:
The cow as a sacred animal; a special day in October for cows; economic necessity compels their protection as providers of calves, milk, fuel, and eventually leather. To harm a cow is as serious a crime as to hurt one's mother.
Hindus do not eat meat. They respect all living things—humans, animals and plants.
Sitting on the floor to eat; the utensils used; Hindu people eat with the right hand only (the left hand is used for toilet and dirty tasks and is considered unclean).
The children discuss the slides and the accompanying information in groups. They make a written and illustrated record of a mealtime for their imaginary Indian family.

(b) Arrange with an agency such as Action Aid to show the children a film and slides of a visit to India. Such topics as farming, irrigation techniques, the various stages of rice growing, village life and the village school can be covered. This will provide the children with much additional information with which to diversify the description of their imaginary Indian family.

It also has the important function of introducing the concept of need. Without over-emphasising famine, poverty, disease and homelessness, a realistic picture of the contrasts in Indian life may be built up. The children may be drawn to respond to the needs revealed and to do something about them.

(c) Group discussions to explore aspects of stereotyping are important. Questions can be raised such as:
Do all Indians eat sitting on the floor?
Do we all eat our meals in the same way?
Do all Indians eat the same kinds of food?
Do we all eat white sliced bread?

C Contrasts

1 *Introduction*

Provide the children with several contrasting views of Indian life. For example:
Show the slides from "Young in India" which depict the house, dress and possessions of the village landlord.

Read and discuss the following extract from *Get Ready for Battle*:
Sarla Devi walked for a long time. She pulled her sari up to cover her head, but still the sun beat down on her and the glare pierced her eyes. Dust and stones from the unpaved roads got into her sandals, and she had to stop from time to time to take them out, sitting on some low wall by the wayside. No one paid any attention to her, she was just one more old woman, in plain cotton sari worn by the poor, sitting resting herself by the road side.

It took her an hour and a half to get to Bund Busti. The colony was just off a busy thoroughfare and she climbed down a bank by a railway bridge. Here there was a sea of huts, side by side, row upon row, tiny squat huts crowded one against the other. The colony was built out of the salvage that came floating down from a more prosperous world—rags and old bicycle tyres, battered tins and broken bricks. Walls were made from dried mud or of tattered matting, roofs were a patchwork of old tiles, rags and dusty sheets of tin held down at the corners by stones.

The earth was streaked with runnels of dirty water, vegetable waste and peels were trodden into the mud and scratched up again by mangy dogs and pigs and a few sick chickens, and the lanes were crowded with people carrying on their domestic lives in public, eating, cooking, washing clothes, carrying water.

Retell some of the stories from *Mother India's*

Children which describe sophisticated family life and values in an urban setting. Support all stories by plenty of pictures, posters and photographs.

2 Group activity

Refer the children back to the work on family routines in Introductory Unit B. After preparatory discussion, they make charts showing the family routine in the lives of the children in their imaginary Indian families.

Give the children in each group an opportunity to summarise their own observations and feelings on India so far, to state what they have learnt and what has interested them. They could try to express these in pictorial form.

3 Assignments

Split the children into groups. Give each group access to as much visual and written material as possible, and set an overall assignment to last approximately three weeks. Each group works on one of the following:

> Houses and huts in villages: materials and methods of construction
> Sanitation and general amenities in the village
> Houses in towns
> Sanitation and amenities in towns
> Roads and transport.

Discuss work achieved and revise assignments as necessary twice weekly. At the end ask each group to choose a few main points from the work it has done and to present a short illustrated talk or demonstration to the rest of the class.

D Stories of India

1 The story of Rama and Sita

Read, discuss and re-read this story so that the children are thoroughly familiar with the names of the main characters and the plot. Help the children to express the story:

> By dramatising key episodes from it.
> By general discussion in groups of their feelings about the characters and main ideas in it.
> By painting or drawing their impressions of it, after they have looked at some visual material (in particular, selected slides from "Main gods and goddesses of the Hindus").

2 The importance of stories

Give the children frequent opportunities to listen to stories, and the freedom to explore them at their own level, taking from them what they will. Help them to appreciate that stories about the god Garuda, or about Krishna, Hanuman or Vishnu, will probably be as familiar to Indian children as some of their own favourite tales are to them.

A sensitive presentation of the story of Sleeping Beauty, with its undertones of good and bad, may help the children to glimpse some of the layers of meaning to be found in it and in similar stories. By this means the themes underlying the Rama and Sita story may be illuminated and amplified.

3 The story of the Blind Men and the Elephant

Read and discuss the story with the children. It can be introduced vividly and appropriately by holding up any object unfamiliar to the children. Ask for their quick reactions; these are likely to be just as varied as those of the blind men.

A long time ago there lived a king who became weary of listening to the so-called wise men. Each of these men of learning had different ideas about the gods and the sacred books, and they used to argue with tongues like razors. One day the king gathered together in the market-place all the blind men in the city. Near them he placed an elephant. Then he told each man to go to the great beast and feel it with his hands. The first blind man advanced to the elephant and felt its head. The second took hold of its ear, the third its tusk, the fourth its trunk, the fifth its foot, the sixth its back, the seventh its tail and the last the tuft of the tail.

"Now then", said the king, "tell us what an elephant looks like."
The first, who had felt its head, said "It's like a pot."
The next, the one who had touched the ear, said "No, an elephant looks like a fan."
"Nonsense!" laughed the man who had fingered the tusk, "It's round, hard and smooth like the handle of a plough."
"Don't be daft!" said the one who had felt the trunk. "The elephant is like a snake."

To cut a long story short, each man described the animal differently. So the foot became a pillar, the back a barn, the tail a rope and the tuft a feather-duster. Each of the blind men was sure that he was right and all the others were wrong. At once a furious argument began. Tempers rose and so did voices. Wild words were flung back and forth. One man punched another. There was a cry of pain. In a few moments the market-place was a tangle of fighting bodies.

The city's learned men looked on at all this, amazed and amused. The king turned to them and said, "I don't know why you're laughing, gentlemen. Your own squabbles are just like the arguments of these poor fellows. You too have your own narrow view of every question and you can't see anyone else's. You must learn to examine ideas all over, as the blind men should have examined the elephant. You'll never understand anything unless you look at it from many different angles."

This story, exemplifying the dangers of adopting a restricted point of view, links well with the question of stereotyping mentioned in Unit B3 Section 4.3.

E   Setting Up a Shrine

For Hindus, building a shrine and performing puja (roughly translated as worship) is a fundamental practice of their religion. It is looked upon as moulding the worshipper's character and disposing his or her mind so that he or she may eventually practise a yoga which will lead to unity with Brahman, the supreme reality. The basic intention is to welcome the god into the home in the manner of an auspicious guest.

1   *Introductory class and group work*

Refer the children back to their imaginary British families: what might be done if a family had to welcome a guest? Children's suggestions will include such things as:

Clean the home.
Prepare a special room and provide soap, towel, flowers.
Cook special food.
Think of things which the guest may appreciate.
Prepare themselves.

In their original groups, the children make a picture or a model of the special room they have prepared (perhaps using cut-outs from magazines). Groups can discuss how they would like to be welcomed to a strange house, and be ready to describe their suggestions to the class as well as explaining their pictures or models.

2   *The simulation*[1]

Point out to the children that the shrine to be set up is only what it might be like in an Indian home, not the real thing. Position a small raised table or an elevated box covered with a cloth in the corner of the classroom. The shrine is to be dedicated to Shiva in his form as Natarajan, the Lord of the Dance, so place an image on the shrine to represent his presence. Several things may now be offered:

*1 An invitation—a mantra to invite the god into the worship. A bell is rung and rice is scattered on the shrine.
2 A seat—a symbolic seat of a flower petal or straw or grass. What is offered depends on the means of the worshipper.
*3 Water—recalling four uses: cleaning the feet (grass or leaves are included); drinking; bathing; general benefits.
*4 Fresh clothes, symbolically represented by a single thread.
*5 Scented paste, spices, etc., placed on the forehead of the god as an honour.
*6 Flowers—usually the flower which is the god's choice.
*7 Incense, burned so as to purify and sweeten the air.

*8 Lamp or burning light—as a comfort and help.
*9 Sweets—offered as specially prepared food for the honoured guest.
10 Betel nut—usually eaten after a meal for cleansing and digestion.
11 A bunch of flowers as a final offering.

If provision of the above is difficult note that the ones asterisked are the crucial ones. Ensure at the very least that 5, 6, 7, 8, and 9 are provided.

3   *Expressive activities*

(a) Hold a short discussion comparing the children's thoughts on welcoming guests to an Indian family's thoughts as they set up a shrine and make their offerings.

(b) Concentrate attention upon Shiva performing the dance of life, exploring such questions as: Why a dancing god? Why the dance of life? Does Nature dance?
Give the children the opportunity to think about all the natural things which "dance with life": leaves on a tree, corn in a field, waves on the sea, clouds in the sky, the earth and the planets rotating, fire, animals, birds, people, sounds. Groups can produce word-pictures of dancing things.

(c) The children express their ideas visually in paintings or by movement, dance and music.

F   The Possessions of Indian People

1   *Introductory activities*

Begin by giving the children some experience in careful observation of articles reasonably familiar to them and in making deductions from what they have seen.

(a) Each child empties the contents of his/her pockets or pencil case on to a sheet of paper. Children then change positions and each makes a list of the objects belonging to someone else. All are asked to consider the questions:
What can you tell immediately from the objects?
Do they belong to a boy or a girl?
Can you tell what they are ued for?
Can you say anything about the home?
After a short general discussion, children note down their conclusions about the particular set of objects in front of them. They then return to their own places, leaving the notes with the objects. Discussion can then follow on the accuracy or otherwise of the inferences drawn by the "visiting" children.

(b) Arrange for a few adults to prepare a set of objects for the children to examine. The children can work in groups, discussing the

---

[1]*The teacher is clearly not "teaching Hinduism", but simply making use of one point of entry into a complex socio-religious culture. The work introduces children to a view of religion (to most Westerners, an abstraction which often seems to be an optional extra to life) as an integral part of normal family life, and to the idea that everyday objects can have special meanings when used in special ways and contexts (i.e. in ritual). The simulation should be an interesting, personally involving and instructive activity for the children.*

possible uses of some of the objects and speculating on what kind of person owns them. The actual owners can be invited into the classroom. Each group can tell the class what they have inferred from the objects; the adult owners can then reveal the actual uses and background details.

(c) Show the children a selection of tools: a shovel, a screwdriver, a foot-pump, some pastry cutters, some secateurs, a paper-knife.

In groups the children consider these questions:

Where would you find these tools?

What are they used for?

What, if anything, can you tell about the physical abilities, interests, skills and occupations of the people who use them?

(d) Suggest to the children that each group's imaginary British family is going into space and will be the first family to colonise a new planet.

Each group has to decide on six objects that its family will take:

Two which will be useful on the new planet.

Two necessities.

Two things of personal or sentimental value.

Each group produces an anonymous list and hands it in.

Announce that the spacecraft has crashed; only the box containing the six special objects has been rescued.

Each group is given one of the lists of objects, but not its own, and tries to work out as much as it can about the family who owned and chose to take them.

An alternative would be for the children to decide what they would put in a box for concealment in the school grounds if they wanted future pupils of a new generation to know what they were like. This could be done on paper or, better, in reality.

2 *The India Box*

Collect in a large box a selection of household and personal articles which exemplify those used by Indian families. Cooking utensils, items of clothing and other artefacts may be borrowed from a local family, or a basic collection may be built up by purchasing from suppliers listed on p. 26. Make sure that the children understand that the articles on view are not typical of all families in India but are simply examples of what may be found.

3 *Group and class activities*

Ask the children to imagine that an Indian family has sent this box over to help them learn about its way of life.

Each group in turn looks at and handles carefully the objects within the box.

Children gather as a class, each group holding an object that interests it and about which it has some ideas.

Each group then makes a further more detailed examination, preparing to answer questions such as:

What is the object made from?

What marks or decorations can you see, and what do you think these represent?

What might it be used for?

What kind of person might use it?

Is it of practical use or for decoration?

Can we learn anything about the place in which the owner lives?

Each group is asked to make a final assessment of the object.

The true function of the objects in the box may be partly revealed by careful observation of selected slides. Otherwise draw the activity to a close by explaining the use and origin of the objects to the children, letting them look at and handle them once again.

The children might later compile a list for a "Britain Box" which would enable the children in their imaginary Indian family to learn about family life in this country.

G **An India Day**

The last day's work on the topic is described by the teacher responsible for it in these words:

To draw this term's topic to a close, I thought it might be fun, and would refresh our minds about the things we learned earlier on, if we had a day when we did Indian things. We should have a day when we wore our saris or dhotis, worked as they might in an Indian school, had an Indian meal, listened to an Indian story and played Indian games. The children thought this was a grand idea.

The furniture in the room was removed, except for the cooker which we needed for the curry and rice. The children put on their saris and dhotis and sat cross-legged on the floor with their slates in front of them.

We studied the Hindu alphabet and number charts, and wrote on our slates the multiplication tables that we knew. We copied some Hindu writing on to the slate. Every now and again, as we went along, we talked about all the different things we had learned.

Our curry and rice we ate outside in the sun.

The afternoon was spent in playing games, "Guli Danda" and "Kotla Chhapai", and listening to the story "The Valiant Chatti-maker".

Guli Danda

Two teams are picked. A long bit of wood (danda) like a rounders bat is used to flick up the 'guli', a

banana-shaped bit of wood, from a small hole in the ground. The first player flicks up the guli as far away as possible, then puts the danda down over the hole. If a fielder catches the guli, the player is out. If it is not caught, a fielder picks up the guli and throws it from where it is so as to hit the danda or land back in the hole. If he succeeds, the player is out; if he fails, the same player can have three more goes. A player who misses the guli three times is out!

When a player has had three goes, the guli is flicked again, and the batting team guesses how many 'bucks' it has fallen from the hole (a buck is the length of the danda). If the fielders agree with the guess, the batting side scores that same number of points. If the fielders disagree, the distance is measured; if correct, the batting team gets the points and the same player starts again. If incorrect, the player is out and the next player is in.

Kotla Chhapai—the hunter's whip
A number of boys sit in a circle. One boy runs round the outside with a whip made of a twisted rag or handkerchief. He is the hunter. If any boy in the circle peeps over his shoulder or feels behind his back before the hunter has dropped the whip, the hunter can run back and give him one stroke. Once the hunter has dropped it behind a boy's back, the hunter tries to run right round the circle before the boy has noticed, pick it up again, and give him three strokes. Then they swop places. If, however, the boy hears it drop or finds it before the hunter has reached him again, he picks it up and runs after him in the same clockwise direction, hoping to catch him up and beat him three times before he reaches the empty place in the circle and sits down. This is a game to keep you alert!
(This game is usually played only by boys in India, but could of course be played by girls as well.)

REVIEW BY THE CLASS TEACHER

The main areas of work undertaken by the class have been described. There were, however, lots of 'infill' lessons, drama work, and visits from local people who had been to India and could tell the children at first hand what it is like to be caught in a monsoon or to bargain in the local bazaars. Pure discussion lessons were held on some of the Oxfam posters, on current affairs in India (a train disaster), on the problems faced by minority groups, on why people in hotter climates have dark skin, and on the use of natural materials for utensils.

I was generally very pleased with the way the children received and responded to the scheme of work. I am, however, aware of some glaring failures. The saddest, and the one I regret the most, was my inability to get Indian people to visit us. The problem mainly was for them to get time off work. The introductory lessons were achieved by inviting a nurse, recently back from nursing for fifteen years in India, to act as a substitute.

I had hoped to arrange for a visit by a group of Indian children from a Southampton school to share games, songs and dancing. This proved too difficult, due to summer term events and transport costs. So, not having sufficient knowledge of Indian dances, I sadly decided to give this area a miss. It was mentioned, but never actually experienced.

I am still not sure whether I got the right balance between the realistic and the romantic sides of India, between wealth and poverty. Generally I tried to put across the idea that the people of India do similar things to us: they work, bring up families, tell stories, laugh and smile and enjoy life and are faced with problems of all kinds irrespective of where and how they live.

This topic excited and stimulated the children. Daily I was asked what we would be doing tomorrow. They looked forward to coming to school. Their interest was sustained by careful planning of the more exciting events—always something else to look forward to! The fact that they were interested and involved meant that I had few discipline problems. The children wanted to know, but there were plenty of creative outlets for the restless amongst them.

I was pleasantly surprised and pleased to see how the children's self-confidence developed over the term when dealing with the many visitors. They proved themselves to be quite charming, responding politely to questions and asking reasonably intelligent questions of the visitors. Even 'thank you' letters were written with a good grace! It was a real social education for them.

Basically it was a term of fun and enjoyment. Each of us shared the information and skills that we had acquired. We admired each others' handicraft, and enjoyed the companionship and sense of "Special Occasion" our Indian meals afforded us. There was the joy of sitting outside in the sun wearing a cool sari or dhoti listening to stories that stretched our imaginations; the wariness of trying strange and often exotic foods; the delight and amusement caused when trying to pronounce Indian names and words; the satisfaction of achieving or producing something to take home to show Mum and Dad; the pride felt when watching the television and being able to say "I know something about that country". Eventually we built up a more complete picture. It was a term which, I hope, has enriched the lives of the children and encouraged them to look more openly at the cultures around them.

The scheme of work for the first year within the school has been outlined in detail. Very little mention of celebration, festivals or rites of passage has been made. This was intentional. Within the topic grid for the school, the middle years have the theme of "Celebrations and Customs". I envisage

the children following on from this term's work by studying again the story of Rama and Sita. This time they will look at it through the celebration of Diwali—a less extensive topic, allowing for a balance of subjects within the curriculum.

In the last year at the school, the children will study, under one of the themes "Growing up", "Journeys" or "Time", some Indian rites of passage. I would include in any of the above themes an Indian wedding ceremony. Rituals relating to the naming of children are also of interest. Whether or not to look at ceremonies relating to death (introducing Hindu ideas of Karma and reincarnation) would depend on the children and on what work had previously been done.

Resources and Addresses

Posters	Individual gods and goddesses (Ganesha, Vishnu, Hanuman, Krishna, Rama and Sita)	Gohil Emporium or Oberoi's Gift Shop
	Hindu Festivals	Pictorial Charts Educational Trust
Slides	Hindu Worship	The Slide Centre
	Durga Puja	Bury-Peerless
	Young in India	UNICEF
	Family in Vadala Village	V.C.O.A.D. or Oxfam
	Transport	,,
	Family in Bombay	,,
	Morning in Zekri Village	,,
	City and Village Trade	,,
	Main gods and goddesses of the Hindus	Bury Peerless
Photopacks	Western India; City and Village Life	C.W.D.E. or Oxfam
	Samanvaya School: an Indian Community Study	,,
Artefacts	Samples of foods and materials	The Commonwealth Institute
	"India Boxes", with selected artefacts	Local R.E. Resources Centres
	General (statues of gods; Diwali cards; dressed dolls; coins; perfumes; spices; saris; begging bowls; etc.)	Articles of Faith, or Gohil Emporium, or Oberoi's Gift Shop

(Family in Vadala Village, Transport, Family in Bombay, Morning in Zekri Village, City and Village Trade — "Western India" Set (superceded by photopack))

Books for the teacher

P. Bahree	*India, Pakistan and Bangladesh: A Handbook for Teachers*	S.O.A.S. 1982
D. Killingley ed.	*A Handbook of Hinduism for Teachers*	Grevatt & Grevatt 1984
H. Kanitkar & R. Jackson	*Hindus in Britain*	S.O.A.S. 1982
Ruth P. Jhabvala	*Get Ready for Battle*	Penguin 1978
E. Rice	*Mother India's Children*	Orbis 1972
	India in the Classroom	Commonwealth Institute

Books for the Classroom

P. Bahree	*The Hindu World*	Macdonald 1985
C. Barker	*Arjun and His Village*	OUP 1975
M. Blakeley	*Nahda's Family*	A. & C. Black 1977
P. Bridger	*A Hindu Family in Britain*	R.E.P. 1975
R. Godden	*The Valiant Chatti-maker*	Macmillan 1983
S. Hobden	*Mother Theresa*	SCM Press 1972
S. Mitter	*Living in Calcutta*	Wayland 1980
J. Solomon	*Bobbi's New Year*	H. Hamilton 1980
	A Present for Mum	H. Hamilton 1981
	Wedding day	H. Hamilton 1981
B. Thompson	*The Story of Rama*	Kestrel 1980
T. Tigwell	*Sakina in India*	A. & C. Black 1982
J. Troughton	*Rama and Sita*	Blackie 1975
	A Hindu Home	C.E.M. 1981

(*Bobbi's New Year*, *A Present for Mum*, *Wedding day* — in "The Way we Live" series)

	How a Hindu Prays *The Story of Diwali* }	Minority Group Support Service
	The Monkey and the Mango Tree *The Tiger's Breakfast and Other* *Stories* *The Story of Mahabharata* *Tales from the Indian Classics* }	Soma Books
Comics	Rama, Hanuman, Garuda, Krishna and Rukmini, Velu Thompi, Panna and Hadi Rani	Soma Books

Addresses of Producers and Suppliers

Action Aid, PO Box 69, 208 Upper Street, London N1 1RZ

Articles of Faith (Mrs. C. M. Winstanley), 123 Nevile Road, Salford M7 0PP

Bury Peerless, 22 King's Avenue, Minnis Bay, Birchington, Kent CT7 9QL

C.W.D.E. (Centre for World Development Education), Regents College, Inner Circle, Regents Park, London NW1 4NS

C.E.M. (Christian Education Movement), Lancaster House, Borough Road, Isleworth, Middlesex TW7 5DU

Commonwealth Institute, Kensington High Street, London W8 6NQ

Gohil Emporium (Indian Arts and Crafts), 355 Stratford Road, Birmingham 11

Grevatt & Grevatt, 9 Rectory Drive, Newcastle-upon-Tyne NE3 1XT

Indian Tourist Office, 7 Cork Street, London W1X 2AP

Minority Group Support Service, Southfields, South Street, Coventry CV1 5EJ

Oberoi's Gift Shop, 101 The Broadway, Southall, Middlesex

OXFAM Education Department, 274 Banbury Road, Oxford

Pictorial Charts Educational Trust, 27 Kirchen Road, London W13 0UD

S.O.A.S. (School of Oriental and African Studies), University of London, Malet Street, London WC1E 7HP

The Slide Centre, 143 Chatham Road, London SW11 6SR

Soma Books (Independent Publishing Company Ltd.), 38 Kennington Lane, London SE11 4LS

UNICEF, 55/56 Lincoln's Inn Fields, London WC2A 3NB

V.C.O.A.D. (Voluntary Committee on Overseas Aid and Development) is now incorporated in C.W.D.E.

Memories and Remembering

Context

The scheme presented here is developed from work done with 8–11 year-olds in a Primary school in a country area. It offers a good example of a multi-disciplinary topic in which R.E. plays a natural and important part, along with Environmental Studies, History, Language and Science. Since it includes suggestions about festivals of Harvest, it would most appropriately be planned for the Autumn term.

Initially, the intention was to devise a scheme focused on "Festivals", and a wide-ranging Topic Web was produced. How was this vast and airy structure to be converted into something manageable, purposeful, and significant to the children? The process was as follows.

The realisation that festivals are, in any community (family, village, church, etc.), occasions for remembering events or myths which have been influential in its origin or growth, led to a new Topic Web with "Memories and Remembering" at its centre; although still too diffuse, this Web contained ideas which related to the children's interests, implied a variety of activities, and made use of resources in the local environment. A large number of practical possibilities had thus far been envisaged.

At this point decisions had to be made as to the aims and objectives which would control both the selection of material and the method of dealing with it. (These are set out overleaf.)

A convergent model, showing the content and activities which various subject-areas can contribute to the topic, was constructed. The chart produced was simpler than that shown overleaf, which has been amplified so as to incorporate material to be found in the fully developed scheme.

A detailed scheme of work was finally produced.

Aims and Objectives

The general aim of the topic is to develop the children's understanding of the nature of memory, and their awareness of its function in their lives and in the life of human communities. The element of "feeling" is emphasised with the intention of increasing children's sensitivity towards realities which are intangible, expressible only partially and indirectly, but nevertheless valued by many people (whether or not they would class themselves as "religious").

More specifically, the scheme has the objectives of enabling the children to:

become more aware of their own senses and capacities;

gain greater insight into their own emotions and into the emotional significance of physical objects and events;

gain greater insight into human relationships, in family, local community, and another culture;

understand the importance of "group memory" within a community;

discover something of the nature of religious celebration in Judaism and in Christianity, and of the meaning of such celebration for the participants.

Books referred to in the text are listed at the end of this scheme.

OVERVIEW

1 Individual Memories
2 Family Memories
3 Remembering and Forgetting
4 Memories around us
5 Celebrations
6 How Jews remember
7 How Christians remember
8 Having a Celebration

1 Individual Memories

Introduce *group discussions* on children's early memories, by reading excerpts from *Cider with Rosie*, for example:

(a) *Lost!* (Ch. 1). *"For the first time I was out of the sight of humans—I put back my head and howled and the sun hit me smartly in the face like a bully . . ."*

(b) *First day at school* (Ch. 3). *"The morning came, without any warning my sisters surrounded me, wrapped me in scarves, tied up my bootlaces and stuffed a baked potato in my pocket. 'You're starting school today.' 'I ain't. I'm stoppin' 'ome'"*.

(c) *Sick child* (Ch. 9). *"Later as the red night closed on me . . . teeth chattered, my knees came up in my mouth . . . my shirt was a kind of enveloping sky wrapping my goosey skin . . ."*

(d) *Mother* (Ch. 7). Mother *"lived by no clocks and unpunctuality was bred in her bones. She was particularly offhand where buses were concerned—not till she heard its horn did she ever begin to get ready. Then she would cram on her hat and fly round the kitchen . . ."*

ENVIRONMENTAL STUDIES

Identifying memorial
  objects (e.g. albums, log-
  books, tombstones) in
  neighbourhood
Discovering information
  contained in memorial
  objects
Interviewing local people
  about their memories
Observing activities at
  Harvest-time
Exploring the local church
  and its services
Historical investigations
  prior to celebration events

LANGUAGE

Listening to stories and
  extracts from books
Contributing orally
Engaging in discussion (on
  stories, growing up, memorial
  objects, dreams, celebrations,
  the Creation story, etc.)
Descriptive writing
Personal writing
Recording information
Compiling lists
Conducting interviews
Writing invitations to a
  celebration event

HOME ECONOMICS

Organising for
  celebration event
Preparing food for
  celebration event
  (Preparing food
    relating to Jewish
    Succoth and
    Christian Eucharist)

MEMORIES AND REMEMBERING

SCIENCE

Experiments on
  ability to memorise
The human body:
  reflexes and automatic
  functions
Instinctive behaviour
  in animals
Memory functions in
  computers

RELIGIOUS STUDIES

Memorial objects
  in the local church
Harvest festivals,
  and beliefs implied in
  them
The Creation story
  in Genesis
The Jewish festival
  of Succoth
The Christian
  Eucharist
Implicitly religious
  material (personal
  identity, relationships
  etc)

DRAMA

Acting scenes from
  early memories
Acting scenes from
  books
Dramatising a scene
  designed to test
  factual memory
"Doing" some of the
  ritual of the Jewish
  festival of Succoth,
  and of the Christian
  Eucharist
Creating, and taking
  part in, a
  celebration event

ART AND CRAFT

Arranging display of
  photographs etc.
Making collage of
  life in the past
Constructing Family
  Trees
Illustrating personal
  writing
Designing a memorial
  object
Building & decorating
  of Succah
Preparing decorations
  etc. for a celebration
  event

Alternative, or additional, material is available in the following "classics", as well as in much recent literature:

Huckleberry Finn Ch. 2	Doing something naughty
Kilvert's Diary: entry for Sat. 16 Jan. 1875	Playing games
Dream Days: The Magic Ring	A visit to the circus
Lark Rise to Candleford Ch. 2	Meeting gypsies and old people
Treasure Island Ch. 1	Fears and fantasies
Past and Present: a poem by T. Hood, in *The Golden Treasury*	Places

Personal writing

Children write, in narrative or poetic form, about some particular experience which they remember. A few suggestions, collected from the class, might act as useful memory-triggers for others: e.g. being naughty; my Grandad; a funny thing happened . . .; being alone; going on a visit. (The inclusion of conversation can enliven a script.)

Several pieces of writing could be grouped into an autobiographical booklet, with an appropriately chosen title ("Myself when young"; "Me once"; "Early days") and illustrations: it could be based on the four *Cider with Rosie* headings above. (One likely result of such work is a recognition by the children of their need for other people, to give them friendship, love and a sense of belonging.)

Group drama

Children work in groups to prepare short scenes based on actual recollected experiences, and present these to the rest of the class. Questioning and discussion follow, on circumstances, characters, reactions and prospects.

Two variations can add interest:
(1) Having introduced the circumstances and the characters before starting the action, stop the action at some critical point, moving straight into discussion, the children speculating on what may happen and what the consequences are likely to be.
(2) Having acted the scene without any introductory remarks, actors join spectators in discussing who the characters were, what was happening, and why.

Scenes from *Cider with Rosie*, or from the other books to which reference has been made, could also be enacted, with discussion following: some children might find this easier than handling personal memories in a public manner.

Display of photographs of the children when younger

The teacher collects, from the children or their parents, photographs taken of them several years previously, and displays these (well spaced out, and numbered) round the classroom. Two possible activities are:

(1) Identity parade. Children move round in silence, listing the photo numbers and writing alongside the names of their classmates; stop when time limit has elapsed, and check the scores.
(2) Each child brings a recent photograph, and places it beside the early one. In small groups, children discuss these pairs of photos of themselves, focusing on how they have changed; individual writing in which "then" and "now" are compared would be appropriate. (See the useful material in CEM's "Exploring a Theme—Myself".)

The teacher could make an interesting contribution by presenting, in photographs and slides, some personal memories.

2   Family Memories

Classroom display

Children bring, and arrange as a display in the classroom, items which are significant in their families as reminders of people (e.g. famous, or infamous, relatives) and events (e.g. weddings, holidays, anniversaries): objects, documents, newspaper cuttings, pictures, albums and tape-recordings may all appear. Each child provides a label for the item brought, and may be asked to say a few words about it.

Make use of some items as stimuli for reflection and discussion, on both
(a) the thoughts and feelings of the people involved in the original experience, and
(b) the value and influence of the item as a reminder.

Who were the people involved? What were they doing or experiencing? Where and when was it happening? What were they thinking and feeling at the time? Why did they choose this particular item as a suitable reminder of the experience? How sure can we be about our answers to these questions?

Does the item serve as a good reminder of the person or event? How does it achieve this? Would something else do equally well? Is the person or event worth remembering? What effect, if any, does the "memory" item have on you? Would you preserve it for the next generation? Why (or why not)?

Children each choose one experience from the past year, and one from a previous year—exciting, comic, interesting, but not necessarily of great significance—and decide on two objects which would help them to recall these experiences. Their choices might be subjects of oral contributions or of written accounts, perhaps after the actual objects have been brought into class at a later date.

Interviews
Anyone who is approachable and co-operative can supply useful material to children engaged on this topic, but the handling of such material can be difficult. Discuss beforehand with the class what areas they will investigate, and how their questions may best be worded; prepare a pro-forma with question headings and spaces for at least key-words of answers received (to be amplified as soon as possible after the interview). Headings might include:

Childhood memories
School: buildings, work, play, teachers
Working life: first job; changes in work
Married life: getting married; bringing up children
War-time: civilian activities and privations; service in the Forces
Leisure activities and interests
Changes: What things do you especially miss? What improvements have you seen? What things do you dislike in today's world? Are there any things which you wish you had done differently?

If possible, tape-record some interviews, for playing back (edited, preferably by the children themselves) in class.

Interviews with members of their own families might lead on to such activities as:

Making individual lists comparing family life 25 or 50 years ago with family life today, using two columns headed "Similarities" and "Differences".
Making a class collage of "Family life 50 years ago" or "When I was your age . . .".
Constructing Family Trees, incorporating summarised information about relatives and ancestors.
Discussing and classifying the kinds of memories most often referred to in the course of interviews.

The interviews—and the experience of interviewing people—will provide plenty of material for worthwhile discussions.

3 Remembering and Forgetting
Experiments on memory
(a) Test children's ability to remember simple information presented orally (e.g. numbers consisting of 4, 5, 6 or 7 digits; a series of objects—the "My aunt went to London and bought . . ." game) and chart the results.

(b) Test children's ability to carry out correctly a sequence of actions in accordance with instructions, and chart the results.
(c) Test children's visual memory. This can be done competitively (as on TV) by showing film clips, each followed by questions on points of detail. "Kim's Game" (displaying a variety of objects for a short time, after which the viewers have to list as many of the objects as they can remember) is always fun, but circumstances may make it more practicable for objects to be held up, one after the other, by the teacher, or even for pictures of objects to be projected on a screen. (Children might be interested to hear the account of the game as originally played by Kim, in Kipling's story: *Kim* Ch. 9).

These experiments, (a), (b) and (c), could all be carried out by the children themselves, working in small groups, findings being shared with the whole class.
(d) Explore the reliability of memory by dramatising a scene, then examining it closely. For example:

A group of children dramatises a robbery;
Another group, acting as a police squad, interviews witnesses (the majority of the class), one at a time and as privately as possible (the "police" group must not of course see the original dramatisation.);
The "police" group presents the "facts" gathered from the witnesses, preferably in both verbal and visual form;
Compare the "facts" (descriptions of the robbers, the course of events, etc.), and discuss why the witnesses do not entirely agree;
Finally, the "police" group could attempt a reconstruction of the robbery.

Discussion on remembering and forgetting
Matters may well be raised in connection with (a) to (d) above which deserve further exploration: for instance, children could profitably discuss, perhaps with reference to some experiences of their own, in what situations exact memorising is important.

Tell a story in which forgetfulness has unfortunate consequences, and consider such questions as: What kinds of action do you forget to do? What kinds of experience do you forget about? What do your parents forget? What do you wish your parents would forget? What would it be like to forget everything? What would it be like to remember everything?

Trying to forget. Read out (after giving any necessary context) a passage such as this from Ch. 1 of *I am David: "David let his head sink upon his chest and tried to fight against the flood of memory that poured over him, the terror, the hatred, the frightening questions that burned like fire within him."* Consider what can be done about unpleasant

memories: can they be consciously erased, or outgrown in time, or rendered harmless as better understanding is gained, or a better personal relationship established (e.g. by an act of forgiveness)?

Trying to remember. Ask the children to contribute ideas about aids to memory, and make a list of these. (Were any children aware of using any such aids during the "Experiments on memory" above?) Introduce the idea of verbal and visual "association"—one word, sign or action takes one on, without conscious thought, to the next. Ask children to give examples, which might include: singing a song; travelling between home and school; performing on a musical instrument. (In these three examples, the "remembering" seems to be done by the vocal cords, the feet, and the fingers!)

Some other areas (more loosely related to the Topic, but by no means insignificant) which might be explored are:

Automatic actions and reflexes in the human body (e.g. circulation of blood; digestive processes; responses to pain; eye adjustment for different intensities of light; the balance mechanism). The very act of remembering may cause an involuntary change (e.g. smiling, blushing).

Instinctive behaviour in other living creatures (e.g. nest building; migration; direction-finding).

Pets. Training them to respond in particular ways. Do they have conscious memories like ours?

Dreams. What experiences seem to be remembered in dreams? Are there some elements which often recur? Are there some elements which occur in many people's dreams? What is remembered of the content of dreams? How can dreams be distinguished from reality? Do dreams "tell" us anything?

"Memory" functions in computers. Are there some things that computers cannot remember?

4 Memories around us

Memorials

Children work in groups to compile lists of memorials (i.e. "memory-banks") of which they are aware, under headings such as: Home and family (photographs, diaries, furniture . . . and people); School (Log book, pictures, articles in store-rooms . . . and people); Neighbourhood (War Memorial, buildings, artefacts, names (people, roads, places), landscape features . . . and people); Church (list of incumbents, windows, memorial plaques, tombstones, registers . . . and people).

Select some of these memorials, and investigate and discuss two questions about them, viz: How did this come into existence? Why was the memory expressed in this particular form?

Each child chooses a personal experience, or an event recently or currently in the news, and devises, describes and illustrates a suitable memorial which is intended to keep the occurrence in the consciousness of the family or the general public. The class as a whole might produce an appropriate memorial for some school event of importance.

What is remembered

Refer the children back to sub-themes 1 and 2 above, in which material was drawn from their personal "memory-bank", from the family "memory-bank", and from various people.

Children (perhaps best working in pairs) discover some of the information held in other memorials, recording it in brief with the aid of the categories previously established in their group work.

Children talk about things which have specially interested them. Their observations are certain to raise questions worth discussing in class; for example:

War Memorial. The number of names for 1914/18 differs greatly from the number of 1939/45—why? How and why are wars remembered?

Buildings. Some are used for other than their original purposes. Why? Should they be preserved?

Tombstones. Discuss the sentiments and symbols found on them. For whose benefit were they erected?

Consider the reliability of the information afforded by these various memorials. Are some kinds of memorial more reliable than others (e.g. stone inscriptions than people's words)? How can we judge? Do different memorials confirm, or contradict one another? Where else might one look for confirmation? Can we ever be absolutely certain?

Many memorials were originally intended to exert some kind of influence on the beholder. (If the children did the work suggested in the final paragraph of "Memorials" above, discuss what influences they hoped their designed memorials might have.) Consider some memorials from this point of view: do they, and the memories they enshrine, affect people at all, and if they do, then in what way? What kinds of memorial might make memories really come alive, with the power to change people's ideas and attitudes? The suggestion may well be made—otherwise the teacher may make it—that only a shared activity (a party, a simulation of the original event, a festival) is adequate; this kind of memorial is explored in the following sections.

5 Celebrations

Birthdays and other special occasions

Tell a story about a birthday (e.g. Eeyore's birthday, in *Winnie the Pooh*; Ben's disappointing birthday in *A Dog so Small*).

Discuss reasons why birthdays are treated as special occasions, ideas being listed on blackboard or sheet of paper. (Not so much remembering the birth—except perhaps for the parents—as expressing love for the person, endeavouring to give happiness and encouragement for the future, and, especially with children, marking a stage of growth; and children may suggest other reasons.)

Working in small groups, children make a list of the ingredients of a "good" birthday (the right presents, cake, no upsets, etc.); then add, drawing on their own experiences, all the elements they can think of which might be present in a larger-scale celebration (music, dancing, processions, decorations, etc.) Build up a public list of these ideas.

Harvest festivities

Display a large calendar, on which Christmas and Easter are marked. Can the children add any other large-scale festivals and celebrations? (It would be sensible to give them a few days notice of this question.) If Harvest is not mentioned now, let it appear naturally as the work proceeds. Show slides of the wheat cycle. What part of the cycle would people be likely to celebrate? Children suggest some ways in which Harvest might be celebrated by the farming community. What types of harvesting might be celebrated by other communities?

Tell the children about beliefs and practices relating to Harvest. People believed that nature was controlled by the Corn Mother or Earth Goddess; if she was pleased, the harvest would be good. The last sheaf of corn to be cut was special, and from it was made a symbol—cross, bell, fan, human image, etc., depending on the region—of the Corn Mother: this "Corn Idol" came to be called a "Corn Dolly". The symbol occupied a place of honour in the Harvest Home supper, celebrated by all the villagers. If possible, obtain cereal for the children to make corn dollies (simple designs, and instructions, are given in *Origins of Festivals and Feasts*, pages 81–83).

Only in the mid-19th Century did the Christian Church in England start holding special services of thanksgiving for the Harvest. Soon, Harvest Festival became part of the Christian calendar, and either incorporated or displaced the Harvest supper. Ask children to talk about their experiences of Harvest Festivals in the local church, and discuss such questions as: Why is the Corn Mother not mentioned? What is the festival intended to bring freshly to the minds of the participants? (Harvest hymns give a clear answer, viz. God's creativity and goodwill, and people's dependence and respon-

sibility to co-operate.) Much useful material can be found in *Harvest and Thanksgiving*.

It would be appropriate here to look with the children at the Biblical source of the beliefs underlying the Christian festival, the Creation story in Genesis Ch.1.1–2.4. One class studied the text, then split into seven groups, each preparing a pictorial representation of one day in the sequence, the seven pictures being joined to form a frieze. In the course of this work many questions were considered, including "Who wrote it?", "When was it written?", and "What was the writer trying to say to his readers by telling this story?". The class went on to explore attitudes of people today towards the created order, and made a scrapbook of materials on various environmental issues, local, national and international. Children became more aware of how people use and abuse, the "given" resources of the world, and of how unequally the earth's wealth is distributed.

6 How Jews remember

Judaism, like Christianity, is a religion which has roots in historical events, events which are re-membered and celebrated in various festivals. One of the major Jewish festivals is Succoth (a word which means "Booths" or "Tabernacles"). This is a joyful festival, linked to the in-gathering of the autumn harvest but primarily, for Jews, a remem-brance of the wanderings of their ancestors in the wilderness, after their escape from slavery in Egypt. In particular they recall God's saving power in protecting and sustaining them during their journey from Egypt to the Promised Land of Canaan.

The observant Jew recalls that period by building a temporary shelter (a Succah), decorating it with harvest fruits, and spending part of each day in it; it is a reminder that all human life is insecure and transitory, dependent on the permanence, stead-fastness and goodness of God.

The work follows naturally from that done in connection with Harvest celebrations; here there is an additional layer of experiences and meanings to be explored. Why is it that Jews go "camping out" in the autumn (not the best time of year)? Would you believe it—the answer is in the Bible! Let's find out—and join them. (In practice, the best starting-point may be to "join them". This is the approach, which has been used successfully with this age-range, recommended here. However, others may prefer to start with one of the other major elements described in the next paragraph.)

The festival of Succoth contains five main elements:

The story

The wilderness wanderings of the Israelites (the ancestors of the Jews): see Leviticus Ch.23.34 and 39–43 for the law about the festival; the long account of the wanderings begins at Exodus 15.22 (a

summary, with Moses' criticism of the people for their lack of faith and obedience, appears in Deuteronomy Ch. 1–3).

Celebration

Building and decorating the Succah.

Special prayers, thanksgivings and songs.

Signs and symbols

Family and friends gathering in the Succah.

Arba'ah Minim, i.e. the four symbolic elements— palm branch, etrog, myrtle, willow (for full explanation of these, see *Understanding Your Jewish Neighbour*).

Customs

Sweet foods.

Pictures of the patriarchs adorn the Succah. to which they are special guests (ushpizim).

Inner meaning

Dependence on God, both in the wilderness and today. The transitoriness and pilgrim nature of human life. (All the patriarchs spent periods with no settled home, as did the wandering Israelites. In later centuries, including our own, many Jews have been refugees.)

The procedure commences with a rather mystifying (but enjoyable) activity, moves into reflection and discussion, and concludes with a little celebration. Ideally, a full-size Succah would be built in the school grounds; if this is not practicable, a small-scale structure in the classroom would have to do . . . small models, on shoe-box bases, only as a last resort.

Give the children the basic instructions for building and decorating the Succah (see below). Discuss these with them, then explore the school grounds for a suitable site. Let building commence! (The children might be left to organise themselves as they think necessary, or could be divided beforehand into groups, each with a specific task such as: collecting materials, building, preparing the harvest fruits, making pictures of the patriarchs, planning and fixing the decorations.)

Ask the children to think carefully, as the work progresses, about what sort of people might construct such a temporary dwelling, and for what reason.

When building and decorating are finished, the children, individually or in groups, list all the questions that occur to them about the activity in which they have been engaged.

In response to these questions, the teacher tells the story of the festival; its meaning, and its significance for Jews today, are further elucidated in discussion.

The class invites groups from other classes to visit the Succah, where they join in simple Jewish songs ('Shalom chaverim' which means 'Welcome friends') and are introduced to the story. Each child is also given a sweet, as a reminder that the Jews eat sweet foods at this season to represent their hope of a sweet year to come.

Instructions for building and decorating the Succah.

(a) Building

The Succah is essentially a temporary dwelling: it should be large enough for a person or small group to stand or sit in. The roof is especially important: it should be possible to see the sky through it. The roofing material must conform to three rules: it must have grown from the earth (i.e. not be quarried or mixed); it must not still be connected with the earth (i.e. must have been cut down): it must not be subject to ritual impurity (i.e. no animal skins). The most suitable materials are branches, straw, bamboo, timber. A Succah built indoors or under a porch or balcony is not valid. The walls can be wood, metal, canvas, brick or stone. Use may be made of an outside house-wall. Commonly, three or four walls are built, with an opening or doorway for entrance.

(b) Decoration

The accent of the festival is on harvest joy. The Succah is therefore decorated with harvest fruits, flowers and other pleasing objects. The names and pictures of the founding fathers of Judaism (Abraham, Isaac, Jacob, Moses, Aaron, Joseph, David) are often put on the walls, as they are invited to join the family in the Succah.

Much useful detail on Succoth is given in pages 126–130 of the comprehensive volume *The Jewish Catalogue*.

7 How Christians Remember

Background for the teacher

Remembering is important to Christians. For most Christians the principal way of remembering Jesus as the Christ is through the celebration of Communion. Just as there are various names for this celebration (The Holy Communion, The Eucharist, the Lord's Supper, The Mass, The Breaking of Bread, The Liturgy), so there are various interpretations of its significance, though the idea of communion (being united) is central to them all. Each name indicates one aspect which is emphasised in a particular tradition:

"The Holy Communion" emphasises that Christians are consciously bringing to mind their unity with their Lord and with one another when sharing bread and wine in this way.

"The Eucharist" (derived from the Greek *eucharisto*, meaning 'I give thanks') emphasises the element of thanksgiving. Christians thank God for the life and death of Jesus, particularly in the prayer of consecration said over the bread and wine (which are thereby set apart to be used only for the act of communion).

"The Lord's Supper" reminds participants of the historical origins of the celebration, in Jesus' own

actions of taking, blessing, breaking and sharing bread, and sharing wine, with the instruction to 'do this in remembrance of me'.

"The Mass": this name may be derived from the Latin words of dismissal at the end of the rite, thus emphasising the sending out of the participants into the world as bearers of Christ in their own lives. For many, however, the emphasis is rather on the re-offering (the re-presenting before God) of Christ's total offering of himself as a sacrifice on behalf of sinful mankind.

"The Breaking of Bread" emphasises the simplicity of the rite, and is a biblical term for the practice of the first Christians.

"The (Holy, or Divine) Liturgy": the term normally used in the Orthodox Churches for the service of Communion. It emphasises worship, according to a prescribed traditional pattern, as the highest expression of Christian faith and unity.

Three principles should be borne in mind when planning work on this subject:

(1) Avoid becoming entangled in the theological and liturgical differences and problems. It is sufficient to point out to the children that there is diversity, e.g. by using slides to show how the setting of the celebration may vary from the simple to the elaborate.

(2) Focus on those elements which relate to the general topic, Memories and Remembering. Establish *what* is being remembered and the common features of *how* the memory is recalled and expressed now.

(3) Identify clearly which elements are accessible to the children at their present stage of development. Identification may be aided by distinguishing four aspects, namely:

(a) The story
The oldest extant document containing an account of the Last Supper is Paul's first letter to the Christians at Corinth (see 1 Corinthians 11.23–26). The Gospels also tell the story: Mark 14.22–25; Luke 22.13–21; Matthew 26.26–29.

(b) Celebration and customs
Although the story is common to all Christian groups, the manner of celebrating is very diverse! However, four central actions are always performed: bread and wine are taken, blessed, broken (in the case of the bread), and shared among some or all of the people present.

(c) Signs and symbols
Again, Christian traditions vary widely, but in all traditions bread (perhaps in the form of wafers) and wine (perhaps mixed with water)

are used. Apart from these, different groups use various symbols to help people to concentrate on Jesus and to worship him, e.g. crosses, crucifixes, altars, incense, candles, holy water, bells.

(d) Inner meanings
Interpretations and emphases differ; but for most Christians the central idea is that by re-enacting Jesus' special acts at the Last Supper the members of the congregation join with Christ and with fellow-worshippers, and with all, both past and present, who acknowledge Jesus as their Lord.

The teacher will find useful material in *The Eucharist*, a book intended for use with Secondary school pupils.

Scheme of work
The theme could be developed from the starting-point of any one of the four aspects listed above: the story; celebration and customs; signs and symbols; inner meanings. Some suggestions follow.

(1) Begin by reminding the children of the topic—Memories and Remembering. Introduce the idea of a meal as a way of remembering some important event, e.g. a family/local/national/international anniversary; the retirement or arrival of a new member of the school; rescue from a fantasy island on which they were all once shipwrecked. Questions to be considered include:

What foods would be appropriate, and why?

How would the food be presented and shared?

What would be done or said at the meal in order to bring the event vividly to mind?

How do the children think they would feel during the meal?

In what ways is the meal unlike an ordinary meal, and thus special?

(2) Focus attention on the symbol of bread[1] (easier to handle than wine!) If possible, make a loaf and create an opportunity for sharing it out (e.g. at an Assembly). Discuss the idea that bread can be a symbol for the most basic things we need. What could it stand for? Food, warmth, love, family . . .? Is bread a good symbol? What might Christians mean when they refer to Jesus as the "Bread of Life"? Explain that the "breaking" of bread reminds Christians that Jesus' body was "broken" on the cross; and that breaking the bread makes sharing possible.

(3) Invite a Christian visitor to the class, to tell the story of the Last Supper and to describe, in

---

[1]*While it is right to focus here on the bread, it should be borne in mind that wine, as well as bread, is an essential element of the celebration. The wine represents blood, that which is the principle of life: participants are not feeding on a dead Jesus, but sharing in his risen life. In the community of worshipping believers, Jesus is being "re-membered", being "put back together" in a "body" which is to express his life, teaching and example; the celebration looks not only (not primarily?) to the past, but to the future and the present. The teacher needs to be ready to say something, in appropriate words, along these lines, even if only in answer to children's questions.*

simple terms, how he/she celebrates the event now. (Brief the visitor concerning the principles set out in "Background for the Teacher" above.)

Use slides, filmstrips, music, personal accounts, etc. to supplement the visitor's presentation, and to illustrate the diversity of ways of celebrating the story and the central features of the worship. Identify with the class some of the ways in which the celebration:

remembers the Last Supper and the life of Jesus;

is a *shared* experience for the community.

(4) Many teachers feel that a simple simulation of a Communion service is valuable. It is important to make clear to the children that they will not be taking part in an actual Communion service, but will be trying to discover what Christians do and to understand what the celebration means to Christians.

In one school, children planned their own service.[2] This gave them an opportunity to use art work, things they had written about Jesus, and music which they had composed. One child read an account of the Last Supper. Blackcurrant juice and bread (in the Autumn, seedless grapes and harvest loaf might have been used) were simply blessed, distributed and consumed. Silence was kept and the children were asked to remember people who were in need of some of the things they could share.

Many questions might well emerge from the children, and lead to fruitful discussion. One group of children asked these questions:

Why are there so many names for the same thing?

What is a chalice?

Why do some have tiny glasses and plates?

Who buys the bread?

What is fasting?

What happens when there is too much bread and wine?

Why are Christians on about blood?

Do Christians have bread instead of photographs of Jesus?

What does it feel like afterwards?

Are people ever frightened about taking part?

Why do people go to it?

(5) Other possible activities (some of which might be incorporated in (4) above).

Imagine that you were present at the Last Supper. Write, to someone who knows nothing about it, your story of what happened.

Make an invitation card to invite someone to a Communion service.

Design a poster announcing the time of the next Communion service.

Compose (or choose) and record a piece of music to be played as people gather for the celebration.

Create a collage showing a variety of people receiving bread and wine at a Communion service.

In all these activities the children should be encouraged to express what they have come to understand about the meaning for Christians of the celebration of Communion.

8 Having a Celebration

The essential here is that the children should plan, organise and take part in an actual celebration: it might take place off the school premises or inside the building; it could constitute, or be held in the context of, an Assembly; it could involve other classes.

It is also essential that the celebration should have a clear focus and a definite purpose, and be an effective conclusion to work on the Topic. The children's own environment will almost certainly offer possibilities: after pooling suggestions (the children's and the teacher's), making a "short list", and giving some thought to the resources needed and to the form of celebration envisaged for each of the short-listed contenders, the class decides. From then on, the class should take responsibility, able to go to the teacher for advice and resources, but genuinely creating the celebration themselves.

It would be reasonable to focus the celebration on some aspect of local life that was not already an object of celebration: resources would be readily available, and the occasion would have meaning and value both for the children and for people in the locality. Some suggestions follow (the first two refer specifically to the past; the remainder celebrate both past and present, change and continuity):

A person who is, or who deserves to become, famous, and who lived in (or wrote about, or painted) the village or its neighbourhood;

An important event which occurred in the neighbourhood;

Local work and activities, then and now;

The school, and the part it has played in the life of the area;

A particular and significant hill, wood or tree: the change it has witnessed (e.g. children's games, modes of transport, fashions of clothing, incidents, etc.) while itself remaining unchanged;

The particular kind of "harvest" which is typical of the area (e.g. coal, plums, plastic goods, oil).

---

[2]*Such a simulation might usefully be preceded by the showing of selected slides, or the video "Christian Worship", accompanied by questions designed to focus attention on particular features; and followed by a second showing of the visual materials, with the children making their own comments on these, in the light of their experience of the simulation.*

Books referred to in the text

M. Domnitz	*Understanding Your Jewish Neighbour*	Lutterworth 1974
K. Grahame	*Dream Days*	P. Harris 1983
J. Harrowven	*Origins of Festivals and Feasts*	Kaye & Ward 1980
A. Holm	*I am David*	Magnet 1980
R. Kipling	*Kim*	Pan 1976
L. Lee	*Cider with Rosie*	Penguin 1983
A. A. Milne	*Winnie the Pooh*	Methuen 1966
F. T. Palgrave	*The Golden Treasury of Songs and Lyrics*	Dent 1983 (pb)
	Exploring a Theme—Myself	O.U.P. 1965
		C.E.M.
P. Pearce	*A Dog so Small*	Puffin 1970
W. Plomer ed.	*Francis Kilvert's Diary*: Selections	Penguin 1984
R. Siegel et al.	*The Jewish Catalogue*	Jewish Publication Society of America. Available from Jewish Education Bureau, 8 Westcombe Avenue, Leeds LS8 2BS
H. Smith and J. Priestley ed.	*Harvest and Thanksgiving* (in *Living Festivals* series)	R.M.E.P. 1985
J. Rankin	*The Eucharist*	Lutterworth 1985
R. L. Stevenson	*Treasure Island*	Puffin 1984
P. Thompson	*Lark Rise to Candleford*	Penguin 1973
M. Twain	*The Adventures of Huckleberry Finn*	Puffin 1983

For biblical readings or references, the use of Today's English Version (published by the Bible Society, sometimes under the title *Good News Bible*) is recommended.

Belonging

INTRODUCTION

Context

This scheme is based on work done in a Junior school in a large and growing town, with a class aged 10+ of mixed ability. It was designed to fit into the school's Topic Grid, which is planned so as to enable key ideas to surface several times during the four years which it covers; thus the children will already have encountered such topics as "Life-styles", "Celebrations and Customs", "Rules and Rituals", and "Communication". The Summer Term Topic "Belonging", orientated towards Religious Education, provided a further oppor-tunity to look at aspects of human groups and communities. The work contributed in many ways to other areas of the curriculum, both as regards content and as aiding the developing of particular skills—most notably in the areas of language and creative expression.

Aims and Objectives

The teacher's general aims are:
- to provide the children with certain insights and skills which will benefit them personally in their experiences both of belonging to groups and of being different from other people;
- to inspire in the children an interest in the Jewish way of life, in the beginnings of the Christian faith, and in the significance of religion for people's lives and relationships.

The guiding principles informing the scheme are three of the objectives for Religious Education in the Middle Years defined in *Religious Education in Hampshire Schools* (1978) p. 18–24 (reproduced in *Paths to Understanding* (1980) p. 33), viz. to help children:
- to understand some features of human groups and communities;
- to appreciate that symbols and artefacts can express human feelings and ideas;
- to extend their awareness that people commit themselves to beliefs and causes.

The teacher's more specific objectives are that the children should gain:
- appreciation of the values and implications of belonging to a group;
- respect for people who are different from oneself;
- appreciation of some of the values and problems of being different;
- some understanding of the faith and life-style of Jews;

- awareness of the sort of impact (albeit described in a fictional narrative) that Jesus could have on people who met him;
- some understanding of the faith and life-style of Christians.

Approach and Methods of Working

The basis of the scheme is the book *The Bronze Bow*; this is supplemented by the book *I am David* (see the "Resources" section below for outlines of the stories).

From the springboard of these books, the children explore their own experiences of belonging and separation, and make discoveries about various aspects of Judaism and Christianity. Activities include visits (to a synagogue and a church), simulations (e.g. Sabbath Eve meal), acting out roles, and making pictures, charts and models. Much discussion occurs, with ideas and conclusions being expressed orally and visually. Use is made, where relevant, of audio and visual means of communication. The co-operation of parents, and of local Jewish and Christian ministers, is enlisted.

The class is often broken down into small groups, varying in size from two to six, especially for discussion and drama work: in such groups, children can pursue a topic more deeply, gain confidence, and take responsibility for summarising and for reporting to the class. For other purposes (e.g. story-telling and sharing the findings of groups) the unit of organisation is the whole class.

Crucial to the success of this way of working is, of course, the relationship which has been established between teacher and class. In a relationship of honesty, trust and openness, children can feel sufficiently secure to give their opinions without fear of being brushed aside or mocked, and to take seriously, without feeling too self-conscious, activi-ties such as role-playing and simulation.

The topic is planned to take up about eight hours per week for half a term. Products of the work might include:
- individual booklets with records of, and com-ments on, the work done;
- various lists, charts and graphs;
- a display of art work and personal (creative) writing;
- a tape/slide sequence on, for example, the visit to the synagogue;
- models of artefacts seen in the synagogue;

an Assembly (perhaps one of a series on Community) in which children present several aspects of the topic.

Resources

The teacher: experience, knowledge, interest, enthusiasm, skills (not least, that of telling a story so that it absorbs the listeners).
The children: experiences, knowledge, ideas, enthusiasms, skills.

Books

(for full references see booklist at the end of the chapter):
The Bronze Bow
Set in the first century C.E., this tells the story of Daniel, a Jewish boy obsessed by hatred of the Roman invaders who crucified his father. Daniel joins a band of young guerillas in order to get revenge; but he hears a preacher named Jeshua, and as time passes he comes to accept his teachings.

I am David

Set in the twentieth century C.E., this tells the story of young David, who escapes from a concentration camp and makes his way across Europe, fearing that at any moment "they" may catch up with him. He eventually comes to learn his own identity and gradually, despite himself, begins to hope, and to lose a little of his mistrust.

If the scheme is to be worked in full, the following items will be needed: for details and sources of supply see p. 47.

Audio-visual resources

Pictures of people of different countries—Unit 1(b).
Pictures showing symbols of belonging and of exclusion—Units 1(b), 2(a), 3(b).
Pictures of people of different appearance, occupation, etc.—Unit 2(b).
Objects relating to various occupations—Unit 2(b).
Flash-cards, with words relating to various occupations—Unit 2(b).
Pictures showing some physical barriers (both natural and artificial)—Unit 3(a).
Pictures showing friendly and unfriendly expressions/reactions—Unit 3(a).
Tape-recordings of people expressing attitudes and feelings—Unit 3(a).
Musical instruments (for improvising expressions of feelings)—Unit 3(d).
Set of slides "The Sabbath in the Home"—Unit 4(a).
Posters showing the Sabbath Eve Seder—Unit 4(a).
Slides showing the interior of a synagogue—Unit 4(b)
Some church magazine and news-sheets—Unit 5(b).

Slide projector and screen.
Tape-recorder and cassettes.

Artefacts

Objects and food relating to the Sabbath Eve meal (Table-cloth, 4 candles, 2 goblets, 2 Sabbath loaves, wine (or blackcurrant juice in lieu), salt, Challah cover, Skull-cap, matches)—Unit 4(a).
Objects relating to synagogue ceremonies and rituals (Menorah, Scroll, Yad, Tallith, Star of David, Kipa, Prayer Book)—Unit 4(b).
Objects relating to Christian ceremonies and rituals—Units 2(c)(ii), 5(a), 5(b).

Places visited

Church—Units 2(c)(ii), 5(b)
Synagogue—Unit 4(b).

Materials for activities

Art materials.
Colour magazines etc. for making collages.
Paper and covering materials for making booklets.
Tools and materials for making models.
Basic props for drama work (especially some hats and cloaks).

Reference materials

Bible (a recent version such as Today's English Version).
A Jewish Family in Britain
Jewish Worship

OVERVIEW

Preliminary   Reading of *The Bronze Bow*
Unit 1   Similarities and Differences:
(a) in the class
(b) in the community at large
(c) in groups to which the children belong
(d) in myself
(e) experiences of being different.
The objectives are observation and awareness; value judgements and stereotyping are to be avoided.

Unit 2   Signs and Symbols of Belonging:
(a) in the children's own experience
(b) distinctive of various occupations
(c) in Judaism and Christianity: the symbolism of water.

Unit 3   Aspects of Separation and Exclusion:
(a) Barriers, natural and man-made
(b) Signs and signals of exclusion
(c) Experiences related to separation and exclusion
(d) Emotions related to separation, isolation and hostility
(e) Making a decision.

Unit 4   Belonging to the Jewish Community
(a) Symbols and rituals in the home
(b) Symbols and rituals in the synagogue

Any study in depth of the separateness, suffering and survival of the Jews is not appropriate to this age-group.

Unit 5   Belonging to the Christian Community:
(a) Admission to the community
(b) Activities within the community

Unit 6   An Experiment in Group Working

Conclusion

Preliminary
In preparation for this topic, the teacher reads *The Bronze Bow* to the class during the preceding term. If necessary, the story could be abridged, the teacher supplying linking passages; but extracts which are to be used in the course of work on the topic should always be read in full, with substantial contexts—lack of detail kills a story.

The aim is simply that children should enter into, and enjoy, the story. At some points clarification might be required, and children might have comments to make or questions to raise; these should be subordinated to the aim of involving the children vicariously in the experiences of the characters in the story.

Unit 1   Similarities and Differences
(a)   *In the class*
Working in groups of 3 or 4, children list what all members of their group have in common. They then focus on differences between them, each member describing (in writing and/or drawing) one other member, with as much information (physical characteristics, interests, etc.) as time allows. Talking within groups will be necessary. Test the adequacy of some descriptions by finding out whether their subjects can be identified by the class.

After re-forming as a class, pool and collate information, converting it into graphs and picto-grams.

Further information may be collected by talking with the children about their experiences, choices, hopes, etc.

Consider with the class what life would be like if everybody was exactly the same. This idea could be the basis for writing a short story.

(b)   *In the community at large*
Display a number of large photographs showing people in various parts of the world.

Several children describe briefly what they can see in some of the pictures—a person's appearance, an activity, the setting, etc. A few points might be taken up immediately for discussion.

Children working in groups of 3 or 4 make lists of the similarities and the differences which they observe in the people pictured. Each group also prepares an answer to the question: "Do you think you can tell, simply by looking at the pictures, anything important about the people shown in them?"

Group findings are shared and discussed. (Did all groups and individual children within groups, "see" the same things? How valid is it to draw conclusions from the evidence of the photographs?)

(c)   *In groups to which the children belong*
Each child makes a list of the various groups to which he/she belongs (family, class, gang, club, team, etc.). They might mark in some way those where a personal choice was involved.

Children discuss in pairs, with reference to several of the groups on their lists, questions such as:
  Does belonging to this group make you think and act in the same way as its other members?
  When in the group, do you try to be a different sort of person from what you are in any other group?
  Does group membership help you to feel that you are more fully "yourself"?
  In the group, are differences between people important? Do some differences seem more, or less, important than others?
Each pair expresses its best insights into the effects of group-membership in two written statements beginning "Belonging to a group makes (or "gives") you . . . ." These are displayed, or contributed orally, and are likely to arouse some discussion.

(d)   *In myself*
Read to the class the poem "I am a being" (written by a Junior child):
  I am a being
  Made up of dreams
  A person real
  Yet who am I?

   I have emotions
   Good and bad
   A happy me
   A me made sad.

  I am of the human race
  In a community I have my place
  A person of reality
  I have my will, for I am me.
Subsequent discussion might touch on the facts that certain circumstances or moods can make people feel different from their normal selves ("He's not quite himself today"; "She's beside herself with worry"), or different from everybody around them; some children may be encouraged by discovering that these are common human experiences.

Each child constructs a "self-portrait", writing personal information round a photograph of himself/herself, on some such plan as this:

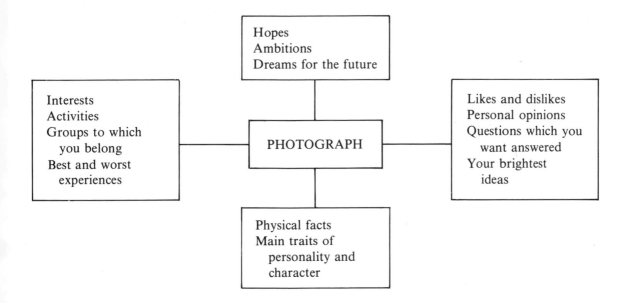

They could mark those items which were different a year ago. If the children were willing (this should be decided in advance) the "portraits" would be displayed in the classroom.

(e) *Experiences of being different*
As a connecting link with the subject matter of Units 2 and 3, read to the class the following passage from *The Bronze Bow* (p. 11) and discuss the feelings of Joel, his sister, and Daniel.

> . . . *From the pocket of the wide striped girdle that bound her waist, the girl pulled a neatly wrapped bundle. Joel produced a small flask which he handed to his sister, then sat down and solemnly held out his hands. With astonishment Daniel watched the girl pour a stream of water over her brother's hands. Hand-washing before a meal–he hadn't given it a thought for five years. He wouldn't have imagined that even a scribe's son would carry water all the way up the mountain just to observe the law. Then the girl turned towards him. He saw the question in her eyes and the slight shrinking, and a stubborn pride stiffened him. He was a Jew, wasn't he? He held out his hands and watched the drops trickle over his blackened knuckles, embarrassed, thinking how the men in the cave would hoot if they could see him.*

Children discuss, and dramatise, experiences such as:
> Joining a new class or club, the routines of which are strange to you.
> Visiting a friend's home for a meal; as you begin to eat, your friend's father starts to say a Grace.
> Going out for the day with a friend's family; you find that you are wearing unsuitable clothes, have an unusual packed lunch, and have not brought any money with you.

Unit 2 Signs and Symbols of Belonging
(a) *In the children's own experience*
Recall the lists made in Unit 1 of the various groups to which children belong. Discuss what, if anything, would enable an outsider to recognise membership of a particular group; ask children to bring, for displaying in the classroom, examples of distinctive uniform, badges, et. Does the wearing of the uniform or badge have any effect on themselves or on other people?

Children working in small groups might design an appropriate badge or crest for their class; individuals might design one for their family. In either case, the design should incorporate symbols which suggest characteristic purposes and features of the group.

Children enjoy inventing clubs and societies with special aims, rules of membership, rituals, badges, passwords, etc. Such an activity could lead to valuable discussion of privacy, secrecy, social acceptability, and related issues. Reference could well be made to the bow of bronze in the story—first a graphic sign (p. 74, 81), then a symbolic idea (p. 115), and finally a real object (p. 138f): children might be able to supply the context for each of these, and to explain the bow's function for Daniel and others, and its meaning.

An Assembly could be organised in which children entitled to wear special uniforms or badges could celebrate their membership of the groups signified. (See the example in *Exploring Primary Assemblies* p. 44).

(b) *Distinctive of various occupations*
Examining visual material (on general display,

and/or issued to small groups) children try to identify groups of people who belong together, according to categories such as:

People who are wearing a particular uniform, badge, etc.

People who meet in special places.

People who have similar interests or occupations. Groups of children report to the class on the types of belonging which they have identified. A list is then built up of all the signs of belonging which have been observed (clothing, buildings, equipment, body ornaments, hair-styles, etc.). Consideration might be given to the fact that certain signs have become powerful symbols, pointing to some larger, more abstract, concept (e.g. a policeman's uniform symbolises authority; a Red Cross symbolises compassion).

Children could devise and play a game, of the "Happy Families" type, in which pictures of objects are matched with various occupations. For example, with the class divided into groups of 4 or 5 children, each group would select one occupation and make 5 cards, picturing a person and 4 objects associated with that person (e.g. chef: hat, apron, knife, sausage: vicar: robe, cross, font, collar). It may be desirable to bring out, in discussion, that the objects indicate the occupation, but do not define the character, of the person.

Two more energetic games, using materials prepared or brought by the children, could be played, the first in the classroom, the second in the playground:

(1) Choose six occupations, and prepare flash-cards containing words, of varying difficulty, relating to these (e.g. carpenter: nail, chisel, plane, rasp, spokeshave, adhesive); add a few irrelevant words as red herrings. Distribute the cards at random round the classroom. Divide the children into six groups, each group representing one occupation. At a signal, children move to collect the set of cards for their group, the first group to report with a complete set to the teacher being the winner.

(2) Choose five or six occupations, and collect six articles associated with each (e.g. nurse: hat, bandages, thermometer, watch, cloak, bottle of pills). Mix these up at one or more points in the playground. At a signal, one member of each group runs to put on, and/or pick up, the appropriate items, and return to the group. List the finishing order. Items are then replaced and re-mixed, and the "race" repeated with different children. From the several lists, an overall winning group can be worked out.

(c) *In Judaism and Christianity: the symbolism of water*

Use the extract from *The Bronze Bow* quoted in Unit 1(e) above to initiate an exploration of the symbolism of water in Judaism and in Christianity.

(1) Judaism

Consider with the class why washing of hands was regarded as important by Joel, Thacia and Daniel. Why did Daniel eventually agree to take part in this ceremonial action? Compare his irritation about hand-washing when in Joel's home, as one who does not really "belong" there (p. 56). The inner meaning of the symbolism may be brought out by reading the incident where Jesus is present at a meal, and someone complains that "no one has provided for us to wash our hands" (p. 84). Was this criticism justified? What do you think the other people present made of Jesus' comments?

At two other points in the story water is significant, viz. p. 36 and 54. Both instances relate to washing the feet of a visitor on his arrival in a house. Might there be more to this action, too, than simply physical cleanliness? These references, and the question, could be discussed, and attention could be drawn to the incidents in Luke 7.36f. (the woman washing Jesus' feet) and John 13.4f. (Jesus washing his disciples' feet).

(2) Christianity

The ritual and meaning of baptism can be of great interest to children of this age-group. If possible, arrange for a visit to a local church and for children to take part in a simulation of the service of Baptism; if such a visit is not possible, simulate a baptismal ceremony in the classroom.

After the event, the children work in small groups, each group producing a four-column chart (perhaps decorated with sketches) setting out (vertically in order, horizontally linked together):

What was done | What was said | What it meant | Questions

These charts could be displayed and looked at by the children; discussion on the questions listed, and discussion on other matters arising, would follow. The teacher might supply some answers on matters of fact, but should not get over-involved in theological issues or presume to correct the children's ideas about what various actions or words meant.

For the purposes of this Unit, the final question to consider is:

What has *changed* as a result of this ceremony? Children can appreciate that the baptised person has been accepted by, and has joined (either by proxy, or by personal decision), a new community; that baptism is a means of "belonging" to the Christian Church.

Unit 3   Aspects of Separation and Exclusion

(a) *Barriers, natural and artificial*

Show, in random order, a number of pictures of

things which cause, or maintain, separation, viz. natural barriers (sea, mountain, river, desert, forest, swamp) and artificial barriers (walls, gates, locked doors, ditches fortifications). Ask the children to group these into the two categories mentioned. Hold a brief discussion on the question "Why do people make these barriers?"

Using more pictures, and recorded material, present examples of human factors which cause, or maintain, separation between people: these would include social factors (language, race, wealth, status, and the distinctive codes and customs of particular groups) and individual factors (pride, fear, selfishness, greed, prejudice, hatred, etc.). Ask the children to identify, and perhaps to classify, these.

In class discussion children share some of their own experiences and consider the separating, excluding and isolating effects of all these "barriers".

Two possible further developments:
> Children, working individually or in pairs, choose two "barriers"—a "thing-barrier" as in the first paragraph, and a "person-barrier" as in the second paragraph—and write, in each case, about the problems posed by the barrier and about how the barrier could be surmounted. For the second piece of writing, children could be encouraged to draw on their personal experience. They could, of course, add illustrations.
> Children working in small groups could choose a picture or episode relating to the category of individual factors and invent a sequence of events to explain the source of the feelings of the people portrayed, to describe the feelings of other people who might be involved, and to suggest an outcome which would overcome the barrier (i.e. some change in attitude, emotions or behaviour). These scenarios could be reported to the class; one or two might be worth acting out.

(b) *Signs and signals of exclusion*
Children are asked to recall, and to observe over a given period, all kinds of "Keep Out!" signs and notices, and to make reproductions of these for a display. They might supplement these with pictures and captions showing various ways in which people signify "You are not wanted!" Reasons for exclusion, and people's reactions to being excluded, would be worth discussing. Have they observed any signs or notices which say "Come in!"?

(c) *Experiences related to separation and exclusion*
Children work in groups to prepare dramatisations on such themes as:
> Being excluded from a game
> Being sent to bed
> Being frustrated in some way, and becoming violent

> Being dared to trespass
> Being unwilling to share something good.
Opportunity should be given for the children to discuss each episode in terms of the emotional and social factors involved.

(d) *Emotions related to separation, isolation and hostility*
Plenty of material on this subject is available in T.V. programmes, newspapers, comics, films, books and personal experiences. The three poems below, written by Junior children, are very specific; children might read and discuss copies of them, then express their own reactions and reflection in one of the following ways:
> pictures or collages which represent the scenes presented in the poems, or scenes which the poems stimulate in their imagination;
> abstract paintings which interpret ideas arising from the poems;
> writing about remembered times of loneliness, anger, isolation, frustration, boredom, etc.
> sound effects appropriate to the emotions involved in the poems or in their own remembered experiences.

Loneliness
How long has she
*   been lying there,*
With broken legs
*   and matted hair?*
"About two weeks"
*   the doctor said,*
"but for one of them
*   she's been dead."*
She must have someone,
*   mustn't she?*
"Who knows?"
*   the doctor said.*
"It matters little now.
*   She's dead."*

Room without Daylight
I sat at my window
Dark was my room
My clock had stopped ticking.
Dark was my room.
Forgotten and lonely
Dark was my room,
Not even daylight peeped
* through the curtains,*
Dark was my room.
Cold and still,
Dark was my room,
Had no more visitors,
Dark was my room.

Anger
1 Revenge, revenge,
*   I'll get my own back.*
*   Revenge, revenge,*
*   I'll smash him in,*

first my right hook,
then my left
anything to get him done.

2   I'm getting wild
    My eyes are red
    My ears go back
    I lower my head,
    I charge towards him
    I'll bowl him over
    And knock him dead.

3   He starts to run
    And I run faster.
    I throw my left
    and get his back.
    I clench my teeth
    My head is boiling
    I'll get him now,
    He's got no chance.

4   Wait a bit
    I'm getting cooler
    And now I don't want to hurt
    The danger's over,
    The heart beats slower,
    My ears no longer steam with heat
    I'm feeling better
    I've relaxed a lot,
    And now my anger's completely
        stopped.

(e)   *Making decisions*
Good illustrations of the need to decide whether or not to belong to a particular group, whether or not to remain separate, are to be found in *The Bronze Bow* and in *I am David*.

By means of questions, help the children to recall events towards the end of *The Bronze Bow*, from the time when Daniel meets Jesus in the upper room (Ch. 21): his conversation with Jesus; his meeting Thacia; his outburst to Leah about Marcus; his hearing about the popular enthusiasm for Jesus; Leah's sickness; the confrontation with Marcus; Jesus' visit to the house. Children discuss in small groups the conflicting ideas and feelings which Daniel has about Jesus, making lists of what they think would be influencing Daniel to decide for, or against, joining the followers of Jesus' way. Their findings are shared and discussed in class. (The teacher might feed in some quotations which show Daniel's state of mind, e.g.: "I don't know where to turn. Everything has failed. Everything I hoped and lived for." (p. 179); "I have to see it through alone. There's no room for anyone else." (p. 186); "There was no friend to fight beside him. There was no leader to follow. There was nothing left to him but his hatred and his vow." (p. 197); "They could not learn to hope again." (p. 198); "One by one they had all left him. Rosh. Samson. Joel. Thacia. Simon. Jesus. Now Leah was slipping

away. With Leah's death he would be altogether free." (p. 199); "We can never know, Simon had said. We have to choose, not knowing." (p. 203)).

Chapter 5 of *I am David* tells of the boy's first experience of living in a house, and of being treated with respect and gratitude (he had rescued the owner's daughter from a fire). The experience delights him—though he has some reservations—but, having overheard a conversation about himself, he decides that he must leave, to continue his lonely journey. Later, he reflects that: "The children and their parents belonged to one another, and David could never belong. He was not . . . *right*. He was different from other children who had not been brought up in a concentration camp. There was nowhere he belonged." (p. 115); now "nothing would ever be the same again . . . because he would always have to remain himself, a boy who belonged nowhere." (p. 116).

The teacher reads after providing necessary background, much of Chapter 5, perhaps summarising the parents' conversation. David's exploration of his own and other people's lives, and his decision *not* to belong to the family which had befriended him, offer many points of contact with the children's experiences, and could lead to fruitful discussion, writing and group drama.

Both stories provide opportunities for considering the familiar, and often destructive, division of people into "us and them", "them" denoting the ill-defined group of those with whom we disagree or of whom we disapprove. In *The Bronze Bow*, Daniel hates "them", the Romans: all alike are "the enemy", until the last sentence of the book: " 'Will you come in to our house?' he asked". In *I am David*, David fears "them", the (unidentified) destroyers of human dignity and life, only one of whom gains his grudging and partial sympathy. Improvised drama could be a useful way of exploring both the creating, and the breaking down, of "us/them" barriers, and of the risks facing anyone who decides to take action to break them down.

Unit 4   Belonging to the Jewish Community
(a)   *Symbols and rituals in the home*
Ask children to make lists of the kinds of activity they engage in at weekends (from Friday evening onwards) which are different from their normal weekday activities. Share a few of the items with the class, and discuss briefly some of the activities associated with Sunday, Saturday and Friday (in that order).

Recall Daniel's visit (in *The Bronze Bow* Ch. 3) to his grandmother's home. What happened there on the *Friday* evening? Read this extract from p. 36:
    The last call of the horn came clearly, announcing
    the start of the Sabbath. His grandmother lighted a
    wick from the lamp and held it to the Sabbath lamp.

"Speak the blessing, Daniel," she said. "It is fitting the man should say it."

He hesitated, then the words came falteringly to his lips. "Praised be Thou, O Lord our God, King of the Universe, Who hast sanctified us by Thy command-ments and commanded us to kindle the Sabbath light."

In Jewish homes today, Friday evening—from the time of sunset, or when three stars can be seen in the sky—starts a very special day, a family day of peace, rest, happiness and celebration.

Use visual materials to present to the children the Sabbath Eve meal, typical Sabbath Day activities, and the restrictions imposed by the Jewish laws.

Arrange to hold a simulation of a Sabbath Eve meal. (For information, and for suggestions about simulation, see *A Jewish Family in Britain* and *Jewish Worship*.)

Children discuss, first in small groups then as a class:

(1) the meaning, purpose and value of the Sabbath rituals. (The point should be clearly established that they affirm that the family belongs together, and is part of a larger "Family" of people who share a tradition and a faith.)

(2) the purpose of the restrictions on working on the Sabbath (when an Orthodox Jew may not, for example, use the telephone, operate electric switches, use money or drive a car). (The point should be made that one is almost forced to 'stop and think' about other things in life, and other values.)

(b) *Symbols and rituals in the synagogue*
Refer back to the children's lists of weekend activities: did any include "Going to church" in Sunday's activities? Do Jews go to church on Sundays? No: they go to synagogue on Saturdays, their Sabbath, which ends on Saturday evening.

Where did Daniel, in *The Bronze Bow*, first see and hear Jesus? Recall Daniel's visit to the synagogue, reading this extract from p. 42:

They were approaching the small stone and plaster building in the center of the village . . . Daniel had to stoop to go through the low doorway. He sidled close to the wall, tensing his muscles, conscious of his shaggy height and his wide shoulders, trying to draw in and make himself smaller. But he soon realized that today there was no curiosity to spare for him.

He was sure that the synagogue had never been so full in his childhood. Close together on the low benches huddled the men of the town, their knees

drawn up almost to their chins. They sat in order of their trades, the skilled artisans nearest the pulpit, the silversmiths, the tailors, and sandalmakers. Farther back sat the bakers, the cheesemakers and dyers, and along the walls where Daniel and Simon had taken their places, stood the lower tradesmen and the farmers. Still others crowded the doorway, and many, he saw, would have to stand outside in the road. By the rustle and murmur behind the grilled screen that separated the women's section, many of the men had brought their wives with them.

"Hear, O Israel: the Lord our God is one Lord, and you shall love the Lord your God with all your heart, and with all your soul, and with all your might—"

The great words of the Shema rolled through the synagogue. For a moment Daniel was caught up by them as he had been in his childhood. But as the long passage of the Law was read aloud in Hebrew and then carefully translated into Aramaic, the lan-guage which the people spoke and understood, his attention began to wander.

Why was there such a crowd in the synagogue on that occasion? Why was it normal then, and still is today, for Jews to meet in the synagogue on the Sabbath? What goes on there? What does it mean?

The children should be able to answer these questions, in part, from the passage quoted; some might add information from their previous know-ledge or experience, while others might have suggestions to make. Answers, and outstanding questions, should be noted, for testing in the light of the work which follows.

Arrange a display of artefacts[1] which would be seen in a synagogue (such as Menorah, Scroll, Yad, Tallith, Star of David, Kipa, Prayer Book). With the aid of other visual material, help the children to get some idea of the use and significance of these.

Arrange for a visit to the nearest synagogue, for a talk and demonstration by an official or member, and a question-and-answer session. If use is to be made of a worksheet, its various items should focus children's attention on features which express the shared traditions, beliefs and aspirations of the Jews, and which are therefore likely to strengthen in those who attend the synagogue a sense of belonging to the Jewish community. A useful book for chidren to read is *Visiting A Synagogue*.

Back in the classroom, the children work in groups to compile lists of all the things in the synagogue which they think would remind a Jew that he/she belongs to the Jewish community, perhaps making models of the most significant ones. In a parallel

---

[1]*Artefacts should act as windows into a religious tradition, real aids to understanding the meanings of the practices and beliefs of its adherents. Thus a protracted focusing on a few objects is to be preferred to a hurried viewing or handling of many, however interesting they may be because of their strangeness.*

column they try to explain why the things would be likely to have this effect. They might make a tape-recording, to acccompany their own illustrations or a selection of slides, and incorporating these ideas, about their visit to the synagogue.

A final discussion would give opportunity for the sharing and clarifying of ideas, and for checking on the correctness of what has been learned and on the adequacy of understanding.

Unit 5 Belonging to the Christian Community
(a) *Admission to the community*
Recap, by means of questions, the work done on Baptism in Unit 2, section (c)(2).

Interest could be stimulated by children bringing to school things (photographs, christening robes, gifts, mementoes) associated with their own baptism, and talking about their parents' memories of the occasion. Discuss why some parents do, and others do not, have their children baptised.

(b) *Activities within the community*
The children explore what goes on within the Christian community (or communities) in the neighbourhood of their school by:
> drawing on each others' experiences (e.g. Sunday activities);
> collecting and analysing church magazines and news-sheets;
> talking with people who belong to various Christian churches;
> questioning clergy and ministers;
> visiting churches;
> participating in services or other church activities.

Their findings are brought together in a booklet, or a series of display panels, with sections (each compiled by a group of children) dealing with:
> activities within the church buildings;
> activities among people of the neighbourhood;
> the work and responsibilities of clergy and ministers;
> activities of all kinds of associated groups (Brownies, bell-ringers, luncheon clubs, young people, etc.).

Two important questions which should be kept in mind by the children during the course of their investigations, and discussed after the work of recording their findings, are;
(1) What seem to be the activities of *central* importance to people?
(2) *Why* do people engage in these activities?
Answers to these questions should be added to the booklet or display.

Ask the children, working in threes or fours, to think about any similarities between activities within the Christian community and activities in their own homes and families, and to jot these down in two columns. Ask them then to underline those which they consider most important as expressing the sense of belonging. The children's lists will almost certainly include "having meals together"— if they do not, the teacher will need to remind them of a central activity which they have forgotten!

Recall the special meal which Jewish families share on the Sabbath (see Unit 4(a)), and compare the meal for which most Christians come together, in countless local groups, more or less frequently, and which is called by various names (Holy Communion, etc.). Make clear, with the aid of visual materials and perhaps of a local minister, what it is that Christians *do* in this ritual meal.

Children might usefully discuss, in small groups, the meaning, purpose and value of the ritual meal, but only briefly; for it will be enough at this stage if children understand that the meal affirms that the participants belong together, and are part of a larger "Family" of Christians who share a tradition and a faith centred on Christ.

It would be appropriate, and could add value to the work in this section, to refer the children back to the questions they were discussing in Unit 1(c), concerning the effects of belonging to a group. Two kinds of question could be considered:
(1) What does belonging to the Christian community do for a person? What difference does it make to his/her ideas, way of life, character, etc.? Answers would be obtained from talking with people—church-goers, and perhaps relatives and classmates—and possibly from TV programmes, magazines, etc.
(2) What do you think belonging to the Christian community *should* do for a person? What difference *should* it make? This would be discussed in small groups, and the findings shared.

Unit 6 An Experiment in Group Working
The children are told that they will be divided into groups of five or six, and that each group will be required to make a model of anything they choose out of scrap materials. They are given until the next day to form their groups.

The voluntary groups are identified and established. After being told that necessities such as paper, adhesives, powder paint and cutting tools will be provided, each group is asked to make several decisions, about:
> What precisely they are going to make;
> A design for their model;
> What materials they will need;
> How they will get the materials;
> How work and responsibilities will be shared;
> When they expect to be ready to start.

Each group is required to keep a record of what decisions it has taken, and of the plans and details of the chosen model. How this is presented, and by whom, will be matters for the group to decide. When all groups are ready to start, a class

discussion may be held on what has happened up to that point. The children will be asked to say what influenced their choice of group, and to raise any problems or matters causing anxiety. The model-making may now start.

After some reasonable progress has been made, each group is asked to discuss the following questions:

Has the question of leadership been solved?

How have any problems or disagreements been handled?

Do any members of the group feel left out of things?

Are there any suggestions as to improving the working of the group?

What are the advantages and disadvantages of working in a group?

When the models have been finished, each group is asked to complete its records of the activity, and to record the views of its members on the task and on the level of their achievement.

Each of the children might be asked to complete a simple form, giving an assessment of the contributions made by each member of his/her group: the form would include no names, and would be filled in privately. A completed form might look like this:

P	A	B	C	D
1		✓		✓
2	✓			
3			✓	✓
4		✓		
5	✓	✓		

Column P Each child in the group (shown by a number only)
Column A Worked hard throughout
Column B Had some good ideas
Column C Helped others a lot
Column D Brought useful material

This form-filling activity should heighten children's awareness of the different contributions, all valuable, which people may make to a group to which they belong, and perhaps of different levels of individual commitment to the group.

A class discussion about the whole "experiment", and what has been learned from it, would be appropriate.

Conclusion
The topic could be rounded off by one or more of the following;

A final discussion about the pleasures and benefits of belonging to a group, and the limitations and responsibilities which belonging entails.

The children, working in fives or sixes, devising a ceremony for welcoming a new recruit to a group (the nature and aims of the group being decided by the children).

An Assembly based on the story of Daniel in *The Bronze Bow*.

An Assembly based on the children's memories of their experiences, hopes and fears on first joining, and their thoughts about soon leaving, the school to which they now belong.

Resources and Addresses

Books (in order of mention in text)

	Religious Education in Hampshire Schools	Hampshire Education Authority 1978
W. Laxton ed.	*Paths to Understanding*	Macmillan 1980
E. G. Speare	*The Bronze Bow*	Puffin 1970
A. Holm	*I am David*	Magnet 1980
V. Barnett	*A Jewish Family in Britain*	R.M.E.P. 1983
J. Rose	*Jewish Worship* (in World Religions series)	Holt, Rinehart & Winston 1985
D. Charing	*Visiting a Synagogue*	Lutterworth 1984
W. B. Griffin	*Exploring Primary Assemblies*	Macmillan Education 1984

Audio-visual resources

Set of slides "The Sabbath in the Home"	The Slide Centre, 143 Chatham Road, London SW11 6SR
	EARO, Ely Resource and Technology Centre, Black Hill, Ely, Cambs.
Slides showing the interior of a synagogue	Education Department, Board of Deputies of British Jews, Woburn House, Upper Woburn Place, London WC1H 0EP
Poster showing the Sabbath Eve Seder (in Poster set "Judaism"— 6 Posters plus Notes)	C.E.M., Lancaster House, Borough Road, Isleworth, Middlesex TW7 5DU
Video: "Christianity through the eyes of Christian children"	C.E.M. Video, 5 Dean Street, London W1V 5RN

Artefacts

Relating to the Sabbath Eve Seder and to the Synagogue	Jewish Education Bureau, 8 Westcombe Avenue, Leeds LS8 2BS

Additional stories and poems which would be relevant

H. Andersen	*The Emperor's New Clothes*	Ref. Unit 1(c): how I appear, or wish to appear, to others
J. Ruskin	*The King of the Golden River*	Ref. Unit 2(c): water as a symbol of life
C. P. Gillman	The Obstacle (in *Evans' Book of Children's Verse*)	Ref. Unit 3(a)
K. Grahame	Its walls were of jasper (from *Dream Days*)	Ref. Unit 3(a)

Additional reference material

M. Domnitz	*Understanding your Jewish Neighbour*	Lutterworth 1974
W. Simpson	*Jewish Prayer and Worship*	SCM Press 1982

Difference

INTRODUCTION

Context

A teacher in a Southampton Middle School, disturbed by the antagonism towards a local gypsy community shown by her class of 11 year old children, decided to organise topic work on the theme of "Difference". She had noted the frequency with which her pupils tended to make premature evaluations and to adopt the pre-judgements of their peers and of the adults they met. The topic was designed, therefore, to encourage the children to explore several aspects of difference, and to look at the causes and consequences of stereotyping and prejudice. Furthermore, it gave the children experience in handling and assessing evidence and in making judgements based upon it.

Objectives

To enable the children:
  to recognise the differences that exist in the society in which they live:
  to appreciate that difference may be a reason for celebration as well as a cause of fear and prejudice;
  to develop an attitude of tolerance and respect for other people's beliefs, customs and ways of life;
  to appreciate the factors which underlie or influence their own and other people's prejudices;
  to cope with prejudice as they may themselves experience it.

Principles and Methods of Work

The topic is expected to last half a term with an allocation of about two hours working time per week. Much of the work is based upon the children's own experience and their observation of people and events around them. Group and class discussions, stimulated by the use of posters, pictures, slides, and information from newspapers and magazines, are used to heighten the general awareness of difference. Individual and group participation in decision-making games, surveys and general activities, designed to make obvious to the children the operation of prejudice and stereotyping, are mingled with expressive work in Drama and Language.

The children are exposed to a wide range of literature and forms of language in an attempt to make vivid the variety of positive and negative points of view which may be adopted in many social, racial and religious matters.

Main Resources

The following items can be prepared before the work begins:
  Posters and magazine pictures showing a variety of people, differing in physical appearance, clothing, nationality, etc.;
  Newspaper cuttings grouped to show different versions of the same event;
  Art paper, paints, charcoal, chalk, clay, wooden discs and cubes;
  Sets of activity cards and duplicated questionnaires.

Books, Poems and Songs mentioned in the scheme of work (for details see Resources section, p. 00) are:

Books	*The Diddakoi*
	Flat Stanley
	Let the Balloon Go
	Blubber
	Web of Language
	The Diary of Anne Frank
	My Mate Shofiq
Poem	The Hunchback in the Park
Songs	Black and White ("The ink is black, the page is white")

A fuller list of useful books, along with suggestions for songs with words particularly appropriate to this topic, appears in the Resources section page 00.

CONTENT

The subject-matter of the scheme is drawn from Literature, Social Studies and History, as well as from R.E. (See top right.)

ACTIVITIES

The Activities involved in this scheme are designed to develop competence in several different areas, viz. language, drama, craft, personal and social. They may usefully be classified under three (somewhat overlapping) headings: the order in which they are given has no significance. (See opposite.)

UNITS OF WORK

A An Introduction to the Idea of Difference
B Coming to Terms with Difference
C Differences of Language: Accents and Situations
D Differences of Opinion: Bias and Evidence
E Differences of Race and Colour: Two Examples of Prejudice
F Differences of Reaction: Prejudice and Propaganda
G Assemblies on the Theme of Difference

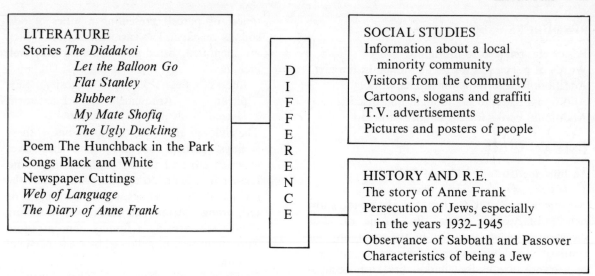

LITERATURE
Stories *The Diddakoi*
        Let the Balloon Go
        Flat Stanley
        Blubber
        My Mate Shofiq
        The Ugly Duckling
Poem The Hunchback in the Park
Songs Black and White
Newspaper Cuttings
Web of Language
The Diary of Anne Frank

DIFFERENCE

SOCIAL STUDIES
Information about a local
    minority community
Visitors from the community
Cartoons, slogans and graffiti
T.V. advertisements
Pictures and posters of people

HISTORY AND R.E.
The story of Anne Frank
Persecution of Jews, especially
    in the years 1932–1945
Observance of Sabbath and Passover
Characteristics of being a Jew

ANALYTIC	REFLECTIVE	EXPRESSIVE
Examining evidence	Observing and listening carefully	Linguistic Engaging in discussion
Following arguments	Interpreting personal observations and experiences	Responding orally to questions
Examining relevance of material to issues being explored	Assessing and interpreting evidence	Summarising discussions etc. Compiling lists Descriptive writing Personal wriring
Discriminating between types of language	Considering causes and consequences of actions	Dramatic Mime, role-play, drama on, for example:
Discerning significant features in stories, events, symbols and people	Determining orders of importance and value Forming reasoned judgements	Aspects of Difference; Aggression and Prejudice; Respect and Acceptance
Discerning significant points made in discussion	Making decisions Forming concepts	Constructive Making pictures and patterns in various media
	Detecting stereotypes, bias and prejudice	Making bar-graphs Making models in clay, plasticine, paper and scrap material
	Self-understanding	Making props and scenery for drama work (e.g. hide-outs)
	Understanding other people's beliefs, attitudes and behaviour	
	Assessing personality and character	
	Considering appropriateness of different types of language for different purposes and situations	
	Discovering forms in which to express the ideals and feelings of individuals and groups	

RESOURCES

Books etc. referred to in the text
Words of poem and songs mentioned in the text
Additional suggestions for drama work
Additional material for thought and discussion
Additional books for the children to read

UNIT A

An Introduction to the Idea of Difference

1 *Discussions*

Arrange a display of posters and pictures to show people of various types. By means of class discussion, arrive at a list of the most obvious similarities and differences in, for instance, outward appearance, expression, nationality, age, occupation and wealth.

Children, in small groups, discuss pictures cut out of magazines. Each group comments on the differences perceived in its pictures.

Read extracts from the early chapters of *The Diddakoi*, the children noting and commenting on the personal and social differences between Kizzy, a half-gypsy, and the other village children. (The story concerns the difficulties of making relationships with someone who is different, and the agonies of being a misfit.)

Children list anything they know about the local gypsy community from direct observation or experience. Alongside this they set a summary of any sayings or traditional beliefs about gypsies which they have come across, any local opinions they have heard expressed, and any information or comment in the local press. A rigorous attempt may then be made to separate facts from suppositions, so that the children's thinking about gypsies may be better founded and more precise.

2 *"Spot the difference" pictures*

The children choose a shape, an object or a person and draw what they have chosen as many times as they like in a haphazard way to cover a piece of paper, using pencil, charcoal, chalk, paint, or a combination of these. They then put in something which is different:
e.g. a white spot amongst coloured spots
    a black person amongst white people
    a square amongst circles
    a fork amongst spoons
Children can both use their ingenuity in disguising the different elements in their own drawings, and enjoy discovering them in others.

3 *How we react to something which is different*

(a) Explore this through discussion, initiated by a stimulus such as: reminding the children of some experience familiar to them (e.g. moving house, changing class, or being faced with unfamiliar food); producing a strange-looking object or parcel; presenting a series of odd sounds on tape. The various reactions which are identified, listed and displayed may well include:

Interest   Fear   Liking   Curiosity   Suspicion   Amusement   Excitement   Hatred   Jealousy   Pleasure

The children are asked to choose one of these feelings (perhaps one they have themselves experienced) and through colour, shape and texture to attempt to express symbolically the impact of these feelings, e.g. hatred might be red, orange, yellow and black, with bubbling shapes representing a fuming concentration. This might well be followed by some personal writing.

(b) Children invent a character which is unusual in some way (behaviour, occupation, personality, etc.), and produce a piece of descriptive writing in which the character's distinctive features are set out. They develop this in a story in which the character brings pleasure through surprise, change, humour, contrast or excitement. Some of these stories are read out, discussion following on the degree of "match" between the events in a story and the expectations which the children had formed when they listened to the initial description of its central character.

(c) A number of pictures, in all of which people who have one characteristic in common (e.g. a smiling face, ragged clothes) are shown and studied. The children are asked to identify the common factor and to say what it suggests to them about the people concerned. They are then asked to judge these people by different criteria, e.g. their health, their occupation, their working skill, their happiness. Discussion follows on the reliability of these comments and judgements.

UNIT B

Coming to terms with Difference

1 *Exploring differences*

The focus is on real people. Differences between them may have arisen from natural causes, may have been caused by human agency, or may have been chosen by individuals. The aim is that children should better understand why people differ, how people are affected by being different, and how people who are different affect others; and that their attitudes and responses should be modified in the light of such understanding.

Suitable stimuli for initiating discussion, either in small groups or with the whole class participating, are:

Posters of a group of distinctive appearance, or of handicapped people, or of people of various nationalities;
The poem "The Hunchback in the Park". (See p. 58.)

Extracts from:

Flat Stanley

This short book amusingly describes the adventures of Stanley who is accidentally squashed flat by a door. As a result of his accident Stanley sees the world from a different perspective and this gives the book its power.

Let the Balloon Go

The story of a spastic boy, John, and the effect of his disability on the family. John is hostile and resentful and his mother over-protective and self-pitying. It is only after John has been left alone for the first time and has abused his freedom that concessions can be made on both sides and the ground cleared for a new start.

Blubber

This book describes the unhappy and tormented life of Linda, a fat adolescent, as she grows up and tries to make sense of the people and events she encounters.

Many children may have only meagre and generalised knowledge about, and understanding of, the more common forms of physical handicap. Either with the help of one of the national societies, or with the co-operation of a local person, present the facts, as appropriate, to the children. Two discussions, one before and one after the visitor's talk, will help the children to perceive the gap between their early generalisations and the informed picture which they subsequently acquire.

Some children may be ready to take a broader view of the factors in life which produce difference. With a particular character, historical or fictional, in mind, they try to discover—or, in the absence of firm information, to estimate—the influences of time, place, heredity, upbringing, environment, intelligence, chance, education, friends, etc.

It might be appropriate for them to reflect on their own lives, each child listing several of his/her characteristics and adding alongside each one, a factor considered to have been influential in the development of that characteristic. These could also be expressed in pictorial form.

Discussion of the questions "Why do people conform?" and "Why do people rebel?" would fit naturally at this point.

It is hardly surprising that children hold stereotyped images of people of other lands; but people close to them—teachers, old folk (especially grandparents), policemen and many others—may also be victims of stereotyping. It is a healthy corrective to invite such people to talk to the children and to demonstrate their interests, skills, hobbies and activities, thus revealing more of their true and complex natures.

2   *Expressive activities*

Children make a "Flat Stanley" (e.g. a plasticine figure squashed flat) and invent a story about the adventures of this figure, relating the story either orally or in writing.

Children select some of the people or groups considered in this Unit and paint pictures of them, to which they add captions; they are encouraged to make their paintings bold and stark, and their captions challenging (e.g. questions such as "Why?" or "Are you against me or for me?"). Personal writing may follow discussion of this art work.

Read extracts from *Let the Balloon Go* as an inspiration for drama or mime. Children take roles of being deaf, blind, or in some way incapacitated; others take helpful or hostile roles. After the children have each experienced at least two different roles, they talk about their reactions, and discuss how it might feel in real life to be insecure or disorientated; it is essential also to consider how personal difficulties and handicaps may be relieved or overcome.

If the teacher thinks it appropriate, and the children are willing, they may discuss in personal terms such matters as dress, possessions, holidays, memories, relatives and visitors. They could write about the ways in which they regard themselves as similar to, or different from, their peers, in these respects, adding comments on any particular pleasures or problems which they experience. In this context the story of Blubber might be used.

Through such activities the teacher can help children to extend their emotional repertory and to appreciate more fully the effort needed to put oneself into other people's shoes. Two examples of pupils' work arising out of this Unit are given below.

Small Paul

I've always had my leg pulled
About being very small,
But through the years I have learned
Not to take any notice at all.

For instance on the bus one day,
When mum offered our fares,
The driver said "No charge for him"—
I was already up the stairs!

One Christmas at nursery school,
With lots of goodies to share,
The magic man chose me to help him—
To see him I'd knelt on my chair!

In the Infant school during P.E.,
When teacher said "Climb the rope",
The top seemed like miles away,
But even with my size I could cope!

Some friends call me "Small-guy" or "Tom Thumb",
Others say "Super Midget" or "Mousie",
I don't care, I pass them off,
I'm good at swimming and Karate.

I like you—you're different

UNIT C

Differences of Language[1]

Children use and listen to language in many different situations. They hear various accents and dialects, and encounter various forms and styles of the written word. Exploring such differences can be of great interest to children; it is also important, for language is all too commonly a factor in stereotyping and labelling people, a cause or an ally of prejudice. Children should become more aware that, while some differences in the way people use language are intentional, others are inevitable and no "fault" of an individual; and that in using or interpreting language the qualities of common-sense, sensitivity and goodwill are needed.

Most of the content of sections 2 and 3 below is imaginatively, and more fully, developed in *Web of Language* and in the BBC Radio series of the same name; the Teachers' Notes (incorporating Pupils' Pages) relating to the broadcasts are recommended.

1 *Speech Identikit*

Record each of the chidren in the class reading (in normal speaking voice) the same piece of prose, or talking about something which interests them. Playback some of these recordings with the class listening and trying to identify the speakers, making individual lists. Select three or four who were correctly identified by most of the class, and build up on OHP or blackboard the features by which they were identified (accent, fluency, emphasis, intonation, vocabulary, accompanying noises, etc.), i.e. their "Speech Identikit". (N.B. No criticisms allowed; no opinions about "right" and "wrong".) A brief discussion of reasons for the observed differences might be appropriate.

Working in groups, children construct Speech Identikit charts for some well-known personalities, using a simple form such as is shown above right, and making the entries in each column as short as

---

[1]*There is enough material here to distract teacher and class from the main theme "Difference": the teacher will need to select rigorously in order to keep this Unit in due proportion in the scheme.*

Name	Typical words or expressions	Accent	Intonation	Accompanying noises (e.g. laughter)	etc. as needed

possible. If each group deals with three personalities, a quick competition between the groups—an "Identify Parade"—could be held.

Some children and teachers might record themselves talking in disguised voices. Children, working in small groups, try to identify the speakers. What features have the speakers succeeded in changing, in order to conceal themselves? What features give them away?

2 Accents, dialects and languages

Prepare a tape-recording with examples selected from various types of "English"—American, Australian, West Indian, Asian, Irish, Welsh, Scottish, English regions and "posh". Invite the children to list those they identify, along with at least one "Identikit" feature which they have observed. Discuss some of the features noted.

One feature likely to have been noted is that in most, if not all, cases some special words are used; sometimes a completely new word, sometimes a word which sounds familiar but which seems to have a different meaning. Choosing one or more of the types mentioned in the preceding paragraph, list a number of such "special" words, setting it alongside a list (in different order) of their equivalents in "received English", giving children the task of equating the items correctly. How do the children react to these "special" words—are they more sensible, more picturesque, more vigorous, misleading or just funny? Children might add examples of regional variations which they have heard when on holidays, and talk about their reactions to these. (It may be worth making the point that language styles adopted by some comedians are the normal language styles, perhaps slightly exaggerated, of ordinary people.)

With the children in groups of 5 or 6, ask them to imagine that one of their number has just moved from home to a distant place, possibly a foreign country, where the environment, the people, their life-style and the way they speak, are very different.

After a short time for planning within the group, role-play a situation in which the newcomer attempts to understand and to communicate with the "strange" people (the other members of the group). Follow up with discussion of the methods used, their success or failure, the feelings of all parties, etc. What would seem strange, to someone coming among *us* from a different area, about *our* use of language? What problems might arise, both for the newcomer and for ourselves?

Three further questions which could be considered are:
(a) What would be gained, or lost, if differences of accent and dialect, and even of language, were eliminated?
(b) Does it really matter *at all* how people speak?
(c) In the light of the ideas raised in discussion of questions 1 and 2, what *does* matter?

The possible effects of T.V. could be discussed. Projects for a world-language, such as Esperanto, could be referred to, examples examined by the children, and the desirability and practicability of such a language discussed.

3 Styles and situations

Illustrate an example of an impersonal style (e.g. read or tape a news item, or instructions about what to do in case of fire), and an example of a personally involved style (e.g. a passionate piece of dialogue from a story or play). Ask one or two of the more extrovert members of the class to present the same materials with the styles transposed or to report a playground fight as plain information (just boring!); and a school Assembly, school dinner, or trying on a dress in a shop, in the manner of a sports commentator (just ridiculous!) How do the children react to these examples? Can they envisage situations in which they might in fact be appropriate (e.g. Head Teacher speaking in Assembly about violence in the playground; a humorous T.V. advertisement for a dress shop)? Ask the children to think of situations in which they were aware that they were using language in a way different from normal (e.g. choosing their words more carefully, or speaking in a different tone of voice). Build their contributions into a list which displays in parallel several types of situation and the styles of language which children have felt appropriate to them. Does the fact that we make such adjustments mean that we shall need to modify our Speech Identikits?

Consider with the children the need to choose words with care, and to think about how to say them, for different purposes. Children work in pairs to improve on the words in the first column, in order to achieve the objectives in the second, in examples such as those shown overleaf.

Listen to some of the suggestions, and discuss what the children have done as regards choice of words. (In the above examples, for instance, the concerns are: tact, perhaps involving euphemism; words with emotive, persuasive force; tact again—not the place for slang or colloquialism; precise, technical vocabulary; avoidance of ambiguity.) The theme of ambiguity could be followed along two lines: (a) It is

You're a liar!	You don't believe him, but you don't want to offend him.
This washing-machine isn't too bad, madam.	You want to *sell* her one.
I've just heard that your grandad has kicked the bucket.	You want to give your friend the news, but to cause as little distress as possible.
Stamp collectors always examine the thing inside the stamp that you can't see, and the wavy bit round the edge.	You want your friend to know *exactly* what to look for when he thinks of buying a stamp for his collection.
She put her hat on her head, and it fell off.	You meant to be *serious*.

to be avoided in scientific descriptions and in instructions: have several children in turn trying to describe quite simple objects (e.g. a fork) while others follow the details as given *but* try to draw the object *wrongly*, as permitted by the describer's omissions or poor choice of words; (b) It is crucial to most comedy: have the children collecting examples, or writing them out, for display in the classroom.

An exploration of differences between spoken English and written English could begin with children making lists of words which they commonly speak, but which they would be unlikely to write in a composition, or perhaps to read in a book; they might include slang words, words used in their games, gang code-words, nicknames, etc. Discuss the reasons for avoiding these in writing. What extra care and attention has to be given to words if they are to be satisfactory in written form?

Along lines similar to those followed in section 1 above (the Speech Identikit), children could try identifying one another from anonymous scripts. They might consider the possibility of constructing "Writing Identikits" for several authors (bringing in the additional features of subject matter and the way in which it is handled), e.g. favourites like Roald Dahl. What are the features that make his books so popular?

UNIT D

Differences of Opinion: Bias and Evidence

1 *Play the game "Goodies and Baddies"*

In this game children, either in pairs or in groups, are given a set of cards on which are written the names of historical or fictional characters, such as: Robin Hood; the Sheriff of Nottingham; Cain; Abel; General Montgomery; General Rommel; Tom; Jerry—a number of stereotyped pairs, within the orbit of the children's awareness. Children sort

the cards, as they think fit, into two piles, "Goodies" and "Baddies"; they might also be asked to write down a reason for each choice. The teacher then suggests that the children consider some of the characters from a different point of view, perhaps giving an example of what is meant (e.g. "Now suppose you are responsible for the safety of travellers in Sherwood forest: what is your attitude towards Robin Hood?") Children make any changes they think necessary in the arrangement of the cards, with a newly introduced third category, a pile headed "We can't tell", being also available.

Children and teacher together examine the criteria of choice; some of the illogicality, the bias, and the preconceived notions in the children's selections may become evident to them. After this discussion, children may wish to rearrange their cards once more.

2 *Newspaper cuttings*

A selection of newspaper cuttings all relating to the same event is examined. Differences of emphasis are noted, and attempts made to separate facts from interpretations and opinions.

Children may enjoy the experience of being given a set of basic facts about an incident, occurring in the school or the locality, which they can write up, offering their own interpretations of what happened, together with comments and opinions.

3 *An Attitude Survey*

Children compile and use a questionnaire to discover preferences, within their class, in matters of food, music, hobbies, sports, school activities, etc. Results are plotted on a bar chart and discussed. It may become apparent during the discussion that some preferences ignore certain relevant factors and thus take on the nature of prejudice. The degree of unanimity about the preferences investigated could

be observed, and questions raised about the rightness of majority views and the desirability of siding with the majority.

Another survey could examine the characteristics of "An Ideal Friend". This would involve compiling a check-list, finding out by questionnaire which characteristics are believed to be the most important, and assessing the extent of agreement revealed.

Throughout this Unit, the teacher seeks to make the children aware that:

(a) they may have preconceived ideas about people and situations, while others may legitimately take a totally different view:

(b) they should always take into account relevant evidence before forming a judgement;

(c) while preferences and opinions are normal and acceptable, they can easily become hard, fixed and unreasonable, turning into prejudice and even intolerance, which are undesirable.

UNIT E

Differences of Race and Colour: Two Examples of Prejudice

1 *Against the Jews before and during the Second World War*

Use visual material to introduce children to the political situations reflected in the story of Anne Frank. (The filmstrip "Prejudice" is recommended but not in the form in which it is presented. For this age range the filmstrip can be cut up and selected slides used. The slides showing grotesque stereotypes of Jewish people stimulate lively discussion and questions as do the slides showing male/female stereotypes.)

Read extracts from *The Diary of Anne Frank*. (Pages 13, 53, 57, 63 of the Pan edition may be the most useful.)

The children can dramatise aspects of the Anne Frank story,
    e.g. excerpts from daily life in the hide-out;
    living in a confined space;
    the observance of the Sabbath and Passover.
The children will undoubtedly enjoy making their own hide-outs. These may be:
    on a small scale, similar to the traditional Easter garden;
    as a desk top model made from scrap material;
    in a corner of the classroom using large cardboard boxes;
    of full scale somewhere in the school environment.
Discussion during and after construction may include:

the differences between the pleasures of voluntarily hiding and the restrictions revealed in Anne Frank's experiences:
the reasons for making places of concealment;
the need for co-operation;
the pleasures of possession, secrecy and cosiness;
the feeling of security against adults, or against specific groups.
Class and group discussions can be held on things which the children take for granted, on the longing for freedom to do ordinary things, and on the inward struggle between hope and despair.

After exploring this historical example, the children are asked to identify some of the characteristics of being a Jew and some of the reasons why Jews were persecuted.[2] Two lists, arrived at by means of class discussion, are put aside for use in the next Unit.

2 *Against minority groups in our own society*

Read extracts from *My Mate Shofiq*, e.g. pages 11–14, 38–41, 66–71, 82–89, 114–17, 137–140. (The story concerns Bernard, an English lad who makes friends with the Pakistani lad Shofiq and discovers that this means sharing his experiences of discrimination.) These are made the basis for role-play, which is followed by reflection and discussion on the feelings and actions of the characters involved. During the period of reflection and discussion, play tape-recordings of "Black and White" ("The ink is black, the page is white"), or equally appropriate songs of more recent vintage, in order to display positive attitudes towards racial issues.

Give children the opportunity to think and talk about their own feelings about people in their society who differ from themselves in various ways; then to become children who belong to a minority group, and to think and talk about their feelings when in that role, experiencing misunderstanding, suspicion and rejection. Actual incidents might be recalled and acted out; alternatively, the teacher, or the children working in groups, might devise scenarios to be presented to the class and discussed.

One child wrote:

I like you—you're different
A small boy stands in the playground,
He stands all alone,
He does not seem to have any friends . . .

I turn to go towards him,
But he edges away.
We just stand looking at each other,
Neither of us sure what to do.
I smile at him and hold out my hand.

---

[2]*Great care needs to be exercised here, since there is a risk that, with insensitive handling, stereotypes might actually be encouraged and prejudices strengthened. It is imperative that children put themselves into Jewish shoes, thinking as from inside Jewish heads; the preceding work on Anne Frank is intended to enable them to do so.*

He smiles back.
Then after hesitating he shakes my hand.
His hand feels the same but is different in colour . . .

I asked where his friends were.
He said to me he did not have any because he was
different,
People did not want to talk to him.
I liked him although he was different.
My friends soon agreed they liked him.

UNIT F

Differences of Reaction: Prejudice and Propaganda

1 *Causes and consequences of prejudice*
In the light of insights gained in the preceding Units, and using the lists compiled in Unit E(1), further discussion in small groups is held. The children try to identify some causes of prejudice, each group making its own list of such factors as fear, ignorance, lack of understanding, insecurity, and group pressure; these are shared, to form a more complete class list. Each group then attempts to rank these in order of importance, group findings being shared and discussed.

The consequences of prejudice (e.g. discrimination and division between people, persecution, violence, and denial of opportunity) are explored in a similar manner, with sharing and discussion of findings.

Children might express two of the consequences of prejudice by representing, dramatically or in any chosen medium (paint, paper cut-outs or silhouettes, clay, etc.) the notions of "avoidance" and "aggression". In the case of the former, one person who is in some way distinctive is surrounded by others who are turning away; the setting might be a disco, a football crowd, the playground, or elsewhere. In the case of "aggression", hateful glances, verbal abuse, threatening movements and actual fighting may all be subjects for representation; aggression between groups, as well as between individuals, should be taken into account.

Further ideas for dramatisation, and pieces of writing for thought and discussion, appear in the Resources section.

2 *Types and uses of propaganda*
A useful introductory exercise within the capabilities of the children is to examine the extent of T.V. advertising, and its effects on them. Over a set period, children make a careful record of advertisements for foods, sweets, toys, games, clothes, gadgets, etc. These records are compared with the actual consumption, possession or use of these items by the children, and with their desire to consume, possess or use them.

Children might also be encouraged to notice and to record various means by which they think prejudiced attitudes might be spread, such as slogans, posters, graffiti, rumours, gossip, cartoons, public speeches, selective reporting, slanted programmes, etc; they might be able to collect examples for display. Discussion on the actual and potential effects of this material would follow. Each child might design a T-shirt bearing a symbol or slogan intended to influence people in a particular way.

3 *Countering prejudice and propaganda*
It would be unfortunate if the children gained an impression that prejudice is inevitable, to be accepted as a fact of life, and that all communication is propaganda, and all propaganda bad in its effects. The activities suggested under section (1) above could be paralleled by others which are more positive: this time, the notions to be represented would be "acceptance" and "co-operation". As regards section (2), children could design propaganda which might change people's attitudes and reduce prejudice.

Finally, work in groups, followed by a sharing of ideas, could lead to a list of prejudices discernible in school and in the locality, together with practical proposals for action which would help to dispel them.

UNIT G

Assemblies on the Theme of Difference
The incorporation into Assemblies of material relating to the topic will help to maintain the interest of the children and will also affirm the value of the work done. Some approaches are suggested below: (1) to (5) are for Assemblies held during the currency of the topic; (6) is for an Assembly which brings the topic to a conclusion.

1 The Assembly is based on a reading of Hans Andersen's story "The Ugly Duckling", which acts as a commentary on the theme of Difference. The prejudice of the other ducks, the turkey, the chicken and the cat is clearly shown. Important too are the effects of their behaviour on the Ugly Duckling, and his eventual joy when he is transformed, and revealed in the beauty of difference.

2 Look at Difference as a matter for celebration. (An example is given in *Exploring Primary Assemblies*, page 49).

3 In a short series of Assemblies, several classes interpret various aspects of Difference: in Music, demonstrating differences of pitch, rhythm, volume, speed and style; in Art, demonstrating differences of colour, texture, perspective and media; in the Natural World, demonstrating differences in weather, season and climate, supplementing visual presentation with poetry and prose; in Language, demonstrating in dramatic episodes differences of approach, style and reaction.

4 An occasion on which children bring to Assembly their own contributions to illustrate Difference. Examples might be: contrasting toys or possessions; an account of something unusual which has been noticed; a mime of an incident which revealed differing points of view or differing emotional responses.

5 Two teachers present the opposite sides of an argument. The children, in groups and with the help of other teachers, formulate and express their views on what they have heard; and each group tries to work out a way by which the two sides might be reconciled, a spokesman announcing the group's suggestion.

6 A display of completed art and craft work, with a descriptive commentary on the general intention of the topic, supplemented by examples of personal writing (reproduced on OHP transparencies) which illuminate some of the key concepts and insights which have arisen during the course of the topic.

Resources

Books

R. Godden	*The Diddakoi*	Puffin 1975
J. Brown	*Flat Stanley*	Methuen 1975
I. Southall	*Let the Balloon Go*	Puffin 1972
J. Blume	*Blubber*	Piccolo 1981
T. Penman & A. Wolff	*Web of Language*	O.U.P. 1982
A. Frank	*The Diary of Anne Frank*	Pan 1968
J. Needle	*My Mate Shofiq*	Fontana Lions 1979
W. Griffin	*Exploring Primary Assemblies*	Macmillan Education 1984

Story

H. Andersen   The Ugly Duckling

Poem

Dylan Thomas   The Hunchback in the Park, in J. Heath-Stubbs & D. Wright eds. *The Faber Book of Twentieth Century Verse*, and   Faber 1975

J. Reeves ed. *Modern Poets' World*. (For the words, see below.)   Heinemann 1967

Songs

Black and White   Recorded by The Spinners Included in *New Orbit*: songs and hymns for under elevens (For the words see below)   Galliard 1972

Radio material

Web of Language (for 10–12): series 2 & 3, with Teachers' Notes   BBC 1982 & 1984

Filmstrip

Prejudice   From Mary Glasgow Publications Ltd., Freepost, Brookhampton Lane, Kineton, Warwick, CV35 0BR.

The Hunchback in the Park

The hunchback in the park
A solitary mister
Propped between trees and water
From the opening of the garden lock
That lets the trees and water enter
Until the Sunday sombre bell at dark

Eating bread from a newspaper
Drinking water from the chained cup
That the children filled with gravel
In the fountain basin where I sailed my ship
Slept at night in a dog kennel
But nobody chained him up.

Like the park birds he came early
Like the water he sat down
And Mister they called him Hey Mister
The truant boys from the town
Running when he had heard them clearly
On out of sound

Past lake and rockery
Laughing when he shook his paper
Hunchbacked in mockery
Through the loud zoo of the willow groves
Dodging the park keeper
With his stick that picked up leaves.

And the old dog sleeper
Alone between nurses and swans
While the boys among the willows
Made the tigers jump out of their eyes
To roar on the rockery stones
And the groves were blue with sailors

Made all day until bell time
A woman figure without fault
Straight as a young elm
Straight and tall from his crooked bones
That she might stand in the night
After the locks and chains

All night in the unmade park
After the railings and shrubberies
The birds the grass the trees the lake
And the wild boys innocent as strawberries
Had followed the hunchback
To his kennel in the dark.

Black and White

The ink is black, the page is white,
Together we learn to read and write . . .
And now a child can understand
This is the law of all the land . . .
The ink is black, the page is white,
Together we learn to read and write . . .

The slate is black, the chalk is white,
The words stand out so clear and bright . . .
And now at last we plainly see
The alphabet of liberty . . .

The slate is black, the chalk is white,
Together we learn to read and write . . .

A child is black, a child is white,
The whole world looks upon the sight . . .
For very well the whole world knows
This is the way that freedom grows . . .
A child is black, a child is white,
Together we learn to read and write . . .

The world is black, the world is white,
It turns by day and then by night . . .
It turns so each and every one
Can take his station in the sun . . .
The world is black, the world is white,
Together we learn to read and write . . .

(The dots indicate that the tune requires the repetition of the last three or four syllables of the even-numbered lines.)

Additional Suggestions for Drama Work

1 *Green face*

One child is to imagine that he/she has a green face . . . or the face might actually be painted green.

The other children play the roles of people met in the course of a typical school day, such as parents, bus-conductor, shopkeeper, lollipop-lady, teacher, classmates.

They act out a sequence of events of the day. Every person the green-faced child meets *must* remark on the change in colour (whether kindly, unkindly, jokingly, nervously or disbelievingly).

Back at home, the child complains to parents, who consult the doctor: there is no cure.

A second stage might be to act out meetings on the following day with some of the same people, the green-faced child this time taking the intiative and trying to explain his/her predicament and to get them to accept him/her.

A third stage might be to move on to the next day again . . . by which time a third of the class have acquired green faces! What changes does this bring about?

After each stage, it would be appropriate to share and discuss the feelings and thoughts of all the children; however, the experience might well carry its own message, which further words would weaken.

2 *New teacher*

The scene is the playground one morning, as the children are arriving for school. Rumours are going round concerning the new teacher who is coming: she is said to be strict and unfair, to dislike boys, to grumble about everything, to be unable to laugh or

smile, and so on. The scene then shifts to the classroom. The new teacher enters, and introduces herself with a smile. During the lesson she has words of praise and encouragement for everyone. She makes the work interesting, and suggests taking the class on an educational outing.

The third scene is the playground at break time, with the children talking about the new teacher, of whom they now have firsthand experience. (2 or 3 minutes should suffice for this.)

In subsequent discussion, attention might focus on three questions:

What effect did the rumours about the new teacher have on you?

Did anyone stop to think about where the rumours came from, or how accurate they might be?

What have been the effects of the lesson with the new teacher?

3 *The big-headed bowler,*

The scene is a meeting, chaired by the P.E. teacher, to select a team for the first cricket match of the season. One boy, newly arrived at the school, impresses the others with his claim to have been a County Junior trialist when at his previous school; the P.E. teacher is persuaded to put him in the team.

A connecting narrative, told by the teacher, describes the practice before the match, and the match itself. In the practice, the new boy's bowling is not impressive: but he has excuses—slippery run-up, ball out of shape, strained wrist (and what others can the class suggest?!)—and declares that everything will work at the match. It doesn't. He is a disaster, giving away dozens of runs.

Scene two is the post-mortem on the match. Who is to blame? How can such mistakes be avoided in future?

The children can scarcely escape the conclusion that the prime need, in countering prejudice, is to discover the facts (as also in (2) above), without which rational judgments about people or situations cannot be made. In this example, the other boys are prejudiced in favour of the new boy (has he some "charisma" in addition to his claims, but irrelevant to his bowling ability?)—a reminder that prejudice is not always hostile.

Additional Material for Thought and Discussion

1 *Two knights, one statue*

Two knights, coming from opposite directions, entered a clearing in the forest at the same moment. In the centre of the clearing stood a noble statue of a former king.

"Well met, Sir Knight" said one. "Did you ever see such a fine golden statue?"

"Well met, my friend" replied the other. "A fine statue indeed—but not *golden*: it is *black*—I see it clearly against the setting sun."

"You are mistaken, sir. It is not *black*, but *gold*."

"*Black*, sir. I do not lie."

Their words became heated. Their tempers were short. The argument turned into a challenge.

They lowered their vizors, put their lances in rest, and charged . . . and missed.

Furiously, at either side of the clearing, they pulled up, turned their horses, and prepared to charge again . . . but instead of charging, they approached each other slowly, each raising his vizor. You would have noticed that both were smiling.

The children, perhaps working in pairs, could invent, write and illustrate their own stories on this theme, viz. the reconciling of perceptions which appear to be in direct conflict.

2 *Going home* (written by an Indian pupil in a Secondary school)

The writing on the wall
I see it everywhere
GO HOME WOGS
And I say to myself
I am gong home
One day

School children chant
As they walk past
GO HOME WOGS
How do they know
The hurt that I feel
How long it lasts
How real
The writing on the wall
GO HOME WOGS
Haunts me night and day
Don't they know I'm just a cog
Don't they know I long to do
Just what they say
The writing on the wall
I see it everywhere
GO HOME WOGS
And I say
As I gulp
And hold back the treacherous tears
I am going home
One day
Do you hear?

3 *Metamorphosis*

Kafka's short story "Metamorphosis" (published, with five other stories, in the Penguin Modern Classics series) begins thus:

As Gregor Samsa awoke one morning from uneasy dreams he found himself transformed in his bed into a gigantic insect. He was lying on his hard, as it were armour-plated, back and when he lifted his head a little he could see his dome-like brown belly divided into stiff arched segments on top of which the bed-quilt could hardly keep in position and was

*about to slide off completely. His numerous legs,
which were pitifully thin compared to the rest of his
bulk, waved helplessly before his eyes.*
The story describes, in typically restrained and
matter-of-fact fashion, Gregor's problems and the
problems which his novel state pose to his family.
To general relief—including his own?—he dies as
the result of an injury, the charwoman disposing of
the corpse. In his insect form, as also perhaps in his
normal existence as the son in a family and as a
commercial traveller, Gregor is at the mercy of
other people, and is (or fears that he is) unable to
communicate to other people his thoughts and
feelings.

Exploring imaginatively the theme of metamorphosis, through discussion and writing and/or
dramatisation, could involve children in considering such questions as:

What does it feel like to be regarded as insignificant, or disgusting, or dangerous, or unable to
communicate with other people?

What things would be specially difficult for you
to do? How would you try to overcome these
difficulties?

If you had become a non-human being, how
would you try to communicate with humans?

How could people show that they still recognised
you, in spite of your transformed state, and that
they still cared for you?

What difference, if any, would it make to you if
you met another creature—perhaps another
transformed human being—like yourself?

Additional Books for the Children to Read

J. Yeoman &
  Q. Blake
	The Wild Washerwomen
	  (For younger children)
		Puffin 1982

B. Ashley	*The Trouble with Donovan Craft* (Black foster-child in family)	Puffin 1977
B. Ashley	*Terry on the Fence*	Puffin 1978
C. Powling	*Daredevils or Scaredycats*	Fontana 1981

L. Fitzhugh	*Nobody's Family is Going to Change*
	  (Racial prejudice and prejudice
	  against women)
		Macmillan Education 1981

J. Needle	*Albeson and the Germans*	Armada Books 1981
A. Schlee	*The Vandal*	Magnet Books 1983
R. Heinlein	*The Star Beast*	New English Library 1978
J. Needle	*A Sense of Shame and Other Stories* (Teenagers in a confusing world)	Armada Books 1982
F. Dhondy	*Come to Mecca and Other Stories*	Armada Books 1978
M. Twain	*The Adventures of Tom Sawyer*	
M. Twain	*Huckleberry Finn*	

SECONDARY AGE-RANGE

INTRODUCTION

Pupils enter the Secondary school with widely varying attitudes towards, and knowledge about, religion. Many view it as a closed system of beliefs, chiefly associated with Christianity, which they either accept, reject or tolerate. Such stereotyping needs to be broken down. The qualities to be encouraged are those recommended by the Agreed Syllabus set out in *Religious Education in Hampshire Schools* (1978), viz. empathy, openness of view, and absence of prejudice. The aim is understanding, which implies appreciation of differences and does not in the least preclude reasoned personal convictions.

The development of understanding requires the active participation of pupils in their own learning process. Thus it is suggested that units of work ought to contain planned opportunities for pupils to discuss in pairs or groups, share their ideas with one another, read together, prepare a class presentation of findings, etc. In all planning, attention should be paid to psychologist J. S. Bruner's words in *Towards a Theory of Instruction* (Harvard U.P. 1966): he points out that individual differences in pupils necessitate the making of a curriculum which contains different ways of activating them, different ways of presenting sequences, and different opportunities for them to engage with materials in order that they may master the "form of knowing" with which they are involved. The notion of "irrigating the imagination" is also one worth bearing in mind.

The development of understanding will be influenced by attitudes which the school, perhaps quite unwittingly, may be inculcating in pupils. The sociologist, T. Husén, in *The School in Question* (O.U.P. 1979), has noted the effects on pupils' attitudes of "classroom instruction of the frontal variety" where the teacher totally controls the material. If teachers expect pupils only to listen, to memorise what has been said, and to ask the odd desultory questions, the hidden message—however much the teacher may talk about participation and dialogue—is that passive acceptance is better than active learning, reception better than participation, and knowledge a gift transmitted by the teacher who knows to the pupil who does not. Husén would see the teacher rather as a planner of experiences, and the pupils as involved in their own learning. Others have observed how the size and structure of a large school tend to cause depersonalisation and alienation, a tendency which may be resisted if pupils are given a more active role in the organisation itself. At a very basic level, a teacher might think about the physical arrangement of the classroom, and ask what account it takes of the needs or wishes of the pupils, and what this particular element of the "hidden curriculum" may be conveying to them (e.g. ranks of front-facing desks, giving prominence to one person).

In relation to the material to be taught in Religious Education, the Hampshire Agreed Syllabus makes a statement of fundamental importance:

> The task of the teacher at this (the secondary) stage is twofold. First, to foster in the pupils a reflective approach to living. Second, to engage the pupils in dialogue with living faiths in such a way that the reflective process is broadened and enriched.

A basic requirement is that pupils should be in possession of, and be interested in, material that they can be reflective about; in the planning of lessons, use could well be made of the four stages recommended by Barnes in *From Communication to Curriculum* (Penguin 1976), viz.: focusing; exploring and manipulating material; re-focusing; public sharing of discussions and findings. If pupils are to be carried to higher levels of reflection, then at some stage they must also involve themselves in the often lonely process of writing, as this is an important way of clarifying thought and of furthering imaginative responses; more disciplined and more demanding than speech, the exercise of writing puts pressure on one to think coherently, logically, and perhaps even creatively. Pertinent questions for the teacher to pose when setting work are suggested by the Schools Council:

> Why are pupils being asked to write?
> What is the writing for?
> Who is the writing for?
> What does the writing achieve?

It is good policy for a Department not only to share in class the work of pupils, but also to photocopy pieces of work which show insight, and to retain them in the Department's resourses. Pupils tend to relate to the work of their peers, and R.E. resources need this type of enrichment.

Classroom Practice in R.E.

INTRODUCTION

Religious Educators have been well served by scholars who have clearly articulated the place of R.E. in the curriculum. *Religious Education in Hampshire Schools* (1978) and *Paths to Understanding* (1980) have given teachers a clear mandate for their professional role. The major task for the next decade is to narrow the gap between statements of ideals and actual practice in the classroom. Making religious insights accessible to pupils of a wide range of abilities and in varying social contexts is a considerable challenge to the teacher.

This article considers firstly what needs to be provided by the school and secondly what methods may be employed by the teacher in order to promote interest and learning. Examples are taken mainly from Christianity, the teaching of which poses, in the experience of many teachers, particularly acute problems at present.

THE LEARNING CONTEXT

Most teachers work hard, often with much ingenuity, to create a good learning environment. Their task would be eased, and their ability to make available to pupils the learning experiences recommended in the schemes in this book would be increased, if adequate provision were made of the following:

Time
The minimum time required if R.E. is to have any real chance of success is 5% of curriculum time (i.e. 2 periods in a 40 period week). In general, double periods would give more scope for the kind of pupil activity recommended in this book. A fair test of adequate provision of time is to count the weekly pupil turnover of each teacher; if this exceeds 400, the teacher is unlikely even to get to know the names of all the pupils for whom he or she is responsible.

Finance
Capitation allowance should be granted to R.E. on a per-capita basis. A quick calculation will reveal the amount of money allocated to teach one pupil for a year. Its adequacy should be measured against an equivalent Humanities subject.

Accommodation
A room with facilities for the presentation, without inconvenience, of visual material is needed, so that full use may be made of resources now available. A simple system of storage and retrieval, for book and non-book material, is essential to the survial of the busy teacher. The basics include a filing cabinet with space for translucent slide containers; plenty of open shelving; easy access to a projector on a stand; an overhead projector on a trolley; display space and a poster rack; a cassette recorder; and tray units for general storage.

The seating plan in the classroom can either help or hinder the teaching style. A layout which enables pupils to communicate with each other as well as with the teacher has considerable advantages: for example the 'conference' style layout below has much to commend it because it enables work in pairs and small groups to occur without disruption, as well as being suitable for more formal didactic teaching.

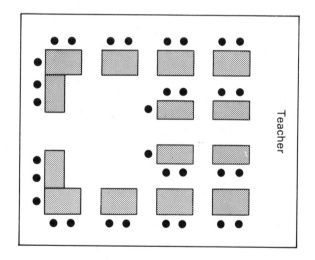

Linking with other subjects
The achievement of the objectives of R.E. will be aided if teachers of the subject can enlist the co-operation of teachers working in other curriculum areas. For example, work on a Christian festival involves becoming familiar with the basic story, looking at various customs and celebrations, thinking about the use of signs and symbols, and exploring inner meanings. If pupils prepare symbolic food in Home Economics, and in Art represent ideas using a variety of media, the work in R.E. is reinforced. Similarly, the development of skills in interpreting myth, symbol, allegory and poetry would be strengthened by the co-operation of the English department. Religious expression takes many forms and logically the exploration of its meaning requires a range of skills to which many colleagues can make a contribution.

LEARNING EXPERIENCES

Most R.E. teachers in documenting the course they offer refer mainly to the content of the course preceded by a general statement of aims and objectives. It would be more useful to teachers if each stage were preceded by objectives specific to it, and if a third section on appropriate learning experiences were added. The school's R.E. syllabus would thus supply answers, relevant to each stage or age-range, to three questions:

Why is this part of the course being taught (i.e. the rationale)?

What content is involved (i.e. the programme)?

How is this content to be made accessible to the pupils (i.e. the learning experiences)?

The third of these questions has perhaps been given insufficient attention both in recent literature about the subject and in documents prepared by individual school departments. The remainder of this article offers some practical suggestions, many of which are expanded and exemplified in later sections of this book.

Thinking Skills

As every teacher knows, the attention span of pupils is limited and variable. Learning processes need therefore to be devised which take account of this fact, and which are likely to engage the attention of all pupils for most of the time. Techniques such as those employed in Edward de Bono's *Teaching Thinking* (Penguin 1979) can be very useful, e.g. working in pairs or small groups to brainstorm a topic; writing down the good, bad and interesting points about a statement or picture; ranking a set of statements in order of their importance. Activities like these can engage pupils more fully than attempting to hold a discussion with a whole class. For example, pupils might be asked to write all they know about "The Bible" or "Jesus": the result will enable the teacher to see areas of need and to match subsequent lessons to these needs. Work on texts can make good use of thinking skills: e.g. pupils might list what they consider to be the good, bad and interesting points about the injunction "Love your enemies"; the exercise challenges them to think, and discussion of their ideas should lead to a deeper understanding of the attitude and teaching of Jesus.

Learning through Visual Stimuli

Most filmstrips and slide sets are too long: the temptation to 'get through them' is strong, but should be resisted, as likely to be unproductive. Presentation of carefully selected slides, accompanied by questions which will engage the pupil with the thoughts, feelings, symbols and actions portrayed, can take the pupil to the central ideas more effectively than if he/she is a passive viewer. The same applies to video tapes: where classes simply watch, the level of understanding achieved is less than when the teacher, selecting significant extracts, focuses attention on central issues and sets appropriate tasks. Pupils can be asked to observe closely certain specified features, which may then be discussed. In a visual presentation of the Christian Eucharist, for example, attention may be directed towards the role played by one particular individual: speculation in pairs about his feelings and intentions can enable pupils to penetrate beyond the outward features of the rite into the meanings embodied in it. Reference to the use of symbolic representation and action in another faith can sharpen awareness still further.

Learning from Visitors

A visitor should be regarded as a valuable resource rather than as a substitute teacher. The ideal is to plan for a series of visitors representing between them a range of commitments. Emotionally charged offerings need not be avoided, for they are an important part of the kaleidoscope of religious expression; but 'blind dates' with people who have some idiosyncratic message to put across are difficult to justify educationally. Visitors should always be clearly briefed, and be aware that pupils will be encouraged to enter into reasoned dialogue with them. Preparation for a visitor is essential, and might well include the gathering of background information and the formulation, after discussion, of key questions to be put to the visitor by the pupils and the teacher.

Learning from Visits

Visits to places of worship can be extremely valuable, but visits to empty, cold churches may be counterproductive (as may tours guided by the minister). Religious buildings, however much they may contain of historic monuments, beautiful artefacts and symbols of the faith, are essentially places used by communities of people trying to live out their faith. Pupils therefore need to encounter people and to question them about what a place of worship and its community means to them. It hardly needs saying that, as far as the building and its symbols are concerned, finding out is better than being told and questions are better answered after they have been asked rather than before. If arrangements can be made for pupils, during their visit, to experience some of the activities typical of the worship of the community, the visit would be more fruitful. (For further suggestions see *Paths to Understanding* p. 27ff.)

Learning from Simulation and Artefacts

R.E. teachers are neither priests nor gurus, but educators. When launching any simulation activity (e.g. baptism, meditation, marriage) they need to make their intentions clear to the pupils. Throughout, they need to act as commentators and to encourage discussion. Religious leaders who have good rapport with young people may be available to help. Religious artefacts can be used effectively to arouse curiosity. The idea that symbols are 'silent teachers' point pupils to the

history and the meanings enshrined in the artefacts as well as to the devotion which they elicit from the believer. In this kind of work emphasis should always be on the meaning which ritual and symbol hold for the adherent, rather than on mere information. For example, reflection about memories and associations could be followed by pupils speculating about the meaning likely to be enshrined in e.g. a rosary, an icon or the burning of incense. If the artefacts can then be discussed with someone for whom they are important, the lesson is likely to develop the pupils' capacity for empathy.

Reading Texts and Story Telling

The impact of a story or text is vital, and it is rarely successful to hand over the task of reading to a class volunteer. Using different versions, telling the story in your own words, and playing tapes of famous actors reading, all have their place. There is a case for 'story time' at the end of a lesson without any reflection or discussion. Usually, however, discussion about interpretations reinforces the essential point that stories have many levels of meaning. The exegesis of texts, a familiar element in courses of study in higher education, may sometimes be appropriate provided that it does not inhibit the more imaginative and divergent ideas which come from some pupils. Teachers with strong yet relaxed discipline and adequate facilities can attempt drama

as a way of deepening pupils' insights into stories. Exploration of the inner meanings of stories or parables in mime, movement or drama is more likely to be effective than a mere telling of the story; e.g. exploring themes such as reconciliation or jealousy may be more effective than acting out the story of the Prodigal Son.

Worksheets

There has been a tendency in recent years to overuse these; and even an imaginatively conceived booklet, produced with the greatest do-it-yourself skill, is hard put to compete with the many cleverly designed materials now commercially available, and to catch the interest of pupils. Where worksheets are used they should direct the pupils to a wider range of learning experiences linked with other resources. It is also useful to check that the cognitive level of operation demanded of the pupil goes beyond mere comprehension, stimulates the imagination, and demands such skills as analysis and evaluation. (Bloom's *Taxonomy of Educational Objectives Vol. 1 Cognitive Domain* (Longman 1965) is still a valuable guide). For example, a worksheet on a puja could involve looking at a slide in a handviewer, identifying the key symbols, and ranking a set of statements about meanings according to their importance.

Visions of Life

INTRODUCTION

This course is planned for the first half-term in a Secondary school, and is inspired by the words of philosopher Philip Phenix in *Realms of Meaning* (McGraw-Hill 1964):

> At the very least, faith refers to an ideal, a hope for maximum completeness, depth and integrity of vision. On these minimal terms, in which no transcendent realities are posited, everyone should be able to acknowledge some religious meaning.

The experiences which constitute Religious Education for pupils in their first few weeks in a Secondary School are crucial: the attitudes, favourable or unfavourable, which they adopt at that time towards this area of study will not easily be changed later. It is imperative that the content should interest the pupils, and should be seen as relevant and important to themselves, therefore deserving of their attention. The course Visions of Life is designed with this in mind: it seeks to employ both a content and a method which will be novel to pupils, and which will not be restricted to the verbal dimension; to draw on pupils' present knowledge and ideas; and to ensure that the subject-matter is of real significance, while intentionally leaving explicitly religious ideas to be raised, if at all at this stage, by the pupils. In addition, the course aims to utilise and develop skills and co-operative activities which will aid the learning process.

To some teachers this course may appear controversial. It is a particular interpretation of the "implicit", or "pre-religious", approach to religion, and is indeed open to debate.[1] The debate might profitably begin with the Schools Council's description of "implicit religion" (Working Paper 36, p. 19):

> Implicit religion resides in those elements of secular experience—like wonder, guilt and love—which evoke questions about life's ultimate significance, its values, meaning and purpose.

The teaching method adopted here is one which starts with the pupils, helping them to reflect on their own experiences and the experiences of others, with the purpose of leading them towards new understandings and into new areas of knowledge.

This method is more often found in First and Middle schools than in Secondary, where the subject-matter has traditionally been regarded as all-important. A guiding principle for the course is in fact one of the objectives specified for the First school age-range, in the Hampshire Agreed Syllabus, viz. that teachers will

> . . . seek to arouse and maintain interest, encouraging and enabling further learning, and closing no doors on the children's own vision and curiosity.

In furtherance of this aim, and in order to approach the task rather differently from a Middle school, the works of an author and of an artist, and a description of man given by a chemist, have been used. The first two examples have been chosen because transcendent ideas are immanent in them, and provide bases for discussion about attitudes and commitments; the third has been included because it is hoped that it will provide the stimulus for further thought about the nature and value of human beings.

Unit 1 Introduction

Pupils imagine themselves to be TV reporters interviewing strangers in the street. Each pupil devises five questions with which to interview one stranger; one of the questions should relate to the stranger's notion of an ideal world. Later, several pupils introduce their stranger to the class.

This procedure serves to:
  break the ice;
  introduce the idea of "vision";
  inculcate the notion that the pupils are important, and that the group is not simply teacher-dominated;
  develop the skill of listening.

Each pupil thinks about the word "vision" and decides what it might mean. Consultation with a friend, or friends, may occur. A dictionary may be used. The best ideas are shared with the whole class, through the medium of the OHP.

Each pupil makes a cover for his/her course-work, entitled "Visions of Life". (The example on p. 66 was done by a 12-year-old girl.)

---

[1]*The important concept of "implicit religion" has been fruitful in developing both the philosophy and the practice of R.E.; it has also been much discussed and criticised. A useful recent article is D. G. Attfield's "Implicit Religion" in British Journal of Religious Education Vol. 7, No. 1, Autumn 1984; see also A. L. Brine's reaction to it in the same journal, Vol. 8, No. 1, Autumn 1985.*

Each pupil writes about himself/herself. If anyone has a personal "vision". such as a view of what he/she would like to be or become, this would be included. Drawings and photographs would add interest. The whole is arranged as the pupil chooses: it is the pupil's own record, not merely something produced for the teacher.

With the pupils' agreement, but not otherwise, their work may be shared publicly. When this happens, the work tends to take on a new importance, for it is seen as a valued communication, relevant both to the teacher and to the rest of the class.

Unit 2   Engaging with the Work of a Writer

The work in this Unit is based on the book *Let the Balloon Go* by Ivan Southall (Puffin 1972). The use of imaginative literature (story, novel, play) in Religious Education is justified on the grounds that it frequently deals with issues which are the life-blood of religion—the conflict between good and evil, self-sacrifice, wholeness, life and death and renewed life—and does so in language and thought-forms familiar to the pupil. There is a strong case for allowing a story to stand on its own: readers or listeners can (as Ted Hughes remarks in the article "Myth and Education" in *Writers, Critics and Children* (Heinemann 1976)) walk round in it, understand its characters, and perhaps grow up a little through it. *Let the Balloon Go* is concerned with such issues and can be used in just the way recommended by Ted Hughes.

This particular book was chosen for several reasons, which it may be wise to spell out clearly:

It connects with the "implicit" approach to religion;

It fosters a reflective approach to living;

It involves pupils in vicarious experience, and develops the skill of empathy;

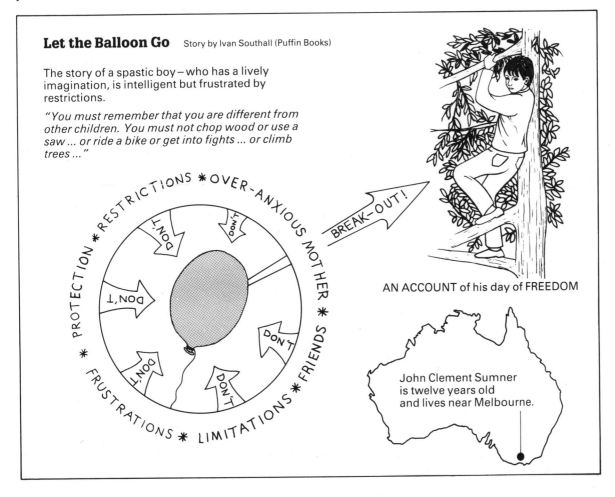

Let the Balloon Go   Story by Ivan Southall (Puffin Books)

The story of a spastic boy – who has a lively imagination, is intelligent but frustrated by restrictions.

"You must remember that you are different from other children. You must not chop wood or use a saw ... or ride a bike or get into fights ... or climb trees ..."

PROTECTION * RESTRICTIONS * OVER-ANXIOUS MOTHER * FRIENDS * LIMITATIONS * FRUSTRATIONS *

DON'T

BREAK-OUT!

AN ACCOUNT of his day of FREEDOM

John Clement Sumner is twelve years old and lives near Melbourne.

It allows a response, while respecting the pupil's autonomy: for preaching does not occur, and the morality is not made too personal by relating it to pupils everyday lives. It thus functions much like myth;

It makes use of a powerful symbolic image (the notion that a balloon becomes itself only by being set free). Since religions convey their meanings through the use of symbols, pupils' insights into the story's symbolism will provide them with a tool for better understanding religion.

The story is of a boy, John Clement Sumner, who is spastic and over-protected. One day, while he is waiting, somewhat miserably, for his mother who is shopping—he seems to spend his life waiting for her—he is given a vision of what life could be like. A stranger says to him: "You can be anything you want to be, a balloon is not a balloon until you cut the string and let it go". When, later, he gains a day of freedom, the outcome is far from expected. (The key ideas of the story may be usefully summarised in a chart, such as that on p. 66, to be issued to the pupils at some stage.)

When this novel was used in a pilot scheme, many of the pupils seemed to live with the boy in his ungainly body; exhausted themselves with him when, on his adventures, he tried to climb a tree; died, as he almost did, thinking freedom had gone for ever. Later they discussed what it meant to be a spastic, or to be disabled in some other way. They thought about society's provision, or lack of it, for the less than perfect in its midst. They thought about themselves, and about what it is to be human and to possess, or adopt, attitudes to life.

The above notes will, it is hoped, be of assistance to the teacher in working out his/her personally appropriate way of handling the book. It is suggested that the Unit might conclude with a discussion about symbolic language: the following procedure has proved effective.

(a) Pupils, working in pairs, discuss the question: The stranger in the story of John Clement Sumner said: "You'll do it, Son. Don't let anything stop you from being the boy you want to be, and the answer's inside you. A balloon is not a balloon until you cut the string and let it go".
Would his words have had the same impact if he had said simply: "Just be the boy you want to be!"?

(b) Each pair compares ideas with another pair.

(c) Some pupils state their answers, and perhaps their reasons for them. A count of opinions might be taken, and a brief report written by each pupil. The report written by a 12 year-old in the top stream was as follows:

These are the class's conclusions:

There were five people in the class who thought the second way of saying it was better, and twenty-five who were in favour of the symbolic way of saying it. The main complaint against the symbolic way was that it was too long and unless you had read the story you would not know what he meant. Others answered by saying that it was not said to anyone, it was said to John who had an extremely fertile imagination and would understand it.

Stuart Pearson (who was for the shorter way) said that a short, sharp sentence was more likely to stick in your mind than anything else. The people in favour of the longer way said it would be easier to remember the long way as it was not everyday that a stranger comes up to you and says something powerful like that. Also, it sends a powerful image into your brain and gives your head something to work on.

My conclusions

I was in favour of the long, symbolic way of saying it. I agree with all the points above, but I also think that the longer way explained to John how to be himself, whereas the other just told him to do it.

The story has stimulated imaginative writing, often deeply felt by the writers and intently listened to by other pupils. The two poems below were the responses of a girl and a boy (not himself disabled) both aged 12:

I Want To Be Free—*the Balloon's Story*

1 *I tug and I pull—*
  I want to be free—
  Tied tight on my strong—
  Won't someone buy me?

2 *The boys on their bikes,*
  How fast they go!
  They weave and jump,
  That's freedom I know!

3 *We fly down the street—*
  I'm tied to his bike.
  Freedom at last,
  I knew I was right.

4 *Freedom I said,*
  But I was wrong.
  The birds they fly free,
  As they sing their song.

5 *My string it has snapped,*
  I fly and feel free.
  The world down below,
  It fascinates me.

6 *I want to fly there,*
   To that fair on the ground,
   But the wind pulls me back
   From the sights and the sounds.

7 *My life goes before me*
   As slowly I die.
   It was freedom I sought,
   But freedom's a lie.

8 *We're all bound by rules*
   And the laws of the land.
   My rules were the wind
   And the string in his hand.

Does Somebody Else Feel Like Me?

1 *Tied up with string,*
   A bird without wing.
   I cannot be set free—
   Does somebody else feel like me?

2 *Stuck at home all day,*
   Nothing with which to play.
   Treated like a baby,
   Do this, or that, or maybe!—
   I wish I could die—
   As every day goes by.

3 *Sometimes in life.*
   I wish I had a knife.
   I just want to die.
   And I think you know why—
   I'm a spastic.

4 *Mum thinks I'm a kid*
   So my tears I've always hid.
   Why can't I be a proper boy?
   I'm just played around with like a toy.

5 *I go to a special school—*
   Not allowed to kick a ball.
   I have to sit in a special chair—
   And always have to take special care,
   Just in case I slip or slide,
   In this chair I have to ride.

6 *BUT I WILL NEVER GIVE IN*
   AND ONE DAY I KNOW I'LL WIN!

Unit 3   Engaging with the Work of an Artist
Many artists, through their works, attempt to express their ideas, feelings and beliefs about life. One such artist was Naum Gabo, who died in 1977. His work is among those explored in B. Lealman and E. Robinson's *Image of Life* (C.E.M. 1980).

Suggested approach
(a) Pupils view three slides of the work of Naum Gabo. These are presented in a setting and manner which will encourage relaxed and concentrated attention. Silence is required while viewing.
(b) Pupils jot down words which they would apply to the works which are being shown. As private and personal responses, each person's contribution is to be respected and valued in its own right; there are no "correct" or "incorrect" responses.
(c) Pupils look with the teacher at an adapted text (the book itself being beyond the ability of this age-group) of relevant sections of *Image of Life*, in order to discover what the artist himself was trying to say. His was a vision which transcended his situation. In the midst of war he created images of good rather than evil, order rather than chaos, life rather than death; in the hope that people might retain a vision of a different, and better, world.

The above activities engage the imagination; encourage sensitivity to, and appreciation of, art forms as means of human communication; and develop the skill of "looking with a listening eye".

Unit 4   Engaging with the Work of a Chemist
A chemist analysed man and found that he consists of:
   enough water to fill a 45 litre barrel;
   enough carbon for 9000 pencils;
   enough fat for 7 bars of soap;
   enough iron for a medium-size nail;
   enough phosphorus for 2000 matches;
   enough lime to whitewash a chicken-coop;
   small amounts of magnesium and sulphur.
Each pupil is issued with a previous pupil's drawing of this analysis (as on p. 69) and examines it.

Each pupil joins with a friend to discuss, and write down brief answers to, the questions:
   (a) What has the chemist done?
   (b) Is his analysis true?
   (c) Is his analysis the whole truth? Or is man more than the chemist says? If so, what more is he?
Ideas are pooled and discussed by the class, pupils' suggestions about the third part of question (c) being listed on blackboard or OHP. Examples (such as those given below) of previous pupils' work in this topic may be used in the general sharing of ideas. Pupils express their responses and thoughts in whatever visual or verbal form they prefer.
   A 14 year-old-girl wrote:

Enough fat for seven bars of soap . . .
Are we not more than that?
Is there hope?

Water enough to fill 45 litres . . .
Is that all they are . . .
The ones who teach us?

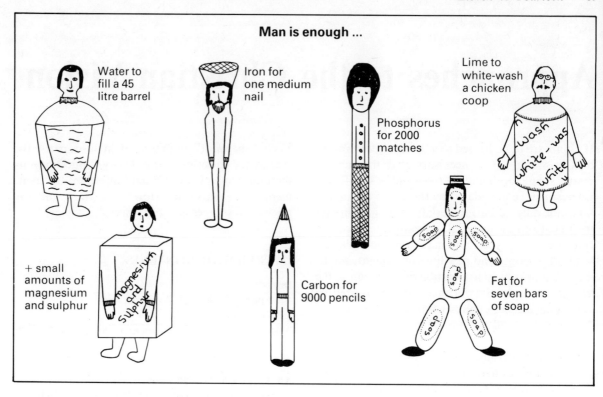

Man is enough ...

Water to fill a 45 litre barrel

Iron for one medium nail

Phosphorus for 2000 matches

Lime to white-wash a chicken coop

+ small amounts of magnesium and sulphur

Carbon for 9000 pencils

Fat for seven bars of soap

No!

Man has senses, eyes and ears:
Man has laughter, he also has tears.
We were made for a purpose, God had a plan . . .
And what is the use of a senseless man?

A 14-year-old boy wrote:

Man is a living, thinking being. He can reason out problems, communicate with his fellow man, discuss different ways of looking at things. He can believe in things and disbelieve in them. He can destroy things and he can create things. Man is more than just a collection of chemicals. The best description of man, is MAN!

Two girls, aged 13 and 14, working together, wrote:

Man has a body,
Man has a head,
Man is born,
But soon he's dead,
And in between,
He feels different emotions,
Of love and pain,
And many devotions,
Man is alive,
He thinks and does.
Man is special,
He has learned how to love.

Personal writing, on the theme "Who/What am I?" or "How I see myself" might be an appropriate conclusion. The following piece of verse (not in fact by a child) could be quoted as one possible treatment of the theme:

Who Am I?

I'm a boy, son of my mother;
To my sister, I'm a brother.
I'm a second year child at school
Where I'm clever, but sometimes a fool.
I'm a nuisance, teacher says,
When she's on one of her off days.
("You're a credit to the class!"
Said Mr. Jones—but he's an ass.)
I'm a real baby in the dark;
But centre-forward on the park,
A scorer in almost every match:
I'm the player they come to watch!
As a fisherman, I land a few.
I'm a keen collector, too—
Fossils mostly. And a radio ham . . .
The more I think, the more I am!

Approaches to the Christian Vision

If pupils are to be helped to a better understanding of Christianity, it is necessary that the subject-matter should both interest them and be significant. Interest can be stimulated by the use of unfamiliar (and not only verbal) material; by an imaginative treatment of that material, a treatment which will challenge stereotypes, and may make possible new kinds of response and new lines of thought; and by the fullest possible participation of the pupils in the learning process. Significance can be ensured so long as the teacher's concern is to answer effectively three fundamental questions,[1] viz.:

(a) What, essentially, is Christianity trying to say? By definition, its focus is Jesus, held to be the Christ, the supreme—unique—embodiment of God's activity in the world.

(b) How is it trying to communicate and preserve its message? Word, symbol, action, and the witness of personal life, are all relevant here.

(c) What kinds of response can its message evoke? Examples of changed lives (new commitments, attitudes, behaviour, aspirations), and of the development of Christian communities and organisations, are manifold.

Most of the suggestions which follow are taken from the introductory section of a 2½-term course on Christianity, undertaken successfully with third year pupils in a Comprehensive school. They offer a series of "snapshots", taken from different angles, of Christian faith and practice. The "snapshots" are grouped (rather arbitrarily) under three headings, viz. artefacts, people, and the Eucharist; and in a logical order which the teacher making use of them is free to ignore. The teacher is recommended to select, and deal briefly with, those adjudged most likely to interest his/her particular pupils, and to explore further one or two which especially catch their imagination and open their eyes to see something of the "vision".

Each "snapshot" is presented in four parts: the reason for choosing it (the "Why?" question); its material content (the "What" question); its treatment in the class (the "How?" question); and any relevant resources and references.

OVERVIEW OF CONTENTS

AN APPROACH THROUGH ARTEFACTS

1 Symbols

Symbols are the typical and indispensable language of religion, giving expression in forms accessible to the senses (tangible, visible, audible) to its central ideas. Christian symbols exist in the pupils'

---

[1] If the pupils, at the end of the scheme, can give reasonably adequate answers to these questions, the teacher will have achieved much. How can the teacher check whether pupils have penetrated more deeply, have synthesised ideas and insights, and have gained some appreciation of the breadth and depth of the total Christian "vision"? One possibility would be to follow each "approach" by asking pupils to write down (perhaps in reply to a questionnaire) the ideas which have impressed them most, and any further prospects which they have glimpsed—or which they think they might glimpse if they sent out "mental probes". Finally, pupils could write answers to the question "What would it mean for you to be a Christian?", giving attention to thoughts, feelings, hopes, attitudes and behaviour: answers might start with the words "If I were a Christian, I would . . . ."

environment, and intriguingly combine the ordinary and the profound.

Among the many symbols that might be explored are:

Fish: a favourite symbol in the early years of Christianity, and still in use today.

Cross: the most familiar symbol, existing in many forms, often in combination with other symbolic elements.

Robes, Vestments, Banners, Shields: symbolism in shapes, colours, patterns.

Rosary: an import from Islam; manual activity as a guide and aid to contemplation.

Suggestions for work on the Fish symbol.

1 Give the class five minutes for each member to jot down, on a piece of paper, a symbol or symbols which he/she knows belongs to Christianity.

2 Teacher to collect the pieces of paper (folded) and then to read them to the rest of the class. Almost certainly the cross will dominate the proceedings; seldom, if ever, does a pupil write "fish".

3 The pupils' ideas about Christian symbols can be looked at and discussed. Interesting discussion may focus on the crucifix and the open cross. (The crucifix reminds the believer of the suffering and death of Jesus. The open cross recalls the resurrection, since the body is no longer fastened to it).

4 (a) Teacher either to pick up a pupil's reference to the fish symbol or (which is more likely) to introduce it to the class by means of a simple diagram:

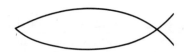

(b) *Either:* Pupils to work with the teacher and explore the possible reasons why a fish might be chosen as a Christian symbol. (See Information Sheet overleaf.)

Or: Pupils to work in pairs using a worksheet such as the following:

WORKSHEET

You are asked to be detectives of the Sherlock Holmes variety and to solve, or attempt to solve, the mystery of the fish symbol. You will find that you have a number of seemingly disconnected pieces of information as you work your way through the sheet, but that is exactly what happens in detective work. See if you can make all the pieces fit together in the end.

1 (a) Make a list of questions to ask about the symbol. e.g. What is peculiar about a fish? What, for example, does it need in order to live?

Are there any references to fish in the story of Jesus?

(b) Keep your questions in mind as you work through the material below.

2 Look up five of the references traditionally associated with the fish symbol. (At first sight some will not appear to have anything to do with fish.)

John's baptising of people, including Jesus: Matthew 3.

Jesus' command to the disciples: Matthew 28.16–20.

The feeding of 5,000 people: Mark 6.30–44.

Jesus' words: John 6.35–40.

The Last Supper: Mark 14.12–31.

Note also the story in the Old Testament (the Hebrew Bible) of the prophet Jonah, who was three days in the belly of "a great fish" (erroneously called a whale) before he was spewed up to safety on dry land.

3 Note that there are two important practices which are common to most churches:

(a) the use of water and words as the way into membership (Baptism);

(b) the sharing of bread and wine (Lord's Supper, Holy Communion, Breaking of Bread, Mass, Eucharist).

4 Look at the words of a third century Christian named Tertullian:

"But we small fishes thus named after our great Ichthus (fish), Jesus Christ, are born in water and only by remaining in water can we live".

5 Look at the following facts:

The Greek word for fish—ΙΧΘΥΣ (ICHTHUS, Ichthus)—provides the first letters in Greek for the following words—Jesus Christ, God's Son, Saviour. It is an acronym, like the word NATO N(orth) A(tlantic) T(reaty) O(rganisation).

Confusing, isn't it?

Have you made any sense of it all?

Teacher and class to listen to, and perhaps discuss, pupil's findings.

Teacher to issue an Information Sheet such as the following, and to go through it with the class.

INFORMATION SHEET: THE FISH SYMBOL

Some people believe that a people under persecution, as the early Christians were, had need of a simple, secret sign. It is thought that the fish may have been one such sign. This idea comes from the fact that the Greek word for fish IXΘYΣ(Ichthus) can be formed from the initial letters of the Greek words for Jesus (I) Christ (X), God's (Θ) Son (Y), Saviour (Σ). So if a Christian met a stranger he/she could determine by means of the fish symbol whether the stranger was a Christian or not.

The fish symbol, however, was for the Christians more than just a secret sign.
A fish cannot live without water, and it is Christian teaching that baptism by water is important for a new start in this life. It is also Christian teaching that it is only by being close to Jesus and following his way that this new life can continue. So eating bread, which he called his body, and drinking wine, which he called his blood, at a service known as The Eucharist, Holy Communion, The Mass, The Lord's Supper, The Breaking of Bread, or The Liturgy, are important ways of remembering and staying close to him. This is no doubt why Tertullian wrote: "But we small fishes, thus named after out great Ichthus, Jesus Christ, are born in water and only by remaining in water can we live".

A wall-painting in the catacomb (underground tomb) of St. Callistis in Rome shows a small basket of loaves standing on a large fish. This drawing is fascinating to those prepared to look with a "listening" eye for it reminds the observer of two stories in the Gospels, one to do with the feeding of five thousand people where loaves and fish were used and all the people were fed, and one to do with the disciples to whom Jesus gave bread to eat in order that they might remember him and live in his way. Since that first giving many thousands of Christians have been spiritually fed in the same manner.

Could the story of the feeding of the 5000 have the latter idea behind it? Could it too be a symbol?

Resource

A. C. Moore   *Iconography of Religions*   (SCM Press 1977)

Research work
Find out about infant baptism and write down your findings in your notebook. You might like to develop your ideas further in a poem.

A 13-year-old-girl wrote:
Baptism is a "rite of passage" of the Christian Church. Baptism is the start of a new life. When small children are baptised it is the occasion when they are named in the eyes of the church, and accepted into the Christian community officially.

The Church of England has Baptism but more popular is the name christening. It is usually practised on small children or babies. When the child grows into a teenager he or she can be Confirmed. In Baptism water is poured over the child's forehead, this symbolises the beginning of a new life. Often a candle is lit from the large Paschal Candle and given to the godparents to light on the anniversary of the baptism to remember "the Way' the child is to follow. I was christened at the age of six months.*

2 Buildings and their Contents
Pupils will be aware of buildings especially set aside for the use of Christians. Visits to such buildings can normally be arranged without difficulty, and may reveal much about the faith of the people who use them.

Christians meet together in buildings of many different styles, e.g.:
     Simple, almost undecorated, halls: emphasising that the faith is maintained and expressed essentially by persons, both individually and corporately;
     Buildings typical of the Free Churches, with a prominent platform for a preacher: emphasising that the faith is based on the Word—of the Bible and, especially, the gospel—and is communicated by the proclamation of the Word;

Churches and cathedrals built according to the medieval pattern: emphasising the value of symbols in forming people's faith and stimulating their devotion (e.g. the cruciform shape; the roof like an upturned boat—the ark of salvation; the altar or table, with Jesus as its invisible focus; the reserved sacrament as a reminder of the perpetual presence of Jesus).

Suggestions for work on a Medieval Church.
The work is based on the idea that the medieval church is a building which tells the Christian story and captures its vision.

Either: Construct a lesson from the information given below.
Or: Give the pupils a worksheet and an information sheet such as the ones below.

WORKSHEET

The picture below is no doubt familiar to you as it is a typical medieval church. What this worksheet seeks to do is to make you look at it more closely in order to decipher its meaning.

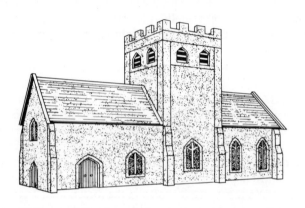

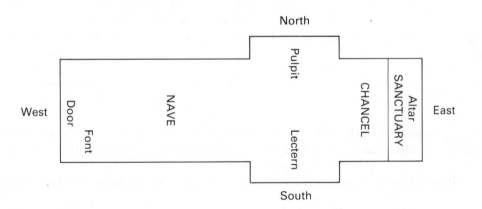

1 Look at the shape of the church.
   (a) What is this shape called?
   (b) Why is such a shape used for a building of this type?

These are easy questions: their answers should be obvious to anyone brought up in, or living in, a Christian culture. The question below may not be quite so easy: as two heads are better than one, work on it with a partner.
2 (a) Look at the labels on the diagram of the church. Make a list of them and write what you know about each. Begin at the west door and work your way up to the altar and the eastern wall.
   (b) Share what you know with your teacher and with the rest of the class. Listen carefully to what is said.
   (c) Improve your notes and retain them.

You have explored your own knowledge; now look at the Information Sheet and see what you can learn.

INFORMATION SHEET

A Building which Tells a Story and Conveys a Message

The Medieval Church

The DOOR stands for Jesus. To enter the church is to enter the home of the community of his people. If you were to look up at the roof, you would observe that it is shaped like a ship: the Latin word for "ship" is the word used for the main part of the building, the NAVE. Actually this shape is a reminder of the ark from the story of Noah. It represents the Christian belief that just as Noah was saved from a storm-tossed world, so man is saved by Jesus from the world of sin.

Near the west door is a BAPTISMAL BASIN or FONT. Admission into membership of the body of Jesus (the Christian community) is through the waters of baptism, from which the Christian steps out into a new life.

At the front of the nave is the LECTERN. This is a reading desk or stand. It is designed to hold the Bible which contains the Christian message. Usually it is in the shape of an EAGLE standing on a SPHERE which is symbolic of the world. Christianity has always been a religion which is concerned with spreading its message. The meaning of the eagle and the sphere is that the message is majestic and is for the whole world. The PULPIT is where the message is taught and explained by the preacher.

Beyond the nave is the CHANCEL. In some churches the chancel is slightly out of alignment with the nave, a fact which has been interpreted as symbolising Christ's head dropping on the cross. Look again at the chancel's position on the diagram, and note where the head would be in this part of the cross shape.

As the chancel is entered, the piece of furniture which catches the eye is the altar which is in the SANCTUARY. This is almost always in the east end of the church for the east is the source of light (the sun rises in the east and sets in the west); it is also in the direction of Jerusalem, the city outside which Jesus was killed. The "source of light" in this world is believed by Christians to be Jesus. The ALTAR reminds them of this fact. If the altar stone is an ancient one, under its cloth five crosses are to be found: these stand for the five wounds of Jesus. A large cross or crucifix is placed centrally on the altar, recalling the sacrifice of Jesus, and the white linen cloth which is generally found as a covering for the altar is symbolic of Jesus' funeral shroud. The candles express the Christian belief that Jesus is alive and is the light of the world.

The sanctuary itself is interesting. The word means "holy place". In the Middle Ages a fugitive from the law, or a debtor, could claim "sanctuary" and take refuge in the church for forty days.

The church may have a SPIRE, which is seen as a finger pointing to the heavens. The whole building is a place for the worship of God, indeed, every church is dedicated directly and solely to God for the word itself means "God's House"; this is so despite the fact that individual churches are given names. The BELLS call the Christian to worship. He or she comes believing that the way of Jesus leads to God.

You will often find a YEW TREE planted in the churchyard where many Christians are buried. The yew is a slow-growing and a very long-living tree, so it is looked upon as a symbol of immortality. It is a suitable symbol for a Christian burial place, as are the daffodils and lilies which are the flowers most frequently found growing around the yew. The bulbs of these flowers look dead before they are planted but new life springs out of them and they blossom into beautiful flowers. This reminds the Christian of resurrection, which is a central belief in Christianity.

Now write your answers to these questions:
1 What have you learned about a medieval church building from this Information Sheet?
2 Which piece of information did you find the most interesting?
3 What knowledge have you gained about Christian belief and one of the ways in which it is expressed?

Some examples of pupils' responses:

I did not realise the symbolism which lay behind a church. I thought the building was just a place designed for worship. Now I understand that the whole church is built to signify something special and that everything in it has a meaning and a purpose.

I found the whole sheet interesting. Now whenever I go into a church I will view everything in it rather differently. I will not just take it for granted.

I have learned that the life of a Christian is meant to revolve around the life, death and resurrection of Jesus and that this is expressed in symbolic form in the church building itself.

(14 year-old girl)

I found the slight misalignment of the Chancel with the Nave very interesting, especially as some say that it symbolises Christ dropping his head on the cross. I would have thought that the "defeat" of Christ is something that the Christian would not wish to reflect upon.

(13 year-old boy)

Christians believe that Christ is the light of the world and that after death they will find new life in the resurrection. They believe that the way of Jesus is the way to God. They express this through symbols.

(13 year-old girl)

Reflection work
Teacher to feed back the pupils' ideas to them and to take up any interesting points made, e.g. the pupil's comment about the "defeat" of Christ.

Resource
F. Bottomley *The Church Explorer's*   (Kaye and
                      Guide   Ward 1978)

3 Coventry Cathedral
The building of the new cathedral at Coventry (adjacent to, and incorporating part of, the old cathedral destroyed in air raids in 1940) is an exciting story; the study of its symbolism takes one to the heart of the practical implications of Christianity. Four aspects on which to focus pupils' attention are:

   The story of the destruction of the old cathedral;
   The rise of the new building as an expression of the notion of the resurrection;
   The charred cross, and the words "Father Forgive", which link the self-giving of Jesus with the Christian response of faith, hope and love;
   The Chapel of Unity, expressing the conviction that all Christians, whatever their differences in certain matters of doctrine or practice, share a fundamental unity in Christ.

Suggestions for work on the charred cross and the words "Father Forgive". (Several copies of *A Guide to Coventry Cathedral*, and a set of slides on the Cathedral, are essential for this unit of work.)

1 The teacher introduces this section by showing three slides:
Slide 1 The city and the cathedral
At the centre of the bustling city of Coventry there stands this place of quietness in which many people regularly find comfort. (A Guide to Coventry Cathedral)
The place spoken about is Coventry Cathedral, a unique cathedral, one which joins a modern building to a ruined ancient one.

Slide 2 The cathedral, ancient and modern
The ruin is the ancient Coventry Cathedral and it bears the scars of a modern war. In the sanctuary there are stains of molten lead—the lead boiled as the cathedral burned. Despite these stains of death the ruin itself is filled with life, for this sanctuary is much used and in it there is a simple altar on which stands one of the most significant crosses in Christendom, the famous charred cross of Coventry.

Slide 3 The sanctuary
Pupils to look carefully at this slide and to identify what they see. They should observe the ruined walls on which the words "Father Forgive" are written. They should also note the altar with its two crosses, one of nails and one of charred wood.

2 Teacher either tells the story of the bombing of Coventry in 1940 or reads the following account and discusses it with pupils.
The 14th-century cathedral church of St. Michael was reduced to ruins by fire bombs during the night of 14th November 1940. This was the night when Coventry suffered the longest air-raid of any one night on any British city during the Second World War. The outer walls and the tower and spire remained intact, but the wooden roof, the heavy oak ceiling, the pews, the floor and the screen were completely destroyed. To some it seemed to be the end of a fine perpendicular church, a building which Ruskin had once admired and which in its richness had been a witness of the prosperity of medieval Coventry.

But two precious relics grew out of the destruction. A few days after the bombing, two irregular pieces of the charred roof beams were tied together by wire and set up at the east end of the ruins. This "Charred Cross" is now world famous, standing behind the stone altar in the sanctuary of the ruins, having as its reredos the carving of the simple words FATHER FORGIVE. The second relic of the ancient church which become a spark of life in the ministry of the new church is the "Cross of Nails". As the roof burned, large 14th Century hand-forged nails which had fastened together its beams littered the ruined floor of the sanctuary. The following morning the inspiration came to form three of the nails into the shape of a Cross.

It was not the only imaginative decision to be made that day. Of far greater importance was the immediate resolve, as the ruins still smoked, to rebuild the cathedral. From that day until the consecration of the new building the life of the cathedral went on in the ruins of the old. The rubble was cleared and two underground chapels were repaired and furnished. Services were held regularly in the open air of the ruined nave, a practice which is being continued, with special services at Easter and Whitsun.

In 1947 the Reconstruction Committee was entrusted by the Cathedral Council with the task of rebuilding and a design competition open to architects of the British Commonwealth was held. There were 219 entries, and the competition was won by Mr. (now Sir) Basil Spence. The work of reconstruction began on 8th June 1954. The laying of the foundations started on 7th March 1955 and the cathedral was virtually completed on 28th April 1962, when the "flying cross" was lowered on to the flèche from a helicopter. The consecration took place on 25th May 1962 in the presence of Her Majesty The Queen.

Hard by the west wall of the new cathedral are visible the bases of some of the massive buttresses which supported the first great cathedral of Coventry. Joined to the new cathedral by the porch are the ruins of the second cathedral church of St. Michael. Hence the third cathedral stands as a massive link between the first and the second—a symbol of the indestructibility of the faith which it expresses (A Guide to Coventry Cathedral)

Reflection work

1 Think about the events of the night of 14th November 1940, and the days which followed. Think particularly of the destruction of the cathedral and the faith of those who created a new sanctuary out of the ruins of the old.

2 Write down their thoughts.

3 Look at the following piece of work which was written by two 14 year-old girls. (Either issue a copy to each pupil or show on OHP.)

The air was filled with death and destruction that night in 1940. The city was destroyed, loved ones lost and the cathedral, like them, was no more. It seemed to many to be the beginning of the end. Faith and hope were brought down with the roof of the cathedral.

The resurrection of Coventry Cathedral shows just how inspiring the Christian faith can be. The cathedral was destroyed but someone made the ancient nails, which had held the roof, into a cross, and someone else made an even larger cross from two charred beams. Both of these were set up in the sanctuary and behind them were written, in charcoal, on the bomb-stained walls, the words "FATHER FORGIVE".

We think this says it all. After all the agony and pain some were still able to forgive the men who had bombed their city and were prepared to find life in the midst of death.

4 Pick up some of the points in what the two pupils wrote. For example, they say that "some were still able to forgive the men who had bombed their city". Consider the words "Father Forgive" in the light of the words of the Cathedral Litany; do you think the words have a deeper significance?

At Coventry Cathedral the inscription "Father Forgive" (the words of Jesus on the cross) is a prayer which acknowledges that everybody is in need of forgiveness—for hatred, envy, greed, prejudice, cruelty. The tragedy of war has been caused by these human failings. The Cathedral litany of reconciliation has been printed on a plaque which stands before the altar, inviting those who look at it to share in its prayer. The litany is printed in many languages and is repeated in the sanctuary every Friday at noon.

The Litany

"All have sinned and come short of the Glory of God."

The hatred which divides nation from nation, race from race, class from class,

   FATHER, FORGIVE.

The covetous desires of men and nations to possess what is not their own,

   FATHER, FORGIVE.

The greed which exploits the labours of men and lays waste the earth,

   FATHER, FORGIVE.

The envy of the welfare and happiness of others,

   FATHER, FORGIVE.

The lust which uses for ignoble ends the bodies of men and women,

   FATHER, FORGIVE.

The pride which leads us to trust in ourselves, and not in God,

   FATHER, FORGIVE.

"Be kind to one another, tender-hearted, forgiving one another, as God in Christ forgave you".

Resources

Books: H. C. N. Williams: *Coventry Cathedral* (Pitkin Pictorials 1966) (for the account of the destruction and the rebuilding)

H. C. N. Williams:*A Guide To Coventry Cathedral* (English Life Publications 1979) (for the Litany)

Slides: Coventry Cathedral Education Department.

AN APPROACH THROUGH PEOPLE

1 Examples of Commitment

Biographical material offers human interest, dramatic narrative, and the opportunity for pupils to experience vicariously what it has meant, in different periods and circumstances, for people to declare, practise and hold firm to their Christian faith.

Time will not permit a full biographical treatment of any one person, and in any case a more effective way of presenting somebody's vision and response is to focus on one or two incidents which highlight them. Restriction to a short list of a famous few is not necessary; the names suggested here include some seldom found in school syllabuses; and there may be excellent reasons for a teacher to select someone who is virtually unknown, but whose life is inspired by Christian faith.

Perpetua and Felicitas. A Roman lady and her slave, living in the second century A.D., and still mentioned in the Roman Catholic Mass in the twentieth century. Both were imprisoned and killed for their faith.

Polycarp. A second century bishop, burned when he refused to renounce his faith: "Eighty and six years have I served him, and he has done me no wrong; how then can I blaspheme my king who saved me?"

Cranmer. Archbishop of Canterbury in the Reformation period. Convicted of heresy, he sought to save his life by signing a document of recantation; at the stake in 1556, the hand that had signed the paper he held in the flames, as the betrayer of his true faith.

Bonhoeffer. Theologian, whose understanding of Christianity led him to political action against Nazism. For his involvement in the plot to kill Hitler he was imprisoned and executed.

Martin Luther King. Pastor, and campaigner for the rights of negroes in the U.S.A., his "gospel" at its most glowing in his famous "I have a dream . . . ." speech. An apostle of non-violence, he was shot by an opponent in Memphis, Tennessee.

Mother Teresa. A Roman Catholic nun, best known for her initiative in opening hostels in the slums of Calcutta, and there caring for the dying poor, whether Christian or Hindu, so that they might "die with dignity".

Suggestions for work on Perpetua and Felicitas.
1 Read the following account.
   A Minority Movement
   Perpetua and Felicitas, c. 203 C.E.
   If you had been in the city of Carthage, on the coast of North Africa, one day in the year 203, you would have seen the crowds hurrying to the amphitheatre to see one of the most sensational forms of entertainment. The Romans loved the games. Most large cities had an amphitheatre—a vast oval building open to the sky, like Wembley stadium, with rows and rows of stone seats round an open space called the arena (from "harena", the Latin word for sand). This afternoon the stone seats were packed with people—Roman nobles and their wives, soldiers, merchants, and huge crowds of common people—all eager for the show. Sometimes there would be athletics, sometimes chariot races and javelin-throwing contests.

But often the sport was cruel and blood-thirsty. Men called gladiators would fight and kill one another, sometimes singly, sometimes in teams of mock battles, while the crowd held their breath or cheered their champion on. Even that bored some of them after a time, and they were always seeking some new form of amusement.

Today there was a special attraction. A number of Christians had been rounded up, and when they refused to call Caesar 'lord and god' they had been condemned to death under a new edict from the emperor, Septimius Severus. They were to face the gladiators and wild beasts in the arena. Soon the talking died down. A number of men and women were driven out on the sand, some quite young, others old and bent, a strange collection armed only with staves. They were to fight some of the young gladiators. The crowds waited, then laughed and jeered because the prisoners would not fight but were killed without a struggle. Then four men were driven out; each in turn had to face a wild boar, a bear, and a leopard. It was not a pleasant sight. The sand was raked over to cover the blood, and the crowd turned to see the chief attraction.

Two women were led into the arena. One of them was a young noblewoman, the other her maid, a young woman of twentytwo, with the name of her master branded on her forehead. She had just had a baby—born in prison a few days before. The two women were to face a maddened cow. The crowd thought this was a huge joke. First one then the other was tossed into the air, but again and again they struggled to their feet and stood together. The noblewoman drew her torn garments round her and attempted with trembling fingers to tie up her dishevelled hair. The crowd roared encouragement. They may have been cruel, but they knew courage when they saw it. At last the cow was driven away and a young gladiator came into the arena. He killed them with his sword as they lay broken, but still alive, in the sand of the amphitheatre.

Who were these women? What terrible crime had they committed? Their names were Perpetua and Felicitas. They were accused of being 'enemies of the human race' because they refused to call the emperor 'lord and god'. We have eye-witness accounts of their martyrdom, including Perpetua's own record of her trial and their time in prison. Her old father begged her, for the sake of her young son, and out of sympathy for his advanced years, to offer sacrifice to the emperor, but she refused. She was asked by the magistrate, 'Are you a Christian?' She replied, 'I am.'

Her maid, Felicitas, was afraid that she might not be allowed to accompany her mistress into

the arena, because the Romans did not execute pregnant women. However, her baby, a girl, was born in gaol. One of her sisters took the little girl and brought her up as her own. The two young mothers, mistress and maid, faced death together.

2 Teacher to supplement the account with the following information:

The early Christians were willing to die for their beliefs. Official persecution began in 64 C.E. under the Roman emperor Nero, and continued intermittently for nearly 250 years. During that time to be a Christian was a punishable offence, so the Christian community beame a public target.

The punishments meted out to Christians were horrific, and women met the same fate as men. Christians were used as scapegoats for anything that went wrong. Indeed, the original persecutions arose because Christians were blamed for a fire which had devastated Rome.

Although persecution was neither systematic nor continuous throughout the first two hundred and fifty years of Christianity, nevertheless every convert knew that he/she might have to die for the faith.

The courage of the early martyrs had a powerful effect in the spreading of the Gospel. It was impressive to see a ragged group of men and women able to raise their voices in a hymn as they faced death. Tertullian, a second century bishop, wrote "The oftener we are mown down by you, the more we increase. The blood of Christians is seed. Many of your own writers teach men to face pain and death bravely, but they do not win disciples as the Christians do, teachers not by word but by deed".

3 Pupils to think carefully about their knowledge of the Christian faith and then to answer the following questions:

(a) Why did Perpetua and Felicitas, knowing the fate that lay in store for them, refuse to call the Emperor "Lord and God"?

(b) Why, when asked directly by the magistrate "Are you a Christian?", did each reply "I am"?

A 14 year-old girl wrote:
Perpetua and Felicitas held in the dock,
Surrounded by people who jeered and mocked,
"Are you a Christian?" the magistrate said.
"I am" each replied,
Knowing soon she'd be dead.

The early Christians used the words "Lord and God" when they spoke of their God, therefore they would not use them to address anybody on earth, not even the emperor. They would not abandon their beliefs for those which they considered to be false. It was their faith in God through Jesus which gave them great courage. If they had denied their belief and faith in their Lord and worshipped the emperor instead, then there would have been no

purpose to their lives in the future, their hopes and aspirations would be lost. Jesus had sacrificed his life for others and they were willing to do the same for him.

Another 14 year-old girl wrote:
Perpetua and Felicitas were true Christians, they would not give up their faith for the emperor. They sacrificed their lives for their religion though others backed down to save their lives, rather than admit to being Christian.

Perpetua and Felicitas were loyal to God and to each other. Felicitas wanted to enter the arena with her mistress and so they died together, leaving their children and families behind.

They were proud to be Christians and not afraid to admit this to the magistrates.

4 Take up and discuss points made by pupils. The discussion should focus on this kind of sacrifice: its meaning and significance, and the dangers inherent in it.

Resource
What is the Christian Church? (Surrey Fine Art Press 1981, for Schools Council).

2 The Pope's Day

Every pupil will surely have heard of the Pope, and be aware that he is an important person exercising both religious and political influence. An account of a typical day in the Pope's life may reveal some surprising facts, and draw pupils into discovering something of the significance of prayer in Christian experience. The following account (from P. Jennings and E. McCabe: *The Pope in Britain* (Bodley Head 1982)) is written in a plain, matter-of-fact style which conveys a sense of the normality of the Pope's day—to a degree, equivalent to the normal experience of pupils themselves, while notably different in other respects.

A Long Day at the Vatican
The Pope usually begins his day at about 5.30 a.m. He is frequently in his small chapel by 6 a.m., where he spends an hour in prayer and meditation before saying Mass. While eating breakfast, the Pope reads the major Italian newspapers. He works in his study until 11 a.m., writing, dictating, and correcting documents and speeches. In 1979, his first full year in office, he is said to have delivered over five hundred addresses.

The rest of the morning is devoted to private audiences with cardinals, bishops, visiting Heads of State, ambassadors, and people from every kind of organisation and walk of life. The Pope often has "working lunches", and if there are no guests he is joined by his two private secretaries. Lunch is prepared and served by the Polish Sisters who look after the Pope's apartment; it usually takes the form of his favourite Polish dishes,

especially when Polish guests are present, although he also eats Italian and other Western food.

Despite his already very long and full day, Pope John Paul does not usually take a siesta, preferring instead to relax by walking in the Vatican gardens or up and down the terraces of the Apostolic Palace above his private apartment. Sometimes as he walks on the terrace he recites the Rosary, or reads. The Pope is fond of singing and music. He also loves to swim when he can, and had a swimming pool built at his summer residence about fifteen miles outside Rome.

During the afternoon the Pope works in his study for two or three hours. He often continues with private audiences for his advisers or people he was unable to fit in during the morning.

For his dinner the Pope prefers a simple, light meal, especially when he is dining alone or with his secretaries. He may watch the television news while he is eating. He loves meeting people, and on occasions he invites friends to supper at the Vatican, often joining in a sing-song afterwards.

Pope John Paul II then spends several more hours working in his study, reading letters and documents. He retires to bed very late, rarely before 1 a.m., having first spent a long period of prayer in his private chapel.

Suggestions for work

Introduce the Pope, if possible by means of some current news-item. Read the account quote above. Pupils work in pairs, discussing the questions:
1 What can one learn about the Pope from this account?
2 (a) What do *you* know about prayer?
    (b) Why, in *your* opinion, does the Pope spend so much of his precious time in prayer?
    (c) What, if anything, do you know of the Rosary?

After the discussion, pupils write their individual responses to these questions.

Some pupil responses to question 2(a) were as follows:

Prayer is speaking to God and listening to God. It can be in our own words or we can use public prayers or the words of other people which seem to say what we want to say. We can pray privately or we can take part in public prayers. We can pray anywhere, not only in a place specially set aside for worship and prayer. Prayer needs time and practice; the willingness to listen as well as speak. God is at the centre of prayer, not ourselves.

Prayer is a way of speaking to God privately. Some people find it comforting when they are worried or frightened. Perhaps when they have done something wrong they feel when they pray their sin has been forgiven.

Prayer is usually said in a chapel or church. People of any religion do it and this means to them that they can communicate with God. A prayer is a sort of religious poem. There are different sorts of prayer.

Prayer is often used for saying "thank you" or asking God for help. Prayers can be said by anyone, anywhere, they do not have to be said or read in a church or other place of worship. Many people think that prayer is stupid today. However, in some ways when you have said prayers you feel relieved. I never usually pray but when I do it is mostly when I am in trouble.

Prayer is a way of talking to God. It is also a way of thinking deeply about yourself and others.

Some pupil responses to question 2(b) were as follows:

The Pope spends so much of his time in private prayer because it is a part of his duty to serve God. It probably helps to give him the strength to work long hours. Also, he has a lot to pray about.

. . . because he feels that he is speaking to God alone and that nobody else can intrude. He obviously prefers praying in private.

The Pope is devoted to God and shows this by praying to him. He might even have a few sins or secrets which he wants to express.

The Pope, as head of the Catholic Church, has responsibility for his flock. He needs to try to know God's will and to be able to interpret it. He has an exacting life and needs to draw strength from God.

3 Miracle on the River Kwai

Ernest Gordon's gripping story of experiences as a prisoner of the Japanese, working on the construction of the notorious railway through Burma, is not a semi-fictional story of the destruction of a bridge, but a true story of the "resurrection" of demoralised men. The Christian dynamic is seen in action, motivating individuals and creating a community of loyalty and hope. Extracts from the book might include:
   p. 59–62: work on the railway and the Kwai bridge.
   p. 75–77: Gordon's letter home, and his determination *not* to die.
   p. 90–92: regeneration begins—new attitudes, new vision.
   p. 101, 102: realisation of the relevance of Jesus.
   p. 107–109: increasing resurgence of life—new legs, lively minds.
   Ch. 7: Church without Walls—fellowship, prayer, symbols, Jesus.
   Ch. 8: Christmas Day, 1943—celebration, hope, a new spirit.

Suggestions for work on the account of Christmas Day, 1943

Pupils are issued with copies of the following extract

from Chapter 8 of *Miracle on the River Kwai*

Christmas Day was going to be something special this year. We were looking forward to it, for the opportunity it would give us to express our feelings about the new insights we had gained. We could only hope that the monsoon rains would not still be falling as they had been on Christmas Day last year, with the skies miserably grey and the camp a wallow of mud.

I had been out of my shack for some months and was living with about two hundred others in the hut for those affected with amoebic dysentery. It was a loose kind of quarantine, chiefly for the purpose of seeing that we used separate lavatories.

A few days before Christmas, Dinty Moore came to visit me. I could tell from his manner that this was no casual call. After we had exchanged greetings, he said with a smile, "I've come to get you all tickety-boo for Christmas." "What did you have in mind?" I enquired cautiously.

"I'm going to shave off that magnificent beaver".

Sadly, I fingered the luxuriant black growth; I was proud of it.

"With what?"

"This." He flourished a kitchen knife.

"Ground to a wafer edge."

He produced a sliver of soap and a rag.

"Sit down," he said. "Let's have a go at it."

I sat gingerly on the edge of my sleeping platform while he worked the soap to a thin lather, rubbed it into my whiskers and went to work. He carved away my beard a patch at a time. The operation resembled some ancient Chinese torture. I was sure the skin was coming off with the whiskers. But so great was Dinty's pride in his talent and his homemade razor that I could only sit tight-lipped and say nothing. He finished at last and, with a flourish, handed me a mirror. He had left me a fine, bushy, upswept moustache; otherwise I was clean shaven. Most of the skin, to my surprise, was intact.

"Now," beamed Dinty, contemplating his handiwork, "you're ready to celebrate."

Christmas Day dawned. Through the door of the hut I saw to my joy brilliant blue skies overhead. Already we had one welcome gift, that of glorious weather.

I looked down the hut. It was hardly recognisable. The ground was clean and neatly swept. The rice-sack bedding had been taken out and thoroughly debugged. The scruffy walls above the sleeping platforms were garlanded with green boughs—the one note of Christmas cheer the jungle offered in abundance. Men stirred, got up and began to move about, wishing one another a hearty "Merry Christmas".

For once we ate our breakfast in leisurely, gentlemanly fashion. Then we prepared for church. We wore whatever was our best, although it may have been no more than a clean loin-cloth.

I went early to church, as I wanted to have a few moments of quiet. I sat on the ground with my back against the trunk of a bamboo. Resting on the Holy Table was a Christmas wreath someone had made from bamboo branches and jungle greens. The green wreath against the ivory-coloured split bamboo made a picture of serenity.

Others had also come for those moments of hallowed quiet and private prayer. Men entered softly. By fifteen minutes before eleven o'clock when the service was to begin, the church was full. Some were sitting on the ground, some on bamboo benches, some on homemade stools. But most were standing along the sides and at the back or front, whichever one might like to call it. Over two thousand P.O.W.s filled the area. But the hush I felt when I first arrived remained unbroken.

Padré Webb entered wearing fresh khaki shorts and shirt, and took his place in front of the Holy Table. He prayed in silence, then he raised his head and announced the first hymn, "O come, all ye faithful, joyful and triumphant, O come ye, O come ye to Bethlehem." He did not need to say the words and have us repeat them after him. Those who knew them sang them; those who did not picked them up from their neighbours.

Bill Maclean, standing beside me, was singing bass and in Latin. We had been at St. Andrews' University together. While we sang, a picture came to my mind of the going-down service before Christmas both of us had attended so long ago. I could see the scarlet-robed students and the yellow lights of the lanterns, making a warm Christmas card picture against the old grey walls of the university chapel.

We sang a second carol, "The First Nowell". Then Padré Webb gave a brief sermon on "The Hope of Christmas." We came to the closing hymn, "Good Christian Men, Rejoice."

We had hardly begun singing it, when we heard the almost-forgotten wail of air-raid sirens. It rose to a shriek, then gradually died away. Far off we could hear a rumble. We exchanged glances. This could not be Japanese. We kept on singing. In the blue sky over our heads we could hear a four-engine bomber flying confidently in the direction of Bangkok. We put all our feeling into that hymn. More lustily then ever, we sang "Rejoice!" Indeed we sang so lustily that the prison guards came charging into the church shouting the Japanese equivalent of "Shut up! They'll hear you."

I had known of the power of praise. But I was not aware that it could soar ten to fifteen thousand feet and be picked up by a bomber crew above the engine noise.

The padré pronounced the benediction and sent us forth in peace. We were barely out of the

church when someone slapped me on the back. "Merry Christmas, Merry Christmas, Ernie old boy!"

It was Bill Maclean, wearing an enormous smile.

"You must have been thinking the same thoughts as myself."

"You mean—that that plane was a symbol of hope?"

I changed my pace to keep step with his, and said, "I wonder if the crew have any idea what they meant to us. Poor blighters. They're no doubt browned off because they've got to fly on Christmas Day."

"Probably a U.S.A.F. plane taking photographs. I hope they saw us."

"If they didn't see us," I replied, "perhaps they heard us, after all."

The happy looks on the faces of the men walking near us and the loud hum of their conversation as they returned to their huts and their Christmas dinners indicated they were all having the same reaction. I remarked to Bill, "This is a merry Christmas—especially when you compare it with last year."

"Last year." He made a face. "That was a ruddy mess."

"It was, indeed! That was just before I got 'dip' and a few other things. It was almost curtains for me."

Bill looked more serious. "We're not out of the woods yet—not by a long chalk. But now there's hope. That's the thing—there's hope."

"There's something else, too, Bill," I said. "There's a new spirit in the camp. Have you noticed how, with many of the men, it's 'You first' now instead of 'Me first'?"

Bill agreed.

Pupils read this extract, moving on when they are ready to the two pieces of work below.

Comprehension work

1 What reason did Captain Gordon give for looking forward to Christmas 1943?
2 What had (a) Dinty Moore done for Captain Gordon, (b) the men done to the camp, before the Christmas celebrations began?
3 Describe: (a) the jungle church on Christmas Day, 1943;
(b) the happenings in the church prior to the Christmas Day service.
4 Give the title of the Christmas Day message and the "symbol of hope" which was seen during the service itself.
5 Write out the words of the first carol which was sung at the service.
6 Describe the "new spirit" which was present in the camp in 1943.

Reflection work

What can be learned, from the description of Christmas Day 1943, about the meaning of Christmas for the prisoners-of-war on the Kwai River? Write down your thoughts in a paragraph or so.

The responses of three pupils were:

The meaning of Christmas shows clearly in the description of Christmas Day, 1943, in the prisoner-of-war camp at the River Kwai. Christmas is something special to be enjoyed by everyone. The prisoners found that it was a time of unity and for helping others. Most of all they found it a time of hope for their future.

(14-year-old girl)

Christmas to the P.O.W.'s must have been a time to forget their position. They made the most of what they had. They entered into the spirit of Christmas although they could not commemorate it as they would have done at home. The aeroplane must have been like the star in the Christmas story, certainly they looked upon it as a sign of hope.

(14-year-old boy)

What I learned from the Christmas Day account was that no one was moaning because they didn't have a Christmas present, and no one was being selfish. And on Christmas day the prisoners-of-war went to church and prayed to God and the men gave thanks for their lives. And instead of the men saying, "Me first, me first", it was "You first" or "After you".

(14-year-old boy)

Resource

Gordon E.: *Miracle on the River Kwai* (Collins Fontana 1963)

4 Communities and Organisations (National and Local)

Christian communities, whether founded centuries ago or in recent years, bear witness to the possibility of people living together in productive harmony, sharing a life-style very different from that of our competitive and alienating society, which they seek in some way to serve and redeem. Pupils should be made aware of the inspiration which Christian faith supplies to such communities, and to many organisations which work for the relief of human need and distress.

Some comunities and organisations which might be included are:

The Society of St. Francis (Franciscan Brothers). Traditional community, its members distinguished by their brown robes. H.Q. in Dorset. Active in evangelism and various fields of social work.

The Community of Taizé (near Macon in Eastern France). Pioneering Protestant community, founded in 1947, now ecumenical. Since the 1960s it has attracted tens of thousands of people, especially young people, of many nations, to share for a week or more its simple way of life, its inspiring worship, its silence, and talks and discussions with the resident brothers.

Corrymeela. Founded in 1965 as a non-denominational community, centred in Belfast, with the aim of bringing about reconciliation between man and man, and man and God: more specifically, between factions in Northern Ireland. Organises conferences, educational programmes and work camps, and actively supports work in the field of community relations.

The Salvation Army. A visible (and often audible!) body of people dedicated to serving and evangelising the disadvantaged in our society. Identifiable by their distinctive uniform.

Christian Aid. One of the largest organisations engaged in raising funds, and arousing practical concern, for the relief of human suffering in many parts of the world.

Any local Christian group would welcome the interest (perhaps the voluntary support) of pupils, and the opportunity to tell them about its work.

Suggestions for work on the Taizé Community
1 (a) Pupils to imagine that they are on a visit to France. This visit is not an ordinary one, as they will discover. They are to go to Taizé, a village which attracts thousands of young people from all over the world. They are to belong for one week to a community run by monks. This community owns a large house and the land which surrounds it. The pupils are given a choice of activity for the week:
   one week of work (either indoor or out);
   ohe week of discussion;
   one week of silence.
   Use could be made of selected slides from the slide/tape programme "Taizé Community". Especially relevant here are numbers 1 (group on the way to Taizé); 2 and 27 (the place); 13 (visitors working); 23, 24 and 25 (discussion groups); 26 (individuals in the "field of silence").
   (b) Pupils to choose one of these three activities, to write it down, and to give reasons for their choice.
   (c) Pupils share their choices and reasons with the whole class, and discuss matters of particular interest.
   (d) Pupils to look at the beginning of Alan Brown's account of his visit to Taizé and his reason for the choice which he made, viz. a week of discussion.

It was the bells which woke me. They were not close but my sleeping brain heard them. I lay awake, I knew it was 7.00 because that was when they first rang for the day. They were waking us, inviting us to worship together at 7.30. I was sleeping in a large hut with about 20 others—it was pitch black in there but now people began to dress and wash. I had only arrived at Taizé the evening before, so had had little time to reflect.

On arrival I had been separated from other members of my party—I was 'old', over 25—and asked whether I would like a week of silence, a week of discussion or a week of work. I had chosen discussion—didn't everyone go to Taizé to discuss?

Then I had bought my meal tickets and been sent to where I was to sleep. The others put up their tents. We had all arrived.

As I walked down the hill to the Church of Reconciliation I looked across the beautiful French countryside. Why had Brother Roger come here? It was a tiny village on a hill, not very different from other French villages. And who was this Brother Roger anyway? As with anything new, my mind was full of questions.

2 Pupils to watch a video of the Taizé community taken from the ITV series 'Believe it or not'. It is a young person's account of the Taizé community and shows it functioning as it generally does in the summer months.
3 Pupils to study Alan Brown's account of the founder of the community, Roger Schutz (p. 2–4), and the founding of the Council of Youth (p. 5–6), and to make notes on each.
4 Teacher and pupils discuss their findings. Teacher to assist with words which may not be immediately understood by the pupils (for example, "reconciliation"). Teacher to bring to the foreground the ecumenical nature of the community.

Reflection work
The Easter "Songs of Praise" television programme in 1985 was broadcast from the Taizé community. One person wrote in to complain, saying that the hymns ought to have been broadcast from an English church and the music ought to have been traditional. The series producer, Stephen Whittle replied (*Radio Times*, May 1985) in the following way:
We felt it important that the Easter "Songs of Praise" should visit a community where the message of Easter is lived as well as preached. Worship at Taizé unites a divided church in a celebration of the risen Christ. For most of our audience this experience proved to be both joyful and uplifting. I am sorry if that was not the experience for them all.
What do you think that Stephen Whittle meant when he talked about, "the message of Easter", this

message being "lived as well as preached", the uniting of "a divided church", and the "celebration of the risen Christ"?

Resources
Book
Brown A.: *Christian Communities* (Lutterworth Education, 1982, for the Chichester Project).

Slide/Tape Programme
Taizé Community (Mowbray 1984)

Video
The Taizé Community, in 'Believe it or not' series (Independent Television for Schools and Colleges).

Booklet
Radio Times (B.B.C. May 1985).

AN APPROACH THROUGH THE EUCHARIST

The act of worship known variously as The Eucharist, Holy Communion, The Mass, The Lord's Supper, The Breaking of Bread, or The Liturgy (for present purposes, the terms may be considered synonymous), is one manifestation of Christian faith. For most (but not all) Christians it is central. As something which is done, and done frequently, by many people in their own neighbourhood, it can be investigated at first hand by pupils. The scheme outlined here attempts to convey some idea of the significance which the Eucharist holds for Christians.[2] Furthermore, an exploration of the Eucharist opens up one avenue towards understanding the central belief of Christians, that Jesus is the Christ, God's agent for renewing the whole created universe.

Two important features of the scheme will quickly become apparent: the approach is indirect, and along several lines; and the Eucharist is presented not in isolation, but in the context of other material relating to Jesus. No attempt is made to give a full account of Jesus, or of the Eucharist, or of Christianity; the aim is to provide a number of significant perspectives on the Eucharist.

Lesson plans make use of the four stages recommended by Barnes, with a fifth stage of writing (see Introduction to the Secondary section, p. 61). The teacher's gifts as a story-teller are employed; so are visual materials, symbols and objects, both for their intrinsic interest to pupils and because they help to explode the commonly held notion that Christianity is wholly a matter of words and beliefs. The pupils' own knowledge and ideas are vitally important resources; on principle, pupils' contributions are received and respected, and embarrassment is avoided or minimised. With their permission, good examples of pupils' work are typed out, and displayed without identification of the authors. The examples of pupils' work quoted in the text which follows are taken from a class in the fifth of eight streams. The teacher will find useful material in *The Christian Faith and its Symbols* and in *What is the Christian Church?* (Refer to Resources on p. 87 for details.)

Unit 1   (3 periods)
Objectives: to enable pupils to appreciate the value of a rite which is symbolic of a complex of events, ideas and beliefs;
to involve the pupils in their own learning.

Introduction of the material (Period 1)
 (i) *Stimulus:* chalice and wine; paten and bread. (These are exhibited on the teacher's desk during every lesson.)
Pupils contribute whatever knowledge and ideas they may have about these objects, and discuss what use is made of them by Christians, and why.
The teacher tells the pupils that they are going to travel through time in search of the meaning of these symbols: first, a journey backwards of 2000 years; then back a further 1000 years.
(ii) *Theme:* a search for meaning.
Set the scene of the Holy Land in the time of Jesus. Bring the description to life with the help of visual material and a well-told narrative. Artists' impressions of Palestine under the Romans are useful; even more so, perhaps, are slides from present-day Israel (e.g. the landscape; the fortifications of Masada and Herodium, which suggest a land that was watched; Roman theatres, symbols and other remains, which indicate a land that was occupied; the models of the Jewish temple and synagogues, which indicate a people who were religious).

---

[2]*The teacher has the task of treating a central Christian rite in a manner which gives no cause for offence to pupils of any other faith or of none, yet which does it full justice; and the latter may be the more difficult part. For most Christians, who worship God as a Trinity of "Father", "Son" and "Spirit", it is pre-eminently by means of the symbols and actions of the Eucharist that the reality of "the Father" is affirmed, the events concerning Jesus are recalled and the beliefs concerning him expressed, and the presence of "the Spirit" is experienced. Facts from the past combine with hopes for the future to strengthen, inspire and unite the participants for living as Christ's people in the present. What the Christian worshipper is seen to be doing (listening, kneeling, eating bread, drinking wine, reciting forms of words, etc.) is, ideally at any rate, only a part of what he is "doing" as a whole person; he is also "putting himself into" the ritual, perceiving meaning in it and receiving benefit from it. A pupil will not "understand" the Eucharist unless he gains some glimmer of all this. How can the teacher try to ensure that such illumination occurs?*
Attention is drawn to Unit 7, "How Christians Remember", in the Primary scheme "Memories and Remembering".

Read extracts (with pupils following in their copies of the text) from *The World of the First Christians* (p. 9: a good summary of the conditions imposed on the Jews by the Roman occupation; not an easy text, but manageable by pupils after the preparatory slides and story), and from *The Bronze Bow* (p. 67–72: Daniel, the hero of this imaginative story of a family suffering under Roman domination, recounts the death of his father).

Development of the material (Period 2)

(a) *Focusing stage*

In response to questions, pupils recall information gained during their first time-journey (in the previous lesson).

The second time-journey takes them to the Israelites' Exodus from Egypt. Again in response to questions, pupils recover knowledge gained in their second-year course on Judaism, concerning this event and its interpretation; the Seder, the Passover meal, is of particular significance.

(b) *Exploratory stage*

Pupils imagine that they are Jews in Roman-occupied Palestine 2000 years ago. They are on the way to Jerusalem to keep the Feast of the Passover. What might they see during their journey? What might they be thinking about the Romans and about the Feast? Pupils discuss these questions in groups of two or three. Ideas are shared with the class.

(c) *Re-focusing stage*

Each group of pupils works out a conversation which they have on the road to Jerusalem, involving their own family situation, the political conditions, and the forthcoming celebration of the Passover Feast.

(d) *Public stage*

Pupils who wish to do so report to the class on the most interesting parts of their conversations. The teacher may give encouragement by mentioning snippets gleaned while going round the groups, and suggesting that pupils might enlarge on these.

(e) *Written stage* (to be done as homework)

Write a letter from Jerusalem to a Jewish friend who has been unable to attend the Passover Feast with you, but has celebrated it at home. In the letter, share your thoughts, fears and hopes for the future. (Responses from pupils who achieve well in this work will be used in the next lesson to help those who found difficulty.)

Two 13-year-old boys (the first a Muslim) wrote as follows:

Dear Friend.

I hope that you are in good health.

Our journey to Jerusalem was quicker than last year as there weren't many Roman guards about. Oh I wish that you had been able to come because this to us was a road to hope for the future! It encourages us to get the Romans out of our country and so bring to a halt the conflict which pains our Jewish community.

When I was walking in the streets of Jerusalem I thought that we could take action like the Zealots—I do hope that they succeed. It is not fair what the tax collectors are doing to us here. We are certainly not free in our holy land!

Let the angel of death deal with the Romans as we get the kid ready. This solemn feast, the Passover, has given me new life and the sense of freedom in my body. The bitter herbs—hatred to the Romans; wine—the experience of my forefathers escaping from the Egyptians. May we too escape.

Yours . . .

Dear friend.

We have travelled well this year but more and more the Romans are around, I feel their eyes upon me.

The meal we hope will inspire us and bring more hope of freedom with it as it did to our forefathers. May it bring luck to the Zealots who I hope soon to join.

Eyes are everywhere, they watch everything that we do. But we must not lose faith, we must smear the lamb's blood on our doors so that the angel of death will pass us by.

I have to go now for a Roman guard is coming to give me a task, but my friend, do NOT give up hope, never give up hope, for the Passover is upon us.

Yours . . .

Recapitulation (Period 3)

Review of written work

Pupils read one another's work, exchanging scripts as they may think fit, without interference from the teacher. (Up to 10 minutes for this.)

The teacher may then identify those letters which he/she finds most interesting and which best illustrate that the first objective for this Unit has been achieved. These may be read out to the class by the authors.

Time should be allowed for discussion, and possibly for some correction or amplification by the teacher on important matters of fact.

Unit 2 (1 period)

Objective: to engage the pupils with some of the teachings of Jesus.[3]

---

[3]*The qualification "some" is important. What appears here, in a plain and direct version, as "The Message" presents only the moral content of Jesus' teaching, not the eschatological: the "Good News of the Kingdom" as proclaimed by Jesus—more so, the full Christian Gospel which includes Jesus—should never be, though it frequently is, reduced to a set of moral precepts.*

Stimulus: "The Message of the New World". (A statement of key ideas in the Sermon on the Mount, cited from the scheme of work on "The Man from Nazareth" in *Paths to Understanding*, p. 94).

THE MESSAGE

YOU are the chosen ones. I want YOU to go and spread my message, the WORD. A NEW WORLD is coming. If you are going to join me in making this NEW WORLD, you must change your way of life, and never return to your old ways.

1. BE FRIENDLY TO EVERYONE, EVEN IF THEY ARE ANGRY AND UNFRIENDLY TOWARDS YOU.
2. DO NOT BOAST ABOUT YOUR GOOD DEEDS. HELP OTHERS, BUT DO NOT ADVERTISE YOURSELF.
3. DO NOT PRETEND TO BE ONE TYPE OF PERSON AND THEN BEHAVE LIKE ANOTHER. THIS IS HYPOCRISY, AND STOPS YOU FACING THE TRUTH ABOUT YOURSELF.
4. DO NOT TRY TO BE WEALTHY. YOU CANNOT LOVE THE NEW WORLD *AND* MONEY.
5. ACCEPT OTHER PEOPLE AS BEING EQUAL TO YOU. DO NOT JUDGE THEIR ACTIONS AS IF YOU WERE THEIR MASTER.
6. IF PEOPLE HIT OUT AT YOU IN ANGER, DO NOT HIT BACK AT THEM.

Tell others of these ideas.
Go and spread the WORD
Help others to join
THE NEW WORLD

Focusing stage
Each pupil is given a folded copy of "The Message". The teacher tells the class that on their papers are written the ground rules for a new society. Pupils then open their papers, and have 5 minutes to read them and think about them, and to decide whether they would accept or reject each one.

Exploratory stage
Each pupil shares ideas with one other.
Each pair then joins with another pair to compare ideas.

Re-focusing stage
The teacher asks one member of each group (of four pupils) to act as scribe and to record the main findings of the group. (5 minutes allowed for this.)

Public stage
Each group in turn reports the most interesting point made in its record. If time allows, discussion will inevitably follow; and there might be opportunities to mention other points made in the groups.

Written stage (to be done as homework)
Write your own thoughts and opinions about the ideas contained in "The Message of the New World".
A 14-year-old boy wrote:
I think that if I joined the New World I could keep the new rules. I believe that eventually everyone would join the New World because thugs and yobs would die out like the Incas did.
The rule which I would find the hardest is, "If people hit out at you in anger, do not hit back" but eventually I would get used to it and there would (or could) be peace—it's food for thought!

Unit 3   (1 or 2 periods)
Objectives: to bring together what has been learned in Units 1 and 2;
to explore some of the ideas which people have, and have had in the past, about Jesus.

Focusing stage
Recalling the work done in Unit 1, the teacher reminds pupils of the political situation in Palestine 2000 years ago, and of the hopes of Jews, expressed in the Passover Feast, for a different world.

Recalling the work done in Unit 2, the teacher points out that "The Message of the New World" contains some of the teachings of Jesus, who came among the Jews proclaiming "the good news of the Kingdom of God". His words and actions made him a centre of attention and the subject of much talk, rumour and speculation; people then and since have viewed him in many ways.

Exploratory stage
The teacher asks pupils to express some of their ideas about Jesus, and, using an overhead projector, builds these into some kind of simple pattern (e.g. spokes radiating from a centre). The teacher then builds a similar pattern (such as the one illustrated) which will show various views of Jesus held by people during his lifetime, as evidenced in the Gospel records. (Gospel material may be elicited from the pupils, or related by the teacher.)

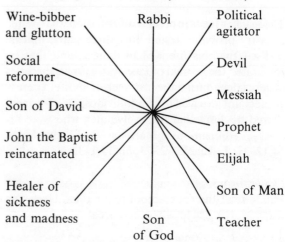

Views of Jesus: (2) In the Gospels

Re-focusing stage
Pupils, working in pairs, make their own pattern of ideas relating to Jesus, and enter it in their notebooks.

Further development
Pupils should also be aware of more recent statements about Jesus, made by people of some eminence, for example:

> *"To me (Jesus) was one of the greatest teachers humanity has ever had . . . In Jesus' own life is the key to his nearness to God; . . . he expressed, as no other could, the spirit and the will of God."* (Gandhi)

> *"If Jesus Christ were to come today, people would not even crucify him. They would ask him to dinner, and hear what he had to say, and make fun of it."* (Carlyle)

> *"Here was more than just a man: here was a window into God at work."* (Bishop J. Robinson)

(These and several other statements are included in "The impact of Jesus", section 9 in *Jesus*.)

A list of such statements could be issued to pupils for reading, as homework, their reflections on them could form the basis for a second period within this Unit.

Unit 4   (1 or 2 periods)
Objectives: to gain knowlege of the last meal which Jesus had with his disciples;
to understand some of the symbolic content of that meal.

Focusing stage
In response to questions, pupils recall facts about the social-political conditions of Jesus' time, about his teachings, and about people's reactions to him. They might have suggestions to make as to ways in which the story might continue. Alternatively, they might consider what Jesus might talk about and do in our present society, and how people might respond.

The teacher feeds in certain information: that Jesus' ministry probably lasted only three years; that he realised that his life was in danger; and that he celebrated the festival of Passover with his disciples in Jerusalem during the last week of his life. There is an account in each of the four Gospels of a meal shared by Jesus and the twelve men who were his closest companions: Matthew 26.17–29; Mark 14.12–31; Luke 22.7–23; John 13.1–32.

Exploratory stage
Pupils read the four accounts for themselves, the teacher giving help where required.

Re-focusing stage
Pupils, working in pairs, are asked to discuss the accounts they have read, and to come to decisions on two matters: whether all the accounts relate to one and the same meal; and which actions of Jesus are symbolic (intended to convey a special meaning).

Public stage
Pupils share with the whole class the decisions which they have arrived at. Drawing on, and supplementing if necessary, the pupils' suggestions, the teacher builds up a clearly visible list of the symbolic actions.

Witten stage (to be done as homework)
Pupils to write their ideas in answer to the question: Jesus meant the disciples to learn, from his actions, some important lessons—perhaps the last that he would be able to teach them. What do you think he meant them to learn from his action in washing their feet?

A 13-year-old girl wrote:

> *What I think that Jesus thought important for his disciples to learn by his actions, and the words which he spoke, is that he was trying to make them help other people who were in need themselves. If he helped them by washing their feet, they would understand what Jesus meant, and then they would do the same, and so on through the generations. You would get on better with people if you all helped each other in different ways.*

Unit 5   (1 period)
Objectives: to gain knowledge and understanding of the Eucharist and of what it means for many Christians today;
to bring together the several threads of the whole scheme.

Visiting a local church
A Methodist church happens to be on the school's doorstep, so a visit can be made within a single time-tabled period. The minister is welcoming, explains things clearly, and makes no attempt to convert the pupils. The church is a tiny, uncluttered building with all the principal Christian symbols visible.

Arrangements have, of course, been made well in advance. The minister has been briefed about the work the pupils have been doing, and has been asked to talk about the meaning of the Eucharist for Christians today. The pupils have been told about the purpose and nature of the visit, and know that they will later be writing about what they have discovered.

The teacher's description of a visit includes the following:

> The minister talks about the importance of meals as times of fellowship, and about how special some meals, such as Sunday lunch or a wedding

breakfast, actually are. He tells the pupils that basically the service means, for Christians, that they are sharing a special meal with one another, and thus sharing in the life of Jesus. The sharing, however, is not meant to stay inside the church: it is meant to be taken out into the world . . . some Christians manage to do this better than others.

He highlights the most important parts of the service, and shows the pupils'some of the prayers. He puts out the symbolic elements of the meal, allowing pupils to examine them. He tells the pupils of some of the differing emphases which are characteristic of other Christian denominations.

It is a delightful visit. The pupils are involved without being put under pressure . . . except by time: we always have to hurry back!

Written stage (to be done as homework)
Pupils are given the task of writing what they know about the Eucharist. (This exercise fulfils two functions: for the pupils, it helps them to clarify their ideas and to remember what they have learned; for the teacher, it provides valuable feedback for evaluating the scheme.)

Four extracts from pupils' responses are quoted below.
> *This is what I know about the Eucharist.*
>
> *When Jesus was having the Passover meal, he wanted the feeling of sharing. By the breaking of the bread and then the sharing of the wine he achieved this. Nowadays in churches when they have this meal which they often call, Holy Communion, the people sometimes have wafers instead of bread. Some churches use little wine glasses instead of one wine goblet. When Jesus did this, he said that the bread was his body and the wine his blood and in some churches today they say that when the bread and wine have been blessed it changes. I suppose its like living Jesus' life all over again.*

> *. . . I think that the meal means that Christians are sharing the life of Jesus and belonging to some part of him.*

> *. . . I think that the meal is a good idea because its like you are actually taking a piece of Jesus' soul and putting it into your own body.*

> *. . . The bread and the wine represent Jesus' body and blood. Jesus told his disciples to keep this custom so that he would be remembered and people would be brought together as one.*

Other Approaches
The several "snapshots" on the preceding pages do not, of course, exhaust the possible approaches to the Christian vision. It is worth asking the question; "Where else may pupils have encountered Christianity, in any guise?" Any such encounter, whatever the attitudes engendered by it, may be the starting-point for a journey from the borderland to the interior of Christianity. A few places where encounter may have occurred are listed below.

Special ocasions, such as weddings, funerals, national observances.

Christian festivals.

Services and activities of the local churches.

News items and TV programmes about conflicts or controversies among Christians.

TV programmes such as "Songs of Praise" and "Highway".

Representations in the media of Christian ministers.

Views about Christianity (including professions of conversion) expressed by famous personalities.

Evangelistic missions in the locality, or at holiday resorts.

For any spark which fires the interest, curiosity or enthusiasm of pupils the teacher has cause to be grateful. The task of turning the energy thus generated to the best advantage will fully test the teacher's skill, but at least the journey towards defined objectives can begin.

Resources

D. Barnes	*From Communication to Curriculum*	Penguin 1976
J. Thompson	*The Christian Faith and its Symbols*	Edward Arnold 1979
Schools Council	*What is the Christian Church?*	Hart-Davis Educational 1981
E. Yamauchi	*The World of the First Christians*	Lion Publishing 1981
E. G. Speare	*The Bronze Bow*	Puffin, 1961
W. Laxton ed.	*Paths to Understanding*	Macmillan 1980
T. Shannon	*Jesus*	Lutterworth 1982

Jesus: An Enquiry

Context

This scheme is developed from work done in a mixed semi-rural Comprehensive school (11–16). It assumes a foundation course which includes work on the language of religion, and was used with second year classes (12+). The school has no pupils from ethnic minorities. Facilities for R.E. are very good—a carpeted specialist room with curtains, so that visual material can be used without undue disruption. The teacher claims that most incoming pupils have little knowledge of Christianity, let alone of other cultures, and are already showing signs of prejudice, especially against Christian institutions. The subject is allocated two periods a week (5% of a 40-period week).

Introduction

Entry to a religious tradition may be made at any one of several points; its heart may be approached by many routes. The decision on where to start may reveal some of the teacher's presuppositions. Both before and after the 1944 Education Act, the Protestant concern with the word of God in Scripture has been dominant in the study of Christianity, although recently the experience of teaching non-Christian faiths has resulted in a more objective look at the phenomenon of Christianity as a living faith and has made possible a greater variety of approaches. Sooner or later, however, the teacher will need to explore with pupils the question of Jesus and his impact on people; and, in an educational setting, he/she will be bound to make use of the tools of historical and literary scholarship.

After a century of intense critical, sometimes hostile, investigation of the sources, there is an almost universal consensus that the presentation of Jesus in the Gospels is at least based on a real man who lived, taught and died in the land that is now Israel. Most Christians would, of course, go much further than this, and would emphasise the historicity of the Gospels and the general reliability of their records concerning Jesus and how people reacted to him; some would insist on their literal accuracy throughout. The teacher has to exercise a responsible caution in teaching what Christians hold to be the historical facts about Jesus, and the revealed truth about his significance as the Christ. Room must always be left for a variety of interpretations and of personal responses.

Pupils at this age can be helped to appreciate that Jesus is presented in the Gospels as a credible figure in a realistic setting, who had considerable—sometimes astonishing—impact on many people, both opponents and supporters/followers. Such was his impact, indeed, that (according to the Gospels, which other New Testament writings support) his opponents had him executed, while his followers, despite that, believed him to be God's Agent for bringing new life and hope to the world, experienced him (so they claimed) as alive among them and within them, and gave him their obedience and their worship. The Gospels were written out of such belief, experience and devotion. The view taken in this scheme is that the prime issue for younger Secondary pupils is the credibility of Jesus the man; while it is fully recognised that at a later stage pupils need to engage more closely with the issue of the Christ of Christian faith.

The scheme is designed to pursue in a constructive spirit an enquiry concerning Jesus. It takes account of the possibility that the enquiry could be hampered by pupils' prejudices, and attempts to challenge these by involving the learner in the solution of puzzles rather than in the passive acceptance of an assumed orthodoxy.[1] The teacher's most difficult task may indeed be to get pupils to suspend their judgement for long enough to come to grips with the material. The teacher may often need to redirect pupils' attention to the limited available evidence, and to encourage the expression of differing interpretations and responses, in order to prevent premature evaluations and the closing of minds.

Objectives

Pupils should be able to give a coherent account of some of the main teachings and events recorded concerning Jesus. (See the first of the objectives for R.E. at the Secondary level in *Religious Education in Hampshire Schools* 1978.)

Pupils should be aware of the kind of impact that Jesus has had on people, an impact not limited to his native country nor to his physical lifetime.

Pupils should understand something of the origins and value of the writings concerning Jesus, especially the Gospels.

---

[1] *The approach recommended here is worked out in more detail in Naylor D. and Smith A.* Jesus: an Enquiry *(Macmillan Education, 1985).*

OUTLINE OF CONTENT

1 The Nature of the Evidence:
   (a) the extra-Biblical evidence
   (b) the four Gospels[2]

2 Jesus the Jew[3]

3 Jesus the Teacher

4 Jesus the Controversial Figure

5 Some Puzzling Stories in the Gospels

6 Crucifixion and Resurrection Narratives

7 Birth and Infancy Narratives

8 The Impact of Jesus

An adequate treatment of this material would probably require two terms. The suggestions which follow are far from exhaustive, and should be taken as examples of effective procedures, specimens of possible learning experiences. It is recommended that the academic year which features a scheme on Jesus should start with the study of another founder (e.g. Gautama Buddha): this would make illuminating cross-references possible.

The Nature of the Evidence

As an introductory activity, to encourage pupils' responses and sharing of ideas, and to provide the teacher with useful information for planning subsequent work, pupils (working in pairs):

(a) Write down anything they think they know about Jesus;

(b) Put in brackets after each item where they got the idea from; mark with the letter S (or underline in red) any ideas they feel sure are correct; put a question-mark (or mark in green) any statement which they think others may not agree with.

(If (a) and (b) are done with water-based pens on acetate sheets, ideas can easily be shared via an Overhead Projector.)

(c) Draw or describe what they think Jesus might have looked like. How sure are they about their versions? Why did they decide on them?

Show the pupils some pictures (e.g. C.E.M.'s "Christ in Art") for them to compare with their own ideas. What different views of Jesus do these pictures suggest to them?

Finally, pupils write down any questions they have about Jesus.

The extra-Biblical evidence

Present some of the evidence from outside the New Testament (e.g. The writings of Suetonius, Pliny, Tacitus, and the Talmud).

Pupils write down things which tell them:
   that Jesus existed
   how his existence can be dated
   the beliefs about him which were held by his followers
   the problems which faced his followers.

The four Gospels

Pupils can start the process of trying to understand what a Gospel is by scanning Mark's Gospel. Refer pupils back to the introductory exercise about Jesus' appearance, and ask them to search for a personal description (one chapter between two pupils). The absence of this kind of information may help pupils to appreciate that Mark's Gospel is not a biography.

An attempt can then be made to locate the Gospels in their setting in the early Christian community. Pupils can be asked to imagine that they have recently (about the year CE 50) become members of a band of Jesus' followers in the town of Corinth, as a result of the teachings of Paul. Working in small groups, they think about the things which would have been typical of their lives as Christians together, and write down their ideas under the three headings:

Actions   i.e. what we did (among ourselves, and in relation to non-Christians);

Words   i.e. what we said and talked about (among ourselves, and in relation to non-Christians);

Writings i.e. what we wrote or collected or preserved.

These ideas can be compared with information contained in the New Testament documents about life in the early Christian community, reference being made to such passages as:

Acts 2.41–47; 4.31–37; 5.42; and Ch. 6.
                     (Actions; words)

1 Cor.11.17 ff. (Fellowship Meal); 1 Cor.16.1.f., 2 Cor.8.2–4, and 2 Cor.ch.9 (Collections for the needy).   (Actions)

1 Cor.11.23–25 (Words used in worship)? (Words?)

General reference to Paul's letters. (Details about his writing of these might interest pupils: see for example Rom.16.22; 1 Cor.16.21; Col.4.18; Gal.6.11).   (Writings)

1 Thess.5.27; Col.4.16 (Letters are to be publicly read, and circulated).   (Writings)

Luke 1.1–4 (referring to earlier writings about Jesus).   (Writings)

---

[2]*A distinctive feature of this scheme of work is that it locates the questions about Jesus firmly within the context of the Early Christian Church's activities, i.e. it treats the Gospels as primary evidence for the Early Church and as secondary evidence about the ministry of Jesus.*

[3]*This and the following six headings are those used in* Paths to Understanding *(1980) p. 57f., where material is suggested for teaching about Jesus with pupils aged 8 to 12.*

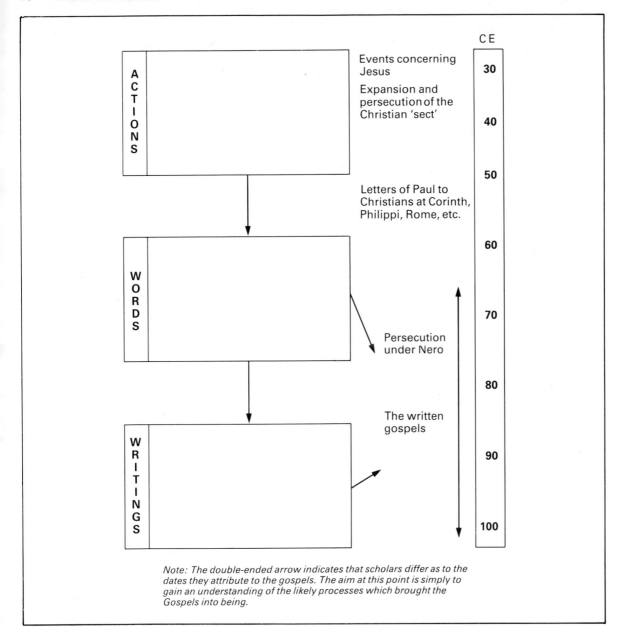

Note: The double-ended arrow indicates that scholars differ as to the dates they attribute to the gospels. The aim at this point is simply to gain an understanding of the likely processes which brought the Gospels into being.

Other important material under the "Words" heading (to be added by the teacher, or looked up by the pupils) includes:

the interpretation of Jesus which is revealed in the accounts of the Apostles' preaching in the early chapters of Acts (the so-called Kerugma);

the arguments (about beliefs, organisation, etc.) and the boastings (about personal holiness) which went on among the Christians at Corinth, as Paul's letters reveal: a useful reminder of the all-too-human realities of the situation!

What has been discovered from the New Testament can be entered in the boxes in the diagram above. The teacher can then move the focus from the period CE 30–50 to approximately CE 100, and, with help from the pupils, build up on OHP the right-hand side of the diagram.

Jesus the Jew

Pupils can be reminded that Jesus was a Jew.[4] They can be asked to make suggestions (giving reasons for them) about:

his home and family

his friends

everyday life and occupations in the first century C.E.

his education

the festivals and celebrations he would keep

the land in which he lived

the social and political context.

The pupils' own ideas can be supplemented by the teacher with the aid of relevant slides, pictures and charts.

Jesus the Teacher

Pupils can be asked to list the qualities they look for

---

[4]*A useful, probably necessary, possibly misleading, and not strictly accurate term, for only after the time of Jesus did the social-cultural-religious tradition to which he belonged come to be called "Judaism", and its members "Jews". The term should be introduced with care.*

in a good teacher, or to rank in order of importance statements (such as those below) written on separate strips of paper:

A good teacher sets a good example;

A good teacher takes an interest in you;

A good teacher praises you when you do well;

A good teacher gets you interested in things;

A good teacher gives you the right answers;

A good teacher makes you want to find out things for yourself;

A good teacher draws attention to your mistakes, but without condemning you.

Two blank strips of paper can be provided for pupils to write statements of their own.

Examples of Jesus' teaching can then be examined, such as:

His reply to the question from John the Baptist (Luke 7.19–35);

A selection of parables which raise questions for the listener;

His answers when questioned in the Temple in Jerusalem (Luke 20).

The qualities of Jesus as a teacher, as revealed in each episode, should be discussed. In each case it will be necessary first to read or tell the story effectively. Pupils can then be asked to try to imagine the setting in the early Christian communities in which this story might have been told.

Jesus the Controversial Figure

A variety of incidents can be used under this heading:

The visit to the synagogue at Nazareth (Luke 4.16–30);

Jesus in the house of Simon the Pharisee (Luke 7.36–50);

Plucking corn on the sabbath (Luke 19.1–10);

Jesus and Zacchaeus (Luke 19.1–10);

Cleansing the temple (Luke 19.45f.).

Small groups can explore questions about each incident. Questions about the first of those listed might be:

What can you learn about Jesus through this story of his visit to Nazareth? (e.g. about his childhood, about the language he used; about his understanding of what he ought to do).

Why were the people of Nazareth upset?

What was Jesus' argument?

How would this story have helped future followers of Jesus?

Further discussion about each incident could be developed by asking pupils to imagine either that they were present at the incident described or had been told about it. Discussion could be based on the following questions:

Which of Jesus' words would you have found praiseworthy? Why?

Which of Jesus' actions or words would you have condemned? Why?

What does this story show about how Jesus' followers thought of him?

Some Puzzling Stories in the Gospels

The title of this section has been chosen to make an important teaching point. It is a fact that the stories commonly known as "miracle stories" are interpreted in widely different ways by Christians. There are four main types of interpretation used by Christians and it is essential to a truly educational approach that several possibilities are explored, e.g:

That the story is a literal reporting of what actually happened (i.e. what a T.V. film would have recorded);

That the story has some rational explanation, in physical or psychological terms;

That the story has been retold in the context of the early Christian church in such a way that an incident has been used (perhaps selectively, or with special emphases, or with added symbolism) as a vehicle for conveying a belief held to be important;

That some original piece of teaching has been transposed into an event so as to communicate it more dramatically.

Pupils may test each of these possibilities, for example on the story of the Feeding of the Five Thousand. A problem-solving approach can be introduced by means of questions, preferably handled in small groups:

What worries or puzzles you about the story?

For what purpose do you think the early Christians told this story?

In what kind of setting might the story first have been told?

What does the story show about how his followers thought of Jesus?

The pupils' responses can then be discussed in the light of the different types of interpretation mentioned above. On the "word for word" or literal view, which will be sincerely held by some pupils and their parents, Jesus possessed special powers which enabled him to increase the quantity of food. On the rationalistic view the event is explicable in terms of normal human experience, e.g. that Jesus' character and attitude inspired people in the crowd to share their food with others—the "miracle" being people's unselfish response to others' needs. The remaining two types of interpretation will require detailed references to earlier lessons on "What is a Gospel?" Exploring these views will mean taking seriously the setting in which the story was used in the early Church, noting how certain references in the story can be linked with features of the Eucharist and pointing to the possibility of the symbolic use of numbers.

Pupils' responses might be given more concrete form by their working in groups to produce specifications for part of a T.V. programme, for which they are responsible, concerning Jesus' impact on people.

Crucifixion and Resurrection Narratives

It is important to recognise the vast range of possible meanings which can be found in the Passion narratives. Traditional statements like "Christ died for our sins" are meaningless to many children. With this age-range the essential task is to handle the narrative so effectively that the story itself becomes the possession of the pupil. Attention could then be focussed on particular characters: for instance, role-playing interviews with Pilate or Judas, Peter or Mary, would help to explore motivation and to uncover meaning. With small group activity of this kind the discussions of groups can easily be tape-recorded and, if suitable, used to compare ideas. Alternatively, certain themes, such as loyalty/disloyalty, justice/injustice, and change, could be explored: some approaches to these are suggested below. With either procedure, the tape-recording of role-play or group-discussion could add interest and facilitate the sharing and comparing of ideas.

Loyalty/disloyalty

Think about Judas' and Peter's different actions. What were the results of their disloyalty?

How do you think Mary the mother of Jesus would feel about these acts of disloyalty?

What might be an early Christian's point of view about Peter's disloyalty?

What do you think Christians would have learned from the story of Peter?

What do you think Christians would have learned from the story of Judas?

Justice/injustice

Pupils working in pairs write down words or sentences which will describe the feelings of Jesus' followers during his trial.

Interview a member of the Sanhedrin about his reasons for wanting to convict Jesus.

Interview Pilate about his view of the situation.

Imagine you are a group of disciples. Jesus has just been sentenced. What are you going to do now?

What were the accusations against Jesus? What evidence was produced?

What coud have been said in his defence? Why did he not defend himself?

Pupils could work on these questions in small groups, and present findings verbally or visually.

Change

From the work done already pupils should have formed their own impressions of the disciples at the time of the crucifixion. We know a little about Judas and Peter and it is possible to speculate about the feelings of the rest who "forsook him and fled". Reference to the early chapters of the Acts of the Apostles, as well as to the existence of the Christian Church in the world, can lead to speculation about what caused the dramatic change from disillusion and fear to confidence and growth. The sequence of events can be represented by a diagram in the form of a calendar from Good Friday to Whit Sunday,

with pupils working in pairs to compose this. The central idea of "change" can be very effectively explored by a careful reading of the "Road to Emmaus" story (Luke 24:13–32). The story itself can be examined thoroughly in small groups using such questions as:

v. 13–14	What do you think they would be saying?
v. 15	What kept them from seeing who was with them?
v. 17	Why were they gloomy?
v. 21	What had they been hoping for? What meanings can you find for the word (used in the New English Bible) "liberate"?
v.22–24	Can you find the story of the women at the tomb in St. Luke's Gospel? What do you think is meant by the term "vision of angels"?
v. 30	Why was Jesus recognised by this action?

The four types of interpretation mentioned earlier can again be explored as in the example given of the Feeding of the Five Thousand. Pupils should be encouraged to imagine the setting in which this story would be told and retold.

Birth and Infancy Narratives

Consideration of these has been postponed to the end of the Unit in the hope that some of the insights into the nature of the Gospels and the various ways in which they are interpreted will make possible a fresh approach to stories which will already be familiar. The early years of the Secondary school are an appropriate time for examining the composite story which most children experience in Junior school nativity plays in order to show that Luke and Matthew offer distinctive and different stories, whilst Mark has none.

An analysis of the different sequences of events, as given in the accounts of Matthew and Luke, can be made in parallel columns, and matters on which the two documents are in agreement underlined. Pupils can then discuss, perhaps in pairs, whether statements such as the following are true or false, and give reasons for their choices:

These stories are accounts of what actually happened:

These stories are based on events which really happened;

The Christians who told these stories wanted to convey to their hearers the significance which Jesus had for his followers;

If someone present had been filming the events, the film would have shown angels appearing to the shepherds and to Mary;

Angels are symbolic figures in the story, expressing the idea that Jesus is important;

Interpretations are as important as facts, because they tell us what people were thinking within a generation of the execution of Jesus.

The Impact of Jesus

Pupils can be asked to find out what two or three people they know think about Jesus.

Using a range of pictures which include representations of Jesus, pupils can try to identify a number of qualities or characteristics of Jesus which artists have attempted to express or to highlight.

With the aid of the filmstrip "The Christian East" (BBC Radiovision 1971) the subject of icons and their use can be introduced. Icons, by means of a formalised symbolism, emphasise the unique and divine character which Christian believers recognise in Jesus; i.e. they focus on "the Christ of faith" rather than on the human Jesus, "the Jesus of history", who has been the subject of this scheme up to this point.

Teacher and pupils can explore attitudes to Jesus on the part of Jews, Muslims and Hindus.

This section can become the starting-point for work on Jesus as the Christ of faith and the Lord of Life, e.g. a study of martyrs and martyrdom. Lives of contemporary Christians—and not only the more publicised "heroes of the faith"—should also be explored, so that pupils can come to appreciate that Jesus is not only a figure from the past to be investigated but, for many people, a living reality in the present.

The impact of Jesus down the centuries is well presented in the BBC Radiovision series "Jesus through the Ages" (1985).

Work on Stories and Festivals

Context

The scheme of work which follows is adapted from work done during a Spring term with pupils aged 11+ in a mixed Comprehensive school in a small town; no pupils in the class were from ethnic minority groups. Pupils come from five main feeder schools, in which Religious Education (with a content that is mainly Christian and largely based on the Bible) is integrated into a Topic curriculum. There is a specialist room with facilities for the use of audio-visual means of communication.

Rationale

The scheme attempts to put alongside each other two elements which are basic to religion:
>   stories: their content, origins and meanings, and how they are preserved and propagated within communities;
>   celebrations and festivals.

These two elements could be expressed, in more technical terms, as "myth" and "ritual".[1]

Stories are at the heart of an individual's identity and of religion. If a person is asked to say something about him or herself, he or she is most likely to tell a story. Religious communities are similar, in that their central beliefs are encapsulated in stories which are told and retold, often in an annual cycle, to generations of believers. These received stories contain many layers of meaning, since each generation coming to them interprets them for itself and, in turn, leaves another layer of meaning for the next generation . . . like a tree which each year acquires a new ring of growth. The capacity to penetrate imaginatively into these layers of meaning is essential to religious understanding. Where the interpretation of stories remains at an elementary level there can be only very limited access to the meanings enshrined in a faith.

Stories are used within religious communities in various ways. Those which have founded and shaped a particular community of faith are normally celebrated in song and symbol, recital and ritual, food and drink.

Using a particular methodology, this scheme explores the Exodus saga and the story of the death and resurrection of Jesus. These have been chosen because they offer opportunities for a wide range of activities connected with the festivals (Passover and Easter) associated with them. The activities suggested allow scope for the development of skills related to the understanding of sign, symbol and ritual as necessary means of religious expression.

A list of recommended Resources is given at the end of the scheme.

Programme: Content and Progression
Stories

An exploration of secular stories, to help pupils to:
>   extend their emotional repertory—ensure that the stories provide material which matches pupils' experiences and feelings;
>   enter imaginatively into the lives of people who live in different ages, places or cultures;
>   appreciate that a story may have several layers of meaning.

Examples of such stories are:

A. R. van der Loeff: *Children of the Oregon Trail* (Puffin 1970)
A true story of a 13 year-old boy who, with his family, sets out in 1844 to open up the frontiers of Western America. His parents die on the journey and the boy John, with his six younger brothers and sisters, leaves the wagon trail and travels uncharted territory to follow his father's pioneering dream. The story shows the immense courage of the children, their physical and inner journeyings, and the indomitable quality of the human spirit.

M. B. Taylor: *Roll of Thunder, Hear my Cry* (Puffin 1980)
The book is based on the author's own childhood experiences in the deep south of America in the 1930's. It traces her loss of innocence as she becomes aware of the great divisions between local black and white communities, of the consequences of prejudice and suspicion for an under-privileged group, and of the capacity of

---

[1] *The story and the festive activities (the "myth" and the "ritual") are vitally connected and mutually reinforcing: the verbal "myth" defines the meanings of the "ritual"; the physical "ritual" enlivens the "myth" as the participating individuals and groups make these meanings a part of their own lives. What is there in pupils' experience which involves them in doing something (occasionally, repeatedly or ceremonially) in order to clarify, internalise or affirm a meaning? In what ways do pupils express "The Story of Me", "The Myth of Myself", so as to preserve identity, recognise dependence, celebrate abilities, and feel that life has meaning and value?*

individuals to have ideals and to fight for principles—"We have no choice of what colour we're born or who our parents are or whether we're rich or poor. What we do have is some choice over what we make of our lives once we're here".

J. Steiner: *The Sea People* (Gollancz 1982)
A parable, or perhaps an allegory, rich with meaning. It is a story of two islands and of the greed and selfishness of the King of the Greater Islands who exploits the people and resources of both his own kingdom and the Lesser Island. Pupils will be able to trace connections between this story and issues, currently being debated, relating to the Third World, to the exploitation of natural resources, and to the quality of man's environment.

Festivals
An analysis of the main elements of the stories, celebrations and customs, signs and symbols, and inner meanings, of the festivals of Passover and Easter.

Passover

Story	Suffering of people
	Call of Moses
	Return of Moses to Egypt
	Conflict with Pharaoh
	Exodus
Celebrations and Customs	The 7-day cycle
	Removal of Hametz (unleavened bread)
	Preparation of Matzah (unleavened bread)
	Attending synagogue
	Songs and Memorial Prayers
	The Seder Meal
	Searching for the Afikomen
Signs and Symbols[2]	Lamb bone; Matzah; Green herbs; Horseradish; Charoset
	Empty chair
	Cup for Elijah
Inner meanings	Slavery and suffering
	Freedom and deliverance
	God active in history
	Spiritual/physical journey
	God's call, people's response
	Community

Easter[3]

Story	Entry into Jerusalem
	Questions put to Jesus
	Last Supper
	Gethsemane
	Trials
	Crucifixion
	Resurrection
Celebrations and Customs	Shrove Tuesday (Mardi Gras)
	Ash Wednesday and Lent
	Holy Week: Palm Sunday; Maundy Thursday; Good Friday; Easter Sunday
	Easter Vigil: the Service of Light (see p. 96f.)
	Pancakes
	Burning of last year's Palm Crosses and marking foreheads with ashes
	Simnel Cakes/Palm Crosses/ Maundy Money
	Hot Cross Buns
	Easter Eggs/Bonnets/Gardens/ Parades/Cards
	Paschal Candle
	Egg-painting and Egg-rolling
Signs and Symbols	Ashes; Fasting; Palms; Hot Cross Buns; Bread; Wine; Water; Candles; Flowers; Eggs
Inner meanings	Conflict of good and evil
	Love
	Sacrifice
	Death and New Life
	Reconciliation
	God's action, people's response
	Community

Process
Stories
Reading aloud to a class the whole text of a book is not recommended; but one or more copies of any book to be used in this scheme should be available in the resource area or library so that pupils who so wish may read the story in full.

Read selected extracts to the class, summarising the intervening parts of the story. Extracts should be chosen so as to give rise to fruitful discussion on important issues, with the aid of questions such as:
What would you have done in this situation?
What would character X feel like?
Have you ever felt like that? When?

---

[2]*It is worth noting that several symbolic objects have particular words—story, prayer or thanksgiving—associated with them, ensuring that they do not lose their meanings.*

[3]*As will be seen, the use of the term here is elastic, taking in the weeks leading up to Easter Day itself, and Holy Week in particular. Some pagan elements relating to celebrating the return of Spring (Lenct, in Saxon) are present, but have been invested with Christian significance; the renewal and transformation of people—Jesus, his individual followers, and the believing community—are the key ideas.*

Why do people behave like that?

What is the author trying to make us see, feel or understand?

What symbols are used to convey impressions, ideas and feelings?

Much of the discussion could best be carried on in pairs or small groups, perhaps with findings being shared in a class discussion. Written work might sometimes be appropriate. Care should be taken not to interrupt the flow of the narrative, by questions or asides, so much that it loses its grip on the pupils' interest and its power to move them.

Festivals

Teaching about religious festivals may be approached from any one of the three perspectives: story; celebrations and customs; signs and symbols. In the following suggestions for teaching about Passover and Easter, the starting points are varied, but the objectives sought are always the same.

Passover

Through music, art, movement and discussion explore the concepts of slavery, freedom and journeying, bringing out both the physical and the inner aspects of these concepts. Negro spirituals such as "Go down Moses" and "Deep river" might be used; also modern songs such as "By the rivers of Babylon" (based on Psalm 137). Link this exploration with the work done on stories.

Recount the story of the Passover, using the book of Exodus. Divide the class into groups and produce a wall frieze of the key events of the story, and/or dramatise some incidents in it.

Discuss the major themes in the story, drawing on previous work which illuminates them, e.g. deliverance from slavery; people responding to the call of God; journeying in fear and hope.

Finding out about the Passover meal

(a) Cook the symbolic foods (perhaps in co-operation with the Home Economics Department in a Secondary school).

(b) Learn songs which are used at Passover.

(c) Make up menus which might be used at a Passover meal by a Jewish family.

(d) Consider how the Passover table would be prepared in a Jewish home.

(e) Simulate a Passover meal with the class, using the food prepared and singing the songs learned.

(f) Discuss the thoughts and feelings aroused by any of these activities, especially (e).

Use filmstrips and slides to study the artefacts and symbols employed by the Jewish community today in re-telling and interpreting the story of the Passover.

By meeting and talking with a Jewish person, try to discover the significance of the Passover Festival for Jews today. (This might be done through private personal contact; or by arranging for a visit to, or a visitor from, a local synagogue.)

Easter

Describe the ceremonies of the "Service of Light", the first part of the celebration of Easter in the Western Catholic Church tradition. (See below for the text of the service, given here because it might be difficult for teachers to obtain.)

(a) Darken the classroom, and perform a ceremonial action of lighting candles, similar to that which occurs in the service.

(b) Discuss the experience of transforming darkness into light.

(c) Compare the ideas and language used in this service with those encountered in connection with work on the Passover (especially the language of the Easter Proclamation).

Tell the story of Holy Week and Easter, referring, as appropriate, to the Biblical narratives, and linking it with stories previously read with the pupils.

Role-play central events such as: Peter's denial; Judas' betrayal; the trials before Pilate; the visit of the two Mary's to the tomb; the meeting with a stranger on the road to Emmaus.

Pupils could write, from the standpoint of one of the participants, to a friend living some distance from Jerusalem, expressing contrasting thoughts and feelings about the events which they have witnessed, or of which they have heard reports.

Using the media of poetry, painting, movement, etc., explore the theme of the transformation of darkness to light.

Consider the link between the "darkness to light" theme and the Easter theme of "death and new life".

By meeting and talking with a Christian try to discover the significance of the Easter Festival for Christians today. (This might be done through private personal contact; or by arranging for a visit to, or a visitor from, a local church.)

Text of the Service of Light

All the lights in the church are put out.

A large fire is prepared in a suitable place outside the church. When the people have assembled, the priest goes there with the ministers, one of whom carries the Easter candle.

The priest greets the congregation in the usual manner and briefly instructs them about the vigil in these or similar words:

Dear friends in Christ,
on this most holy night,
when our Lord Jesus Christ passed from death to
    life,
the Church invites her children throughout the
    world
to come together in vigil and prayer.
This is the passover of the Lord:
if we honour the memory of his death and
    resurrection
by hearing his word and celebrating his mysteries,
then we may be confident
that we shall share his victory over death
and live with him for ever in God.

Then the fire is blessed.
Let us pray.
Father,
we share in the light of your glory
through your Son, the light of the world.
Make this new fire holy, and inflame us with new
    hope.
Purify our minds by this Easter celebration,
and bring us one day to the feast of eternal light.
We ask this through Christ our Lord.
Amen.

The Easter candle is lighted from the new fire.

The procession may follow immediately . . . or the
optional blessing of the candle may follow.

Optional Blessing of the Candle.
After the blessing of the new fire, an acolyte or one
of the ministers brings the Easter candle to the
celebrant, who cuts a cross in the wax with a stylus.
Then he traces the Greek letter alpha above the
cross, the letter omega below, and the numerals of
the current year between the arms of the cross.
Meanwhile he says:
Christ yesterday and today
the beginning and the end
Alpha
and Omega;
all time belongs to him,
and all the ages;
to him be glory and power,
through every age and for ever. Amen.

When the cross and other marks have been made,
the priest may insert five grains of incense in the
candle. He does this in the form of a cross, saying:
1 By his holy
2 and glorious wounds   1
3 may Christ our Lord   4   2   5
4 guard us   3
5 and keep us. Amen.

The priest then lights the candle from the new fire,
saying:
May the light of Christ, rising in glory,
dispel the darkness of our hearts and minds.

Procession
Then the deacon or, if there is no deacon, the priest
takes the Easter candle, lifts it high, and sings alone:
Christ our light.
(All) Thanks be to God.

Then all enter the church, led by the deacon with the
Easter candle. If incense is used, the thurifer goes
before the deacon.

At the church door the deacon lifts the candle high
and sings a second time:
Christ our light.
(All) Thanks be to God.

All light their candles from the Easter candle and
continue in the procession.

When the deacon arrives before the altar, he faces
the people and sings a third time:
Christ our light.
(All) Thanks be to God.

Then the lights in the church are put on.

Easter Proclamation
When he comes to the altar, the priest goes to his
chair. The deacon places the Easter candle on a
stand in the middle of the sanctuary or near the
lectern . . .

The priest sings the Easter proclamation at the lectern or pulpit. All stand and hold lighted
candles . . .

Short Form of the Easter Proclamation (Exsultet)
Rejoice, heavenly powers! Sing, choirs of angels!
    Exult, all creation around God's throne!
    Jesus Christ, our King, is risen!
    Sound the trumpet of salvation!

Rejoice, O earth, in shining splendour,
    radiant in the brightness of your King!
    Christ has conquered! Glory fills you!
    Darkness vanishes for ever!

Rejoice, O Mother Church! Exult in glory!
    The risen Saviour shines upon you!
    Let this place resound with joy,
    echoing the mighty song of all God's people!

The Lord be with you
(All) And also with you.
    Lift up your hearts.
(All) We lift them up to the Lord.
    Let us give thanks to the Lord our God.
(All) It is right to give him thanks and praise.
    It is truly right
    that with full hearts and minds and voices
    we should praise the unseen God, the all-
        powerful Father,
    and his only Son, our Lord Jesus Christ.

For Christ has ransomed us with his blood,
and paid for us the price of Adam's sin
to our eternal Father!

This is our passover feast,
when Christ, the true lamb, is slain,
who blood consecrates the homes of all
believers.

This is the night when first you saved our fathers:
you freed the people of Israel from their slavery
and led them dry-shod through the sea.

This is the night when Christians everywhere,
washed clean of sin
and freed from all defilement,
are restored to grace and grow together in
holiness.

This is the night when Jesus Christ
broke the chains of death
and rose triumphant from the grave.

Father, how wonderful your care for us!
How boundless your merciful love!
To ransom a slave
you gave away your Son.

O happy fault, O necessary sin of Adam,
which gained for us so great a redeemer!

The power of this holy night
dispels all evil, washes guilt away,
restores lost innocence, brings mourners joy.

Night truly blessed when heaven is wedded to earth
and man is reconciled with God!

Therefore, heavenly Father, in the joy of this night,
receive our evening sacrifice of praise,
your Church's solemn offering.

Accept this Easter candle.
May it always dispel the darkness of this night!

May the Morning Star which never sets find this
flame still burning:
Christ, that Morning Star, who can back from
the dead,
and shed his peaceful light on all mankind,
you Son who lives and reigns for ever and ever.

(All) Amen.

Resources

Books for the classroom

O. Bennett	Exploring Religion series	Bell & Hyman 1984
	Festivals	
	Signs and Symbols	
	Religions of the World series:	Macdonald 1984
A. Brown	*The Christian World*	
D. Charing	*The Jewish World*	
C. Knapp	*Simon, Leah and Benjamin*	Black 1979
C. Lawton	*I am a Jew*	Franklin Watts 1984
	Matza and Bitter Herbs	Hamish Hamilton 1984
	Living Festivals series:	R.M.E.P.
	Shrove Tuesday, Ash Wednesday, Mardi Gras	
	Holy Week	
	Easter	
	Passover	
T. Shannon	*Christmas and Easter* (Chichester Project No. 7)	Lutterworth 1984

Books for the teacher

V. Barnett	*A Jewish Family in Britain*	R.M.E.P. 1983
B. Carr & P. Oberman	*The Gourmet's Guide to Jewish Cooking*	Octopus Books 1973
C. Lawton	*The Seder Handbook*	Board of Deputies of British Jews, Upper Woburn Place, London WC1H 0EP 1984
F. Nesham & H. Kilminster	*The Christian Year Cookbook*	Mowbray 1980
M. Palmer	*Faiths and Festivals*	Ward Lock Educational 1984

Booklets from C.E.M.

The Jewish Home
Christian Objects
Christian Worship

C.E.M., Lancaster House,
  Borough Road, Isleworth,
  Middlesex TW7 5DU

Posters

Judaism
Celebrating Easter (Primary
  and Secondary)
Jewish Festivals
Christian Festivals

C.E.M.

Pictorial Charts
  Educational Trust
  27 Kirchen Road,
  London W13 0UD

Slides

Christian Worship—Holy Week

The Slide Centre,
  143 Chatham Road,
  London SW11 6SR

Celebration Meals

B.B.C., 35 Marylebone
  High Street,
  London W1M 4AA

Artefacts

Christian: from "Articles of Faith",
  Mrs C. M. Winstanley,
  123 Nevile Road, Salford
  M7 0PP
Jewish: from Jewish Education Bureau,
  8 Westcombe Avenue,
  Leeds LS8 2BS

Videos

Judaism through the Eyes of
  Jewish Children
Christianity through the Eyes
  of Christian Children

C.E.M. Video, 5 Dean
  Street, London W1V 5RN

Approaches to the Hindu Vision

Context

This scheme of work is a development from one which has been used in a variety of schools and was devised and shared on an in-service course. The outline given here is aimed at third year Secondary pupils but with appropriate modifications it has been used with pupils as young as top Juniors. If pupils with origins in the Indian sub-continent were present in the class, the possibility of sharing ideas and insights would be a bonus.

While the form of the scheme is an exploration of the main ideas and practices of Hinduism, it is important to acknowledge the wider culture within which these beliefs, values, customs and rituals have their place.[1] With the younger pupils more emphasis would be placed on this wider social context. (Too often Westerners separate out religion from culture in their study of Hinduism and India: on the whole, it is preferable to think of the people rather than the "-ism".)

Three books which provide invaluable background information and are referred to in the text which follows, are:

H. Kanitkar and R. Jackson: *Hindus in Britain* (1983). (Available from the School of Oriental and African Studies, Malet Street, London WC1E 7EP). Detailed information about Hindu life in contemporary Britain, with some suggested teaching schemes.

D. Killingley (ed.): *A Handbook of Hinduism for Teachers*: Grevatt and Grevatt, 9 Rectory Drive, Newcastle-upon-Tyne NE3 1XT (1984). A comprehensive book with useful stories, discussion of key concepts, and outlines of main practices and patterns of Hindu life.

V. P. Kanitkar: *Hindu Festivals and Sacraments*. (Available from the author, 83 Bulwer Road, New Barnet, Herts.). A practical survey of the main patterns of festival worship and rites of passage.

Objectives

The intention of the scheme is not primarily to convey a body of general knowledge about Hinduism. Emphasis has been placed on establishing a number of central concepts and eliminating superficial, stereotyped judgements about the religion. There are now significant numbers of Hindus in our society and their beliefs are often seriously misunderstood: charges that Hindus worship idols is one common misrepresentation. The plurality of gods, and the absence of a historical reference point like the Buddha or Jesus, make for difficulties in designing a framework of study. The scheme offers direction in overcoming such difficulties.

Three features of Hinduism, which render it a particularly valuable subject for study, are worthy of notice. Many of the stories and celebrations are vivid and colourful; the openness with which Hindus approach other religions is often attractive to pupils; and the diagnosis of the human condition which is offered can be very stimulating.

At the end of the course pupils should:

Have explored their own attitudes towards, and understanding of, Indian culture, in order to identify areas of stereotyping and misjudgement and to develop an attitude of openness towards Hinduism;

Have developed a knowledge of the central concepts and actions in the religious life of a Hindu;

Have entered as deeply as possible, and without premature evaluation, into the feelings, beliefs and actions of Hindus;

Have applied some of the insights gained from the study of Hinduism to their own concerns.

OUTLINE OF CONTENT

Unit 1 Background work on Indian Culture

Unit 2 God and the gods of Hindus

Unit 3 Central ideas in Hindu thought—karma, dharma, samsara, moksha, bhakti, yoga

Unit 4 Patterns of worship—
in the home—Puja
in the temple
at a festival (Divali)

---

[1] *It is tempting to arouse pupils' interest by emphasising the oddness of the beliefs and practices of people of a different culture. The temptation must be resisted. The teacher must, to the best of his/her ability, do justice to what is a normal component of life for millions of people, presenting it as normal, and helping pupils towards fresh perceptions, so that they may recognise its reasonableness, significance and attraction for those millions.*

Unit 5   Hindu social patterns

Unit 6   Gandhi

Unit 7   Conclusion

CLASSROOM APPROACHES

Unit 1   Background Work on Indian Culture

(i) Pupils, working in pairs, *either* write down all
they know about India, *or*
write down the words which come into their
minds about India.
Discuss where these ideas have come from.
How many of the ideas refer to "problems",
"disasters" or "underdevelopment"?
Think carefully about the list that has been
made, and mark with a ? any idea or word
about which you feel doubtful. Share findings with the class, and identify any stereotyped ideas.

(ii) Show selected slides of village and urban life.
Good sets are available from C.W.D.E. and
from OXFAM (e.g. "City and Village Life").
Pupils write down good/bad/interesting
points about each slide.
Compare points with the original list of ideas
about India.
Use the slides to illustrate (a) diversity and contrasts in Indian culture, and (b) the
continuity of traditional elements.
Draw attention to aspects of Indian life which
break the stereotypes—art, architecture,
industrial development.

(iii) Aspects of Indian life:
Music: listen to tabla and sitar;
Dress, jewellery, etc., demonstrated by a visitor
if possible;
Familiar objects in an Indian home;
Food: types of food, symbolic use of food, food
taboos.

Unit 2   God and the Gods of Hindus

Three key themes can be explored:
The significance and meaning of specific gods;
The relationship between the multitude of gods
and the idea of one supreme reality;
The use of images by Hindus.

The significance and meaning of specific gods
Different Hindus will select different gods for special attention in their worship. Pupils should understand that this selection is not exclusive. A shrine to
Krishna, for example, might have many pictures of
other gods and saintly figures—including those we
associate with other traditions (e.g. Jesus, Muham-
mad, Mary, etc.). A visit to a local temple, if one can
be arranged, will make this obvious. Alternatively,
the familiar story of the Blind Men and the Elephant
will clarify the idea that for Hindus the gods are not
exclusive.

To develop an understanding of the place of the
gods in Hinduism, a programme of work in three
stages can be undertaken.

Ganesha, the Elephant God
Select one god as a simple illustration.
Ganesha, the elephant god, is a good choice. He is a
very popular Hindu deity, and some key aspects of
his symbolism can be easily grasped.
The central notion to emphasise is that Ganesha is
the "overcomer of obstacles".

Some questions for discussion, and some activities,
are suggested below:
What "obstacles" in their own lives can pupils think
of, and how would they try to overcome them?
Why is the symbol of an elephant as obstacle remo-
ver a good one?

Examine a picture or statue of Ganesha.
Pupils write down their observations and feelings
about the image.
How could the objects Ganesha holds (i.e. a flower,
an axe) be seen as obstacle removers?

Identify his mount—a small rat! (All Hindu gods
have some kind of vehicle which reflects the deity in
some way).
Pupils can speculate about the appropriateness of
the rat. (Some obstacles can only be moved deli-
cately and carefully, not by the use of force.)

Pupils choose or invent a symbolic figure to represent their own obstacle-remover.

Read and discuss some of the stories associated with
Ganesha (especially how he got his elephant head)
and consider the ways in which he is used in Hindu
homes, shops and temples, e.g. at a wedding, a
house-warming, the opening of a shop or the beginning of a new task. Why use the obstacle-remover
on these occasions?
(see Killingley op cit. p. 58 for relevant material.)

The three-fold cycle: Brahma, Vishnu, Shiva
The symbolic nature of the Hindu deities having
been established, the class can proceed to study the
more significant deities—the three-fold cycle of
Brahma (the creator), Vishnu (the preserver) and
Shiva (the destroyer).

After discussion about the life-cycle creation—
destruction—re-creation, pupils work out their own
visual or dramatic representation of this cycle.

Study carefully the symbolic representation of
Shiva as Lord of the Dance (see Killingley op cit. p.
67f.). Pupils in groups can try to identify and interpret the various features of the image.

Discuss with pupils the idea of life as a "dance".
What patterns of creation—destruction—rebirth

Shiva as Lord of the Dance

can they identify in life around them? What sense can they make of worshipping a god of destruction (Shiva)? After discussion, pupils may consider examples to illustrate the Hindu view that creation and destruction are dependent on one another.

Supply pupils with a variety of pictures or statues of Vishnu and Shiva. Ask pupils to identify the symbols, gestures, vehicles, etc. which characterise each of them. Pupils should then apply their findings to further representations of the two deities.

An Avatar of Vishnu (Rama , Krishna, etc)
Introduce the notion of an Avatar: the Preserver (Vishnu) sometimes finds it necessary to come to earth as an incarnation (e.g. as a fish or tortoise or, most importantly, in human form as Rama, Krishna or Buddha, for example). In his incarnate form Vishnu fights to overcome evil and suffering on earth. Highlight the Hindu openness both to Buddha and to Christ.

Select one Avatar (Rama or Krishna is the most obvious choice).
Outline the story of the Avatar, and discuss its meaning (basically, the overcoming of the force of evil).
Discuss the role of the consort of the Avatar (i.e. Radha or Sita) in the story, and the ways in which she is represented visually.

Pupils, after discussion in small groups, decide what kind of Avatar is needed in today's world, and how to represent this Avatar symbolically. Their ideas may be expressed in written or visual form. They might also consider how best to represent the force of evil today.

The choice of Avatar can be used again in the work on Hindu worship (Unit 4).

The relationship between the multitude of gods and the idea of one supreme reality
Various aspects can be explored:
(a) Consider the fact that a person can be seen from many perspectives, can have many attributes, can play many roles—yet is one reality. Each pupil makes a list of statements about himself/ herself, beginning "I am a . . .";
(b) The importance of opposites—life/death, light/darkness, good/bad, joy/sadness, creation/destruction, etc., each term in a pair implying the other;
(c) The idea that there are more than 330 million gods—a vast incalculable number!—i.e. that everything is part of the one supreme reality, and can therefore be used to represent that reality. Discuss what this would mean for a Hindu's view of life around him;
(d) The concept of Brahman, the supreme reality. The goal of life is to discover and experience the identity of oneself (Atman) with Brahman.

The use of images by Hindus
(a) Hindus have different levels of understanding concerning the status of the gods and their representation. For many, an image helps to focus the mind on a particular god, or on his attributes, and is thus an aid to worship; few, if any, could be said to worship the image, the material object itself.
(b) The link between visual images and that which they represent (cf. photographs kept as a memory—the memory is important, *not* the photograph itself). The image can be regarded as a "silent teacher".
(c) The notion of statues as pointers. It is that to which the statue points that is important. Once you see what is pointed to, the pointer can be discarded. Beyond the form of the statue (whether male or female, human or animal, or a combination of both) is the all-pervasive Brahman, the reality which is sought and worshipped.
(d) The common Indian tradition of throwing statues away each year to ensure that everyone remembers that the statue is disposable. (But not all Hindu groups do this).
(e) The story about idol-worship on p. 263 of W. Owen Cole ed.: *Religion in the Multi-Faith School* (Hulton 1983) can be discussed.
(f) Able pupils might go on to explore the idea that the gods themselves represent aspects of the one supreme reality.

Unit 3   Central Ideas in Hindu Thought
Some key ideas—especially karma, dharma, samsara, moksha, bhakti and yoga—may be introduced at this stage. They should be treated with respect and sensitivity, and an attempt should be made to relate them to the pupils' own experience. It should be kept in mind, and made clear to pupils, the Hindus differ among themselves

in their familiarity with particular concepts, and in the interpretations and emphases which they put on them.

The human condition

(a) *Karma.* The word means both "action" and the way in which actions shape a person's destiny. A good or bad life will be the result of good or bad karma. Since Hindus believe that we go through a series of rebirths, some actions may only bear fruit in a later existence: this helps to explain apparently undeserved good or bad fortune.

Pupils could consider examples of personal experiences which Hindus would explain by reference to the concept of karma.

(b) *Dharma.* Dharma comprises everything a person should do in life, given his or her particular situation. To pursue one's dharma is to have good karma. Dharma is determined by various factors such as gender, financial circumstances, and family background. For many Hindus, caste is an importnt aspect of one's dharma.

Pupils could consider what they think influences their dharma. What factors are, or are likely to be, most important in influencing the direction of their lives and the achievement of success and fulfilment? Share some answers with the class, discuss their similarities and differences, and explore the reasons for these.

(c) *Samsara and Moksha.* Samsara is the belief that one's present life is only one of a series of lives, the nature of which is determined by karma. The goal, for the Hindu, is to achieve liberation (moksha) from the cycle of birth—life—death—rebirth.

Pupils could discuss the idea of samsara, bringing in any apparent evidence which may have come to their notice. Imagining the nature of their past and future lives, with a serious attempt to link these to characteristics of their present existence, could lead to personal insights and further discussion.

Paths to salvation

The goal of a Hindu's life is moksha, libertion from the cycle of rebirths. There are several ways whereby a Hindu may try to achieve this. The most basic is simply to follow one's dharma and thus to produce a good karma: this involves living positively and fully, in a manner appropriate to one's nature, social status and occupation.

Many Hindus also engage in special practices to help them towards liberation. Three principal ones are:

(a) *Bhakti.* Bhakti, the expression of devotion to a personal deity, is the most popular and widespread form of religious activity among Hindus.

Two good examples of bhakti ideas which could be examined are the pattern of love between Radha and Krishna, and the triumph of good over evil in the life of Rama. (See Killingley op cit. index for references to Rama and Krishna.)

Material in Units 2 and 4 is relevant.

(b) *Meditation and reading of the scriptures.* Pupils should at least be introduced to the principal Hindu Scriptures, viz. the Ramayana, the Bhagavad Gita, and the Puranas, and gain some idea of their nature and contents. The more able pupils could find interest and value in reading and discussing selected sections of these works.

(c) *Yoga.* Yoga, for Hindus, is a highly developed pattern of physical training which leads to mental discipline, and perhaps to higher levels of spiritual awareness and insight. It is not to be confused with western forms of yoga, practised only for physical exercise or health.

A teacher familiar with the Hindu forms of yoga, or with access to a knowledgeable visitor, could introduce pupils to some elementary postures, breathing techniques and mental exercises to illustrate this form of religious practice. Pupils could consider the differences between the goals of popular western yoga (e.g. the improvement of one's appearance) and the goal of yoga in Hinduism.

Unit 4 Patterns of Worship

The Hindu way of life is experienced and absorbed from an early age through observation of, and participation in, rituals: in the daily worship at the household shrine, in the temple, and in special worship conducted by a priest on the occasion of a public festival such as Divali. These three aspects of worship are treated separately below. It should always be remembered that there is great variety in patterns of Hindu worship; whatever example they study, pupils should be aware that it is only one detail in a complex picture.

In the home—Puja

To help people to experience and understand the supreme reality and their relationship to it, Hindu wise men of the remote past devised upasana: this is a combination of prayers; offerings of fruit, flowers, incense and light; and meditation. For success in meditation, some symbol is needed to concentrate one's mind on the infinite Brahman; images are meant to perform this function. (See Unit 2 on the use of images.) Puja, the daily act of worship in a Hindu home, makes use of this pattern.

A home shrine will be dedicated to one of any number of deities, male or female. It will incorporate statues, pictures and symbols of the chosen god and of other gods (Hindu gods are not jealous!), and other artefacts and decorative items.

As preparation for understanding and appreciating the significance of Puja, pupils should work on two themes:

(a) how we decorate places (bedrooms, classroom, etc.); why we decorate them; and what our style of decoration indicates about ourselves and our main commitments;

(b) how we might prepare a welcome for a special guest.

After pupils have (by personal research, perhaps assisted by the showing of slides or film—e.g. the C.E.M. Video "'Hinduism through the eyes of Hindu children", or the Slide Centre's set "Hindu Worship") gained the necessary basic information, and have obtained materials from Indian shops or families, a shrine can be set up in the classroom and Puja can be demonstrated. (The activity is a demonstration, not an act of worship.)

During the demonstration pupils could consider these questions:

> What does each offering mean?
> What might a Hindu be thinking as he or she makes these offerings?
> What does the ritual suggest about how the Hindu feels about the god?
> If the god is a symbol, what might the Hindu think the symbol is pointing to?
> What is it reminding the worshipper of?
> What rituals do I take part in?

The basic idea of the worship is to welcome the god into the home in the manner of a special guest. The pictures or statues represent the god, whose reception is symbolised by various objects and actions, as listed above in the topic 'An Approach to India', p. 22.

(See Kanitkar op cit., for more details about Puja.) Follow up, if possible, with a visit to a Hindu temple.

In the temple
A visit to a Hindu temple (mandir) is invaluable. In preparing for a visit, the teacher should discover what form of worship is used; it cannot be assumed that it will conform to any presupposed pattern. (See the set of useful guidelines in *Hindus in Britain* pages 24–25).

Among the topics which can profitably be explored are:

> Different forms of worship: arti; prasada; communal prayers; the singing of bhajans; private meditation; celebrating rites of passage;
> The role of the priest, who will often, but not always, be a brahmin. (This could serve as an introduction to the topic of caste.);
> The symbolism of the temple: the shrine; pictures; the sound-symbol OM;
> The use of the temple as a social and communal forum for the local Hindu population. (This could serve as an introduction to the life of Hindus in Britain.)

At a festival—Divali
A familiar and popular festival, Divali, the festival of lights, celebrates the story of Rama and Sita, and, for many Hindus, marks the beginning of the New Year. (See Kanitkar and Jackson op cit. for more details.)

Approach the festival from any one of five aspects: story; celebration; customs; signs and symbols; inner meanings.
Story Rama and Sita. The capture of Sita by the demon Ravana and her rescue by Rama. The final return by the united pair, greeted by the lighting of many candles or 'deva' lamps.
Celebration Worship in the temple: special prayers to Lakshmi, goddess of wealth, at the onset of the New Year; special offerings (arti); prayers to Lord Rama.
Customs Divali cards. Cleaning of the home and carrying out financial accounting in preparation for the New Year. Mehendi hand decoration. Dancing. New clothes. Rangoli patterns. Family gatherings. Presents.
Signs and Symbols Deva lamps. Cards, often with representations of Ganesha (to remove obstacles for the New Year) and Lakshmi (hope for good fortune).
Inner Meanings Triumph of good over evil, light over darkness. The cycle of life, death and rebirth in the marriage, loss and recovery of Sita.

Pupil activities
Recreate the story in pictures, drama or slide-tape sequence and relate it to the idea of an Avatar.

Design their own Mehendi and Rangoli patterns.

Make Divali cards, inventing their own symbolism to express the underlying meanings.

Compare the Divali celebration with their own New Year experiences, and devise their own way of marking and celebrating New Year.

If possible, pupils find out about the specific form of the celebration of Divali and New Year in a local community, and its meanings for the participants, inviting members of the community to the school.

Other festivals which could be explored in a similar way are:

> *Holi:* a joyful and colourful celebration of Krishna's love for Radha.
> *Navaratri:* a festival, of varying significance, which is focused on the female deities of Hinduism.

(See Killingley op cit. and Kanitkar op cit. for details of these festivals.)

Unit 5 Hindu Social Patterns
Any generalisations about Hindu social life are likely to be as inaccurate and inadequate as

generalisations about most other aspects of Hindu culture and religion: variety, and the capacity to contain difference, are noteworthy features. There are other features of Hindu life which pupils may find it difficult to consider seriously or to reflect upon without pre-judgement. One such is the matter of caste; before condemning the system, pupils might consider how far, in what ways, and on what criteria, our own society creates and maintains social divisions. Another such feature is the arranged marriage; pupils will probably be unaware of the care that parents put into the "arrangement".

One possible approach to the study of Hindu social patterns is to explore the typically Hindu ideal of human life as comprising four fairly well-defined stages ("ashramas").

Pupils can be introduced to this by examining their own lives and ambitions, guided by such questions as these:

How do you see the pattern of your future life?
How far can you choose and determine your own future?
Are there any clearly marked stages in the life you foresee?
Are these stages (or could they be) marked in any way?
What will be your greatest responsibilities?
Which period of your life do you most look forward to?
What is your goal for life?

Pupils can then compare their answers and ideas with the four-fold pattern of life which a Hindu expects to follow:

1 *Student stage* (brahmachari): a period of study and preparation for life, initiated by the thread ceremony;
2 *Householder stage* (grihastha). The stage after marriage when the Hindu takes on the responsibilities of work, home and family;
3 *Hermit stage* (vanaprastha). When responsibilities are reduced in later life, the Hindu can withdraw (traditionally, to the forest) to meditate and to read the Scriptures;
4 *Monk stage* (sannyasi). To become a sannyasi, a Hindu has to be initiated by another sannyasi. The sacred thread is discarded, and the Hindu concerns himself solely with salvation; poverty is

regarded as an ideal at this stage. Few Hindus reach the final stage in this life, but would hope to achieve it in some future existence.

Other themes on Hindu social life could be considered along similar lines, i.e. by pupils looking at their own lives and their own society, and making comparisons with Hindu culture:

Caste (varnas);
Vegetarianism and diet;
Non-violence (ahimsa) and pacifism;
The place and role of women (both in social life and in mythology);
The family: marriage patterns, family roles, education, rites of passage;
Death and associated ceremonies.

Unit 6   Gandhi

Use of the film "Gandhi' (now available on video) is recommended, although the accuracy and balance of its representation of Hinduism are questionable. Selected scenes could be used as a basis for a study of Mahatma Gandhi, and could provide a useful focus for further exploration of many of the themes already introduced, for example:

Reverence for life; non-violence; poverty (an ideal or a problem?);
Caste and untouchability;
The role of women, and the significance of Hindu marriage;
The worship of Rama (Gandhi's chosen deity);
The unity and diversity of India: spinning-wheel and salt-march as symbols.

Unit 7   Conclusion

Each pupil could make a diagram or chart to illustrate what he or she has learned about Hindus.

Pupils working in small groups could prepare displays or presentations on Hinduism and the Hindu way of life. They could try to identify how and why their ideas have changed since the beginning of Unit 1.

Pupils could play "The Hindu Game of Life", published in the C.E.M. magazine *RE Today* (Autumn 1985 issue). This would serve as a means both of revision and of further insights.

Approaches to the Buddhist Vision

Context

This scheme of work, designed to occupy one term, was used with a group of third year pupils in a large Comprehensive school in an urban area. The pupils approach Religious Education with about the same degree of openness to influence as they do any other Humanities subject. Though the department is well stocked with textbooks, it is under-resourced on Buddhism. Measured by the enthusiasm of the pupils the scheme was successful, and it is intended to build up a wider range of resources in future years.

Objectives

The impact of Buddhism in the Western world is quite considerable. By now there are nearly 100 Buddhist groups in the U.K. Buddhism provides interesting contrasts to British culture, which derives its main views of the world and man from the Hebrew-Christian tradition. Buddhism's non-theistic nature and its doctrines of man and salvation sharpen the questions which confront the student of religion at any level. The pupils in this school found the notion that it was possible to be "religious" or "spiritually inclined" without a belief in God fascinating. Buddhism, having a historical reference point in Gautama Buddha, is more accessible to pupils in this age-range than Hinduism, where a framework of ideas is more difficult to establish.

At the end of the course pupils should be able to:
  Give a coherent account of the main teachings of, and events concerning, Gautama Buddha;
  Explain to another person such key concepts as buddha, dharma, sangha, karma, samsara, nirvana;
  Describe some ways of worship of Buddhists and the meaning which these have for the Buddhist;
  Apply some of the insights gained from the study of Buddhists to their own concerns;
  Have an attitude of openness towards Buddhist views of the world.

The content of the course is drawn mainly from the Theravada tradition. It is not the intention of the course to amass information. A central concern is to cultivate the skills of suspending judgement and to engage pupils with ideas from a culture different from their own.

OUTLINE OF CONTENT

Unit 1   The Buddha
(a) The Buddha Image
(b) The Story of Siddhartha Gautama
(c) How the Buddha is worshipped (saluted)
(d) The Buddha and The Christ

Unit 2   The Dharma (Teaching)
(a) The Buddha's method
(b) The First Noble Truth
(c) The Second Noble Truth
(d) The Third and Fourth Noble Truths
(e) The Noble Eightfold Path
(f) The concepts of Samsara and Karma
(g) Summing up

Unit 3   The Sangha (Community)
(a) The concept of the Community
(b) The Ten Precepts
(c) The Three Refuges
(d) The site of the Temple or Monastery
(e) Daily life in the Sangha

Unit 4   Meditation

Unit 5   The Festival of Wesak

Unit 6   Concluding Exercise

CLASSROOM APPROACHES

Unit 1   The Buddha
(a) *The Buddha Image*
Pupils divide into six groups. Each group is presented with a different image, real or visual (examples appear below), of the Buddha (see Resources item 10). Pupils discuss their impressions of the image and collect information about it. This procedure is repeated with three other images (the teacher instructing the groups when to exchange images) and the different impressions are compared. Each group is asked to decide:
 (i) what are the common features of the Buddha images;
 (ii) what are the major points of difference;
 (iii) what feelings the images together evoke.

In the course of discussing these questions, the meanings underlying various features are explored, inevitably bringing to light some ideas central to Buddhism. Groups report their findings to the class.

1 Buddha
    expounding the
    Dharma (Japan,
    12th. Century).
    Right hand thumb
    and ring finger form
    the wheel[1] of the
    teaching.

2 Meditating Buddha
    (Thailand).

3 Earth touching
    Buddha (Tibet).

4 Serpent-king
    sheltering Buddha
    (Cambodia/
    Kampuchea).

5 Standing Buddha
    (Mathura, India).

6 Buddha setting the
    wheel[1] of the teaching
    in motion (Sarnath,
    India, 12th. century).

7 Walking Buddha
    (Thailand).

8 Reclining Buddha in his
    parinirvana
    (Sir Lanka).

[1]*The Wheel is a central symbol in Buddhism; perhaps originated by the Buddha himself, it has been widely used by his followers to depict a great many important teachings. It incorporates both human life in all its aspects (birth, feelings, desires, evils, sufferings, death, rebirth, etc.) and the content of the Dharma (which holds out the hope of enlightenment and deliverance—see Unit 2 below).*
Pupils might construct their own pictorial ''Wheels'', showing in them the context and course (past, present and projected) of their own lives, their fears and hopes, the restricting forces and the possible means of escaping or overcoming these, and so on.
(For an example of the Wheel, see p. 21f. of item 1 in the Resources.)

Written exercise
Pupils are told:
You have come across an image of the Buddha in a place where you did not expect to find one. Describe, in either poetry or prose, the image and how it made you feel.

Pieces of work which come near to the "feel" of Buddhism are shared with the whole class. A 13 year-old in the top stream expressed her response in a poem:

Caught up in city rush,
no time to stop and think.
I work as a robot,
my feet and mind compelled
to do the work of day.
No time "to stop and stare"
in my waking hours.

Then I caught his eye,
My vision . . .
I had to stop, I had to know
if calmness and peace
of first sight were true.
I looked hard, I looked long
at the Buddha of tranquility.

So strange to see something
to make you halt.
A mystical power which works
even in our modern age.
The Buddha will always be
a stopper of mankind . . .
a stopper to make man think!

(b) *The story of Siddhartha Gautama*
The story is read or told by the teacher—the impact of the story is frequently lost if pupils read it themselves, either silently or aloud. The sketches opposite may be photocopied (titles having been obscured) and cut out so that pupils can arrange them to tell the story. The words are included to help the teacher.

After rearranging the episodes, pupils are asked to select the one they consider to have most importance for them and to give reasons for their choice. The following questions may also be explored:
What festival is linked with episodes 2, 8 & 9?
Where did 7 happen?
What is the significance of the elephant in episode 1?
What made Gautama leave the palace in 5?
(For the story, see Resourses, items 1 and 2 and for information on festivals, see item 9.)

(c) *How the Buddha is worshipped (saluted)*
A table covered with a piece of beautiful cloth is set up in the classroom, with a Buddha image placed on it along with flowers, a holder for a lighted joss-stick, and simple lamp. It is important to make it clear to pupils that this is not intended to be "real" worship but simply to show what Buddhists do.

The teacher places the flowers on the table, telling the pupils that when Buddhists offer flowers they say:
I make offering to the Buddha with these flowers
And through this merit may there be release.
Even as these flowers must fade
So my body goes toward destruction.
He then lights a joss-stick, telling the pupils that when Buddhists do this they say:
To him of fragrant body and face, fragrant with infinite virtues, to the Buddha I make offering with fragrant perfume.
He then offers a small lamp or candle, telling the pupils that when Buddhists do this they say:
With this lamp which shines brightly, destroying darkness, I make offering to the truly enlightened lamp of the three worlds, who dispels the darkness (of ignorance).
These words are projected on an O.H.P. or handed out so that pupils can discuss the following questions in pairs:
(1) What is the meaning of each of these offerings?
(2) What might a Buddhist be thinking when he or she makes offerings?
(3) Is ritual activity important?
(4) What ritual activities do I take part in?
Finally, pairs join together, and each group of four devises a ritual intended to bring to mind the qualities of someone who is not with them.

(d) *The Buddha and The Christ*
A detailed comparison at this stage is not recommended. It is useful, however, to make simple points, e.g.

Personal Name	Family Name	Title	Dates (approx.)
Siddhartha	Gautama	Buddha (the Enlightened one)	563 to 483 BCE
Jesus	bar-Joseph	Messiah or Christ (the Anointed one)	5 BCE to 30 CE

The Story. Pupils bring out similarities and differences in the stories, e.g. birth (prophecies, sense of destiny), temptation, marriage.

Unit 2 The Dharma[2]
(On the Buddha and his teaching, see Resources, items 3 and 8.)

(a) *The Buddha's Method*
   (i) Pupils discuss in pairs the qualities they look for in a good teacher, and make a list of these.
   (ii) Teacher tells the Parable of the Mustard Seed (a version is given in item 4 in the Resources). Discussion in small groups of (a) the meanings in the story (all the stories have

The Conception

The Birth of Gautama

The marriage of Gautama

Leaving the Palace

The Ascetic Life

The Temptation

The Enlightened One

The Pari-Nirvana

The Story of Siddhartha Gautama

[2]*Translations such as "the teaching" or "the doctrine" do not adequately convey the depth of meaning in this concept. "Dharma" comes from a root meaning "to bear, support, uphold", and signifies "that which is", i.e. the Eternal Truth. (A Burmese translation of the prologue to the Fourth Gospel uses it for the Word, the Logos: "In the beginning was the Dharma".) It was this dharma that the Buddha perceived, embodied, and made available in his teaching.*

many layers of meaning), and (b) the Buddha's method of teaching. Compare the findings under (b) with the qualities listed in (i).

(b) *The First Noble Truth*
  (i) Show a series of contrasting slides from contemporary life, e.g. brand new cars/scrap yard; baby/old person; party/aftermath of party; new house/derelict house.
  Discuss in small groups implications of the slide sequence, then share ideas in class discussion.
  (ii) Write a poem or a piece of prose entitled "If only . . ."
  These two exercises can be used as a stimulus for the exposition and discussion of the First Noble Truth, which involves some understanding of:
  Anicca—impermanence
  Dukkha—unsatisfactoriness
  Anatta—no permanent self.
  It is useful to use here the notion of the Buddha as the doctor who begins by making a careful diagnosis of the human condition. These three concepts are central to his diagnosis and need careful discussion in order that they may be well understood. Translations of such concepts are always too crude. The opportunity should be taken here to introduce the Pali or Sanskrit words. Two particular notes of caution are worth mentioning. First, attempts should be made to avoid the over-simplistic assumption that the First Noble Truth is pessimistic. Buddhists would claim that it is *realistic*, in that unless reality is accurately analysed, unhappiness arises because of a distorted view of the world. It is useful to remind pupils that the Buddhist greeting "Sabbe satta sukhita hondu" means "may all beings be happy!" and if they can meet Buddhists during the course of this piece of work the notion that Buddhism is pessimistic will quickly be dispelled. Secondly, the concept of Anatta is not easy to understand. At this stage, however, it is sufficient to discuss the ways in which we all change constantly, not only in our physical make-up but also in our personality.

(c) *The Second Noble Truth*
  This truth explains the cause of Dukkha, and is usually translated "craving' or "thirsting". It comprehends all desires and attachments, whether pleasure, possessions, self-esteem, long life, or any other supposed "solid joys and lasting treasures".
  Ask pupils to collect from colour magazines pictures of what advertisements say will make us happy and satisfied. Discussion can be initiated by placing a Buddha silhouette over the pictures.

(d) *The Third and Fourth Noble Truths*
  The Third Noble Truth is that emancipation from Dukkha—an end to unsatisfactoriness, a cessation of suffering—is possible. The Fourth Noble Truth shows the way to attain this.
  The idea of the Buddha as the doctor can be raised again, and pupils can formulate and discuss *their* prescriptions for putting the world right. These prescriptions could be classified into categories, such as personal, political, social or apocalyptic.

(e) *The Noble Eightfold Path* can then be introduced; it comprises:
  right understanding . . . right thought . . . right speech . . . right action . . . right livelihood . . . right effort . . . right mindfulness . . . right concentration.
  Discussion can take place in pairs on the meaning of each of these elements in the Buddha's prescription for living, and comparisons can be made with their own ideas previously discussed.

(f) *The concepts of Samsara, Karma and Nirvana*
  This is an appropriate point at which to introduce these key concepts.
  Samsara (the cycle of birth—life—death—rebirth) can be discussed in relation to pupils' own experience; some of their ideas might be expressed in symbolic pictures. Discussion could follow on the idea that "craving" or "thirsting" bind a person to this cycle, and on the purpose of Buddhist teaching and ritual, as means of bringing about the extinction of desires, and thus the ending of the cycle. (See note on p. 107.)
  Karma (very roughly translated as "the law of cause and effect") can also be discussed in relation to pupils' experience. How do our actions affect others? How do they affect ourselves? For example, the person who treats others with violence, in thought, word or action, may be damaging not only his victims, but also himself.
  Nirvana, to which enlightenment and the following of the Eightfold Path opens up the way, is the only worthwhile goal: an experience of tranquillity, in the absence of desires and strivings. (Parallels with "Heaven" or "Paradise" are likely to be misleading.) What views do pupils have about a "worthwhile goal", an "ideal state of being"? Has any experience of theirs come near to it?

(g) *Summing up*
  The line drawings on the following page may be photocopied for use, perhaps on an O.H.P. transparency. The transparency could be cut into eight pieces (three pictures and five words), and the picture of Buddhism (as studied up to this point) could be built up. By putting the

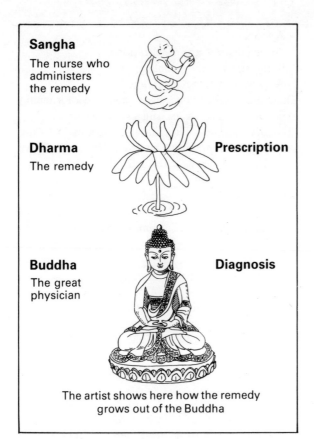

Sangha
The nurse who administers the remedy

Dharma
The remedy

Prescription

Buddha
The great physician

Diagnosis

The artist shows here how the remedy grows out of the Buddha

concept of the Sangha (the community of monks) last of all, a transition can be made to the next Unit of the scheme.

Unit 3 The Sangha

(a) *The concept of the community*

Pupils can be invited to invent the kind of community in which they think the Buddhists' way of life could best be practised, giving consideration to such questions as:

What would be the community's guide-lines for the conduct of its members?

How would it be organised and led?

What ceremonies (if any) could be devised for people joining the community?

What ceremonies could be devised for marking the death of a member of the community?

The life of a boy joining the Sangha in Sri Lanka can then be described.

(b) *The Ten Precepts* can then be compared with the guide-lines devised by the pupils.

(c) *The Three Refuges*, the basic creed of the community, can be discussed in relation to what the pupils rely on or put their trust in.

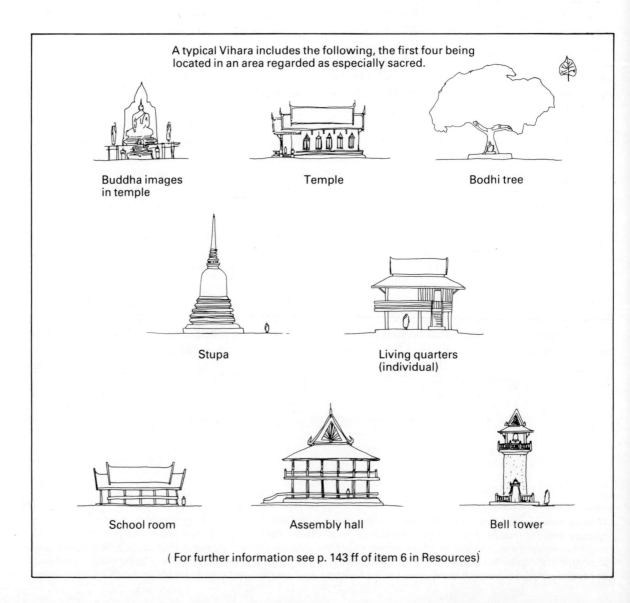

A typical Vihara includes the following, the first four being located in an area regarded as especially sacred.

Buddha images in temple

Temple

Bodhi tree

Stupa

Living quarters (individual)

School room

Assembly hall

Bell tower

(For further information see p. 143 ff of item 6 in Resources)

(d) *The site of the temple or monastery*
The diagrammatic sketches of what one would find in a typical Vihara (monastery or temple site) can be used to show the ways in which the monks (bhikkhus) function.

(e) *Daily life in the Sangha*
Daily life in the Sangha can be discussed. Pupils are divided into groups of 5 or 6. Three of them take on the role of Rahula (a boy entering the Sangha), Gunapala (his father), and Chandrani (his mother). These three are interviewed by the others in the group, and the interviews are recorded on tape if possible. Questions should be devised in order to bring out their attitudes and beliefs.
(See Resources, items 5 and 7.)

Unit 4   Meditation[3]

In dealing with meditation it is important for the teacher to be clear about his or her role. He or she is not a meditation master or guru but an educator charged with the task of helping pupils to understand the meanings which Buddhism has for its adherents. It is only legitimate, therefore, to invite pupils to try to think like a Buddhist in the same way that a teacher of English literature invites his or her pupils to stand in the shoes of a particular character.
Metta (Loving-kindness) meditation can be introduced by asking pupils to think about people—people they love, people they know as acquaintances, and people they do not like—and to think kind thoughts towards them.
Samatha meditation can be introduced by simple breathing exercises. Pupils can be encouraged to watch themselves breathing and to let go of any other thoughts which intrude. This can simply be presented as an aid to self-understanding.
Vipassana meditation. A plain description will probably be adequate. (See Resources, item 5).

Unit 5   The Festival of Wesak

Because it celebrates the birth, enlightenment and death of Gautama Buddha, work on the festival of Wesak can focus some of the ideas already introduced. Like the festivals of other faiths, Wesak has four main ingredients:

A story
Some customs and celebrations
Some signs and symbols
· A variety of inner meanings.
These elements can give rise to a variety of learning experiences, such as are suggested below:
(i) *Story-telling*—The Jataka stories of the Buddha's previous birth can be used. They show his growth towards the perfection of enlightenment.
(ii) *Customs*—Wesak cards depicting the birth enlightenment and death of the Buddha can be made. Models of Lumbini garden (the birth place) could be attempted if time allows.
(iii) *Signs and Symbols*—The meanings of the following symbols can be discussed:
Lotus flower—symbol of purity. Grows out o mud and slime but is unstained by it;
Buddha—symbol of stillness and calm;
Bodhi tree—symbol of enlightenment;
White elephant—symbol of royalty. Arising from legends surrounding the birth of Gautama;
Monks' robes—symbol of renunciation. Made from pieces of cloth given to them—often pieces taken from dead men's clothes. (See the explanation given by a Buddhist monk Resources, item 11.)

Pupils can be encouraged to create new symbols based on the central ideas involved.
(See Resources, item 6.)

Unit 6   Concluding Exercise

Work in pairs, with one pupil taking the role of a Buddhist boy or girl, the other taking the role of interviewer, concerned to discover, by asking appropriate questions, as much as possible about the Buddhist faith and way of life. Questions, and the main points of replies, should be recorded in some way (a basic pro forma, agreed by the class beforehand, could perhaps be produced and information entered on it).

Two or three of the more articulate pairs might repeat their "interview", outside the lesson, for the purpose of recording it on tape. Play back extracts from these in class, for discussion in pairs, a brief reporting to the class, and final comments by the teacher.

---

[3]*The relevance and value of studying Meditation could be enhanced by asking pupils to think about, and to discuss in small groups, their own emotional states and how, if at all, they try to control them. What do they do in order to concentrate their attention on something? How do they attempt to cope with disturbing feelings (anger, shame, etc.)? Have they ways of putting themselves into a particular frame of mind (e.g. generous, courageous or receptive)? What have they experienced of stillness and silence, and how have these states affected them?*

Resources
Books etc. referred to in the text

1 Schools Council	*Buddhism* (in series Journeys into Religion)	Hart-Davis 1981
2 E. Conze	*Buddhist Scriptures* (p. 34 f.)	Penguin 1969
3 W. Rahula	*What the Buddha Taught*	Fraser 1978
4 H. Lefever	*One Man and his Dog*	Lutterworth 1973
5 H. Sadhatissa	*The Buddha's Way*	Allen & Unwin 1971
6 W. O. Cole & P. Morgan	*Six Religions in the Twentieth Century*	Hulton 1984
7	Topic Folder No. 5: Buddhism	C.E.M.

Filmstrip with Cassette

8 What Buddhists Believe   From Audio Learning, 183–189 Queensway, London W2 5HL.

Charts

9 Buddhist Festivals   From Pictorial Charts Educational Trust, 27 Kirchen Road, London W13 0UD.

Artefacts

10 Images of the Buddha   From Articles of Faith, 123 Nevile Road, Salford, M7 0PP.

11 Extract of letter from the British Mahabodhi Society, London Buddhist Vihara, 5 Heathfield Gardens, London W4 4JU, to a R.E. teacher.

In the Buddha's time and since, the monks used to receive pieces of cloth from the laypeople. These pieces were of varying sizes and used to make up into a large Robe. The Buddha gave the design of these Robes—they were to be laid out like the fields of Kapilavastu, his birthplace (in present day Nepal). The orange colour is used to dispel mosquitoes and gadflies and other insects—also, the design and colour tends to make robes useless to laypeople—thieves used to steal robes of better cloth and colour so the Buddha prescribed the way the robes are made nowadays, exactly as they were in his day. Robes have been called the "Banner of the Buddhist Saints"—so many monks became saints as a result of their quiet lives and renunciation of the world and worldly things.

From the Ven. Dr. H. Sadhatissa, Head of the Order of Buddhist Monks.

Books for the classroom

J. Ascott	*Our Buddhist Friends*	Denholm House Press 1978
A. Bancroft	*The Buddhist World*	Macdonald 1984
A. Bancroft	*Festivals of the Buddha*	R.M.E.P. 1984
C. Barker	*Ananda in Sri Lanka*	Hamish Hamilton 1985
C. Hardy	*Buddha*	Holt, Rinehart and Winston 1985
T. Ling	*Buddhism*	Ward Lock Educational 1970
P. Morgan	*Buddhism in the Twentieth Century* (reprint from *Six Religions in the Twentieth Century*)	Hulton 1985
P. Morgan	*Buddhist Stories*	Available from: Mrs. P. Morgan, Westminster College, North Hinksey, Oxford OX2 9AT
D. Naylor	*Thinking About Buddhism*	Lutterworth 1976
D. Naylor & A. Smith	*Buddha: A Journey*	Macmillan Education due 1987
M. Patrick	*Buddhists and Buddhism*	Wayland 1982
F. W. Rawding	*The Buddha*	C.U.P. 1975

Filmstrips/Slides

Encounter with Buddhism	B.B.C. Publications, 144 Bermondsey Street, London SE1 3TH
Life of Buddha	Hulton Educational Publications Ltd., Raans Road, Amersham, Bucks. HP6 6JJ
Buddhism in Sri Lanka	Ann & Bury Peerless, 22 Kings Avenue, Minnis Bay, Birchington, Kent CT7 9QL

Moral, Social and Religious Education with Older Pupils: Guidelines and Resources

RATIONALE

Religious Education in Hampshire Schools (1978) states:

"Religious education frequently makes a contribution to programmes of social education or health education, and in some schools forms part of an integrated or inter-disciplinary course of study. There is much to be said for such courses, but it is essential that within them the religious education component is identifiable, clearly defined, and related to the total scheme of work in the school".

The literature of Religious Education at the beginning of the 1970s stressed the independence of Moral Education. More recently attention has turned to the fact that every aspect of school life and each component of the curriculum have contributions to make to the moral education of pupils and to the nurture of social responsibility. The recognition that there is no such thing as a neutral school or a neutral teacher is leading to a more careful scrutiny of questions about values in the planned curriculum and in the context within which it is carried out. Teachers of science and physical education will increasingly be asked to take some responsibility for their pupils' moral development.

The Religious Education teacher is well placed to make a significant contribution to personal and social education. Although it is possible to have moral education without reference to religious sanctions and presuppositions, there is no morality which is entirely devoid of presuppositions. An important aspect, therefore, of the courses we are considering is that of learning to identify the presuppositions and value judgements which lie behind moral claims and examples of behaviour. This is an area in which the religious educator has distinctive skills. Systems of belief or world views, and the moral codes which derive from these, are the subject matter of Religious Education, and neither can be studied in isolation. In practical terms these considerations mean that the following components must be present in the examination of issues where moral choices have to be made.

Facts

A knowledge of the facts of the case, so far as these can be ascertained. For example, a study of sexuality would include cultural and physiological data; and an examination of the issue of pollution would include data on the causes, extent and results of pollution.

Opinions

An appraisal of possible responses to the above in terms, for example, of personal relationships or social responsibility.

Commitments

An examination of underlying presuppositions or commitments and the difference these make. Hence, for example, questions concerning sexual relationships would involve not only an exploration of personal and social consequences, but also an examination of the way in which men and women are regarded in religious traditions. Similarly a consideration of ecological questions would require an exploration of views of the creation and of man's place within it. This is the component to which the R.E. teacher will have a distinctive contribution to make.

Action

The skilful teacher will keep these three essential components in balance, but will want to go further. The course could be sterile if it dealt only with theoretical aspects. Pupils will also need to have the opportunity to make moral decisions and to learn from the consequences of their decisions. It is for this very good reason that many teachers have involved their pupils in a wide range of community service activities.

PROGRAMME

Programmes of Social and Moral Education in the Fourth and Fifth years usually include such areas as the following:

MYSELF	Personal decision-making; smoking; alcohol; drugs; sexuality (including abortion/homosexuality/S.T.D. including AIDS): honesty; racialism; prejudice; health.
THE FAMILY	Different family structures (e.g. gypsies; Indian extended family

systems; eskimos; Japanese families); relationships in the nuclear family; love; sex; marriage; divorce; child development; handicap; rites of passage; old age; death.

THE COMMUNITY Law and Order; policing society; local government; community care groups; (un) employment and leisure; conservation ; the multicultural society; the media.

GLOBAL ISSUES War and peace (nuclear issues); world development; conservation of the planet; racial harmony; space exploration.

The issues raised under these headings should be planned so that each of the four components outlined above has its place.

LEARNING PROCESSES

Success or failure of the programme will to a large extent depend on the learning processes involved. Members of the team responsible for the teaching often come from a variety of subject areas and, as H.M.I. Survey (1985) of R.E. in Years 4 and 5 of the Secondary School points out, they will appreciate guidance on methodology as well as on the content of the course. Helpful advice about active learning methods can be found in the booklet "Discussion Methods" available from Moral Education Centre, St. Martin's College, Lancaster.

Many pupils of this age are unlikely to respond to a direct presentation of issues which the teacher regards as important; but if the issues are transposed into story form, involving real characters with real dilemmas, then it is possible for pupils to take on roles in order to explore the different sides of a question. Assuming the role of one who holds certain beliefs about the nature of the world and man's place within it will sharpen awareness of the third component mentioned in the rationale above. Debate can similarly be stimulated by asking pupils to rank a set of statements or solutions about a particular moral or social issue.

Encounters with visitors can also provide stimulus to the course. Maximum benefits can be obtained from inviting visitors if the principles outlined in the article on p. 120f. are followed. Similar principles apply to the use of video. Pre-viewing the film, and selecting parts relevant to the objectives of the lesson, are essential. The 'Panorama-style' commentary rarely makes demands on the viewer and judicious use of the pause button or turning off the sound may be more effective in involving pupils.

In addition to newspaper and magazine cuttings and television to give up-to-date information and opinion on current issues, the following list of resources may be helpful. Resources of this nature increase daily and are rarely panaceas; if, however, they are used and supplemented in accordance with the rationale presented in these guidelines they can be invaluable for the teacher.

RESOURCES

An annotated list compiled by Ken Oldfield, Director, West London Institute of H.E., Borough Road, Isleworth, Middlesex, follows.

Resources for the Teacher
Personal, Social and Moral Education: A Source Book, Brian Wakeman, (Lion 1984)
Practising, experienced, Christian teacher surveys both theory and practice scenes honestly and intelligently. Particularly useful sections on assessment and "tools for the job".
World Studies 8–13: A Teacher's Handbook, Simon Fisher & David Hicks, (Oliver and Boyd 1985)
Ideas, activities and resources can be adapted for all age-ranges from this creative, stimulating handbook.
The Development Puzzle, Nancy Lui Fyson, (Hodder and Stoughton, 7th edition 1985)
Many new entries in this excellent, vast resource book, chiefly concerned with Development Education in its widest sense.
Amnesty International: Education Pack
Available from:
    Amnesty International British Section,
    5 Roberts Place,
    off Bowling Green Lane,
    London EC1 DEJ
An annually updated resource list for teaching and learning about Human Rights, along with ten excellent units on relevant topics.
World Religions: A Handbook for Teachers, Alan S. Brown ed., Commission for Racial Equality/Shap Working Party (1986).
Articles and comprhensive resource lists over a vast subject area.
Religion in the Multifaith School, Owen Cole ed., (Hulton 1983)
Articles and resources recommended by practising teachers, covering a wide age and subject range.
World Concerns and the United Nations, U.N. Information Office/H.M.S.O. (1983)
Model teaching units for Primary, Secondary and Teacher education. Not all the models will be useful but the publication has value.
India, Pakistan and Bangladesh: A Handbook for Teachers, Patricia Bahree (S.O.A.S. 1982)
A comprehensive resource manual for many aspects of teaching related to the sub-continent.
An Introductory Manual for Peace Education, Development Education Project (1985)
Available from above,
    c/o Manchester Polytechnic,
    801 Wilmslow Road,
    Didsbury, Manchester M20 8RG

How to be a peaceful teacher, John Wingate, (Friendly Press 1985)
Available from:
 Friendly Press,
 61 New Town,
 Waterford,
 Ireland
Concise but fine material to help the teacher's own outlook and balance.
Alcohol Education Syllabus 11–16
Informal Methods in Health and Social Education, Bill Rice
"Free to Choose" Drug Education Pack, Bill Rice
Smoking Teaching Pack, Bill Rice
Health Education 13–18, H.E.C.
Life Skills Teaching Programmes 1 and 2, Hopson and Sealy
All available from:
 Tacade,
 2 Mount Street,
 Manchester M2 5BG
Tacade, with the Health Education Council, produce excellent materials in this sphere of which the above are a few of their most recent.
Ways and Means: An Approach to Problem Solving, Kingston Friends Workshop Group (1984)
Practical exercises in conflict resolution for secondary children.
The Ethical Dimension of the School Curriculum, Lionel O. Ward ed., University of Swansea (1982)
Excellent collection of relevant articles by the theorists, Hirst, Wright, Wilson, Pring, Kohlberg et al.
Values is a new magazine for teachers involved in social and moral education edited jointly by the staff of the Moral Education Centre at St. Martin's College, Lancaster, and the newly established Centre for Social and Moral Education, University School of Education, 21 University Road, Leicester LE1 7RF.

Video and film resources
A central resource for presenting complex issues coherently in this field. The most comprehensive and interesting catalogue is that of
 Concord Films Council Ltd.,
 201 Felixstowe Road,
 Ipswich, Suffolk IP3 9BJ.
 Telephone: 0473 715754
which is updated with regular supplements. A few films are available on free loan.

Some social and moral issues are tackled by
 C.T.V.C. (Church Television Centre)
 Video and Film Library,
 Beeson's Yard, Bury Lane,
 Rickmansworth,
 Herts WD3 1DS
 Telephone: 0923 777 933
and it is worth looking at their catalogue.

Both B.B.C. and I.T.V. are increasing their output in schools broadcasting in the P.S.M.E. area. The B.B.C. "Scene" programmes are particularly outstanding in this field and the quality of many Yorkshire T.V. programmes is very high.

Designated Channel 4 broadcasts can be taken off air by schools who pay a small fee. For information about this contact:
 T.V. Recording Licence Dept.,
 Guild Sound and Vision Ltd.,
 6 Royce Road,
 Peterborough PE1 57B
 Telephone: 0733 315315.

People are often the best resource for these courses. Many organisations have qualified regional staff keen to contribute to programmes of work. They often have access to the latest resources in the field and are willing to share in the preparation of units of work. Teachers do well to build up their own lists of valuable names, telephone numbers and addresses of:
 Local clergy and ministers; local Council of Churches Secretary
 Oxfam: Christian Aid; Action Aid; Save the Children: local reps.
 Local Health Education Council; Health Education Officer
 N.S.P.C.C.; R.S.P.C.A.; National Children's Homes; Barnardos: local reps.
 Help the Aged; Age Concern; Local Hospice: contacts
 Council for Alcoholism; Alcoholics Anonymous: contacts
 The Samaritans; The Simon Community: contacts
 Local Marriage Guidance Counsellors
 The Police Schools Liaison Officer
 Friends of the Earth; World Development Movement; Greenpeace: members
 Amnesty International: local secretaries
 Leaders of local Interfaith Groups
 The Salvation Army; C. of E. Children's Society; Shaftesbury Society: contacts
 Local M.P.; local County and Parish Councillors

Drama, games, simulations and computer programmes
It's Not Fair! A Handbook on World Development for Youth Groups, Christian Aid
Valuable publication which suggests a number of games and simulations.

Starpower, Obtainable from Christian Aid.
A simulation game for 25–35 players, suitable for senior pupils. A low mobility three-tier society is simulated to explore the relationships between the powerful and the powerless.

Drama for Justice, Christian Aid
Helpful suggestions for role play, posing difficult

problems faced by large numbers of people on our planet.

Values Auction, Christian Education Movement
This game on values and ambitions has been transformed into a computer programme by C.E.M.—available under the title *What's it Worth?*

The Farming Game, Oxfam
Simulates problems faced by West African subsistence farmers. Easy to run and very effective.

Slick, B.P. Educational Services (1983)
BBC B 40-track computer programme. Well-packaged with good graphics offering challenging ideas about the oil industry which holds the attention of students.

Books for Students (series)
Textbooks are not a good investment in this area because they date rapidly. However, the following provide background facts and may stimulate ideas when constructing a programme:
Patterns of Living series, Olivia Bennett, (Macmillan Education with Save the Children, 1982)
4 titles: City Life, Village Life, Family Life, Learning in Life. Full colour photography, clear text; international outlook.
Debate series, (Macdonald 1985)
Race, Disarmament, Rich world, Poor world, Law and Order, World Conservation Drugs. New series using double page spread format, b/w photos. Useful.
Standpoint series, various authors, (Oxford University Press 1976)
Death, On the Warpath, All in the Mind, Don't Shoot the Goalkeeper. Attractively presented b/w books which do not pretend to be impartial. Strong views expressed which gain good responses from pupils.
Communities in Britain series (Batsford 1984)
The West Indians, The Chinese, The Jews. Heavy, unattractive presentation but a very informative, promising series.
People, Politics, Power series (Wayland 1981)
U.N., Arms Race, Human Rights, Media, Trade Unions, Political Parties, Terrorists and Freedom Fighters, A Woman's Place. Useful, informative series, giving facts about forces at work in today's world. B/w photographs and short readable entries.
Today's World series (Batsford 1984)
Race and Race Relations, Apartheid, Islam, Terrorism, The Welfare State, Space Exploration, The Superpowers. Heavy Batsford b/w presentation but useful.

Checkpoint series (Edward Arnold)
A wide range of relevant issues: Growing Old, Death, Marriage, Trade Unions, Prisons, Police, Men and Animals, Women, Human Rights. Attractive easy reading, drawing on many sources. Magazine format stimulates discussion and opinion.
In the News series (Wayland 1983)
Violence, Families, Addiction, Race, Old Age, Self Help, Leaving Home, Health Care. Double page illustrated magazine-type spread, raising different aspects of the topic.
Counterpoint series (Harrap 1978)
The Media, Crime and Punishment, Medicine and Morality, People and Politics, Prejudice and Discrimination, Work and Leisure. Cartoon format for a series popular with less able students and good for discussion.
Modern World Issues series (Cambridge Education 1982)
The Arms Race, Society and New Technology, Human Rights. A commendable series for older students.

Individual textbooks
Christianity in the Modern World, David Field (Hulton 1983)
Christian ethics in today's world. For "O" level and G.C.S.E. syllabuses.
Frontiers: An issues resource book, Ralph Gower (Lion 1982)
Personal, Social, International issues tackled from a largely Christian standpoint, although there are statements from selected world religions on some topics.
Perspectives: A Handbook of Christian Responsibility, M. A. Chignall, (Edward Arnold 1981)
Dull, unattractive, heavy textbook for students, but teachers may find some content useful.
Real Questions, David Field and Peter Toon (Lion 1982)
Christian approaches to life and faith questions.
Religion and Social Justice: Ethics in a changing society, J. St. John (R.M.E.P., 1985)
Problems of social morality are explored, drawing on a wide range of contemporary and historical opinion. Broadly Christian outlook. For the more able pupils.
Thinking about Life: Exercises in moral and religious education, Tom Gardiner (Edward Arnold 1984)
Well presented series of questions, exercises, assignments and dramas, intended to stimulate discussion.
The United Nations and its Agencies, R. J. and J. Owen (R.M.E.P. 1985)
A source book with examinations in mind, along with lists of resources and addresses. Useful, if dull.

GENERAL ARTICLES

Religious Studies 16–19: Objectives

Arrangements for General Studies in this age-range vary considerably between institutions. Much depends on whether the institution considers itself to have a continuing responsibility for the general education of its students. Where such a concern exists, problems of provision still remain, with further problems caused by the attitude of many students towards areas of study not directly related either to examinations or to vocational skills. *Paths to Understanding* (1980) includes some interesting programmes of work being carried out in Sixth Form Colleges. Experience has shown that students do respond to a stimulating and sensitive presentation of significant material, and that they are of an age to benefit from such work.

Many students are involved at this period of their lives in a search for meaning and an attempt to discover and establish an identity. An enquiring approach to the answers which some people have found, as expressed in and through the main religious traditions, can inspire and promote the quest. Such an approach must be genuinely open, affording students opportunities to articulate their own questions, to criticise received standards and traditions, to evaluate the beliefs and practices of others, and to move towards personal conclusions and decisions.

The objectives set out below can serve as a useful check-list for the teacher of 16's to 19's. They were originally compiled by a working party in the London Borough of Hillingdon, and were edited by Warren Laxton to match the philosophy and style of *Religious Education in Hampshire Schools* (1978). They are reproduced here by permission of Hillingdon L.E.A., of whose Agreed Syllabus they form a part.

GENERAL OBJECTIVES

To enable pupils:
(1) to gain a more comprehensive and coherent understanding of the religious traditions already studied, in respect of their central beliefs and practices, and of their historical context and development—so that they could for example:
  (i) discuss and compare beliefs about God and man in the religious traditions they have studied, and the ways in which these beliefs are expressed in ritual observances;
  (ii) grasp and discuss intelligently the content and course of some recent theological debates within Christianity.

Illustrative material:
(a) *Concepts of God or gods, evil and "salvation" in, for example, tribal societies, Hindu societies and Christian societies;*
(b) *The nature of religious language and the claims of religious dogma (e.g. the concept of "myth" in relation to the Gospel birth-narratives and the doctrine of incarnation);*
(c) *Some recurrent difficulties of Christian belief (e.g. the concept of "miracle"; the resurrection of Jesus; the relationship between "the Jesus of history" and "the Christ of faith").*

(2) to encounter, understand and evaluate a variety of contemporary religious phenomena—so that they could, for example:
  (i) better appreciate the influence of religion in the lives of human groups and individuals;
  (ii) explain the principles and appeal of sects and cult-movements of a religious or quasi-religious nature;
  (iii) appreciate the experiments and problems involved in attempts to establish good relationships between religions and between denominations;
  (iv) be aware of changes, and understand the reasons for change and for resistance to change, in such matters as religious observance, organisational structures and the communication of a faith.

Illustrative material:
(a) *Current events (e.g. as in the 1980s: Militant Islam; the Just War; Northern Ireland; Liberation Movements in South America; the growth of Pentecostalism);*
(b) *The beliefs and practices exemplified in Jehovah's Witnesses, the Unification Church, Transcendental Meditation, Spiritualism, forms of Occultism, etc.;*
(c) *The work of the World Congress of Faiths, the Council of Christians and Jews, the World Council of Churches, the British*

Council of Churches and local Church Councils.

(d) *Experimental forms of worship (e.g. the Church of England's Alternative Services Book 1980); Christian communities; religion in the mass media; missions; modern versions of the Bible.*

(3) to compare religious and non-religious stances for living—so that they could, for example:

(i) describe the characteristics, implications and effects of a religious interpretation of existence;

(ii) give a coherent account of the characteristics, implications and effects of at least one non-religious stance for living;

(iii) appreciate some of the sociological and psychological factors involved in religious thinking and behaviour;

(iv) individually formulate, or articulate more adequately, some consistent set of beliefs and values which is felt to provide a reasonable, significant and provisional element of personal integration.

Illustrative material:

(a) *A study of specifically religious terms and ideas drawn from differing religious traditions (e.g. sin, karma, forgiveness, transcendence, nirvana, worship, islam);*

(b) *A study of humanist and/or atheist beliefs, values and practices;*

(c) *A study of a Hindu Sadhu or Sannyasi, a mystic or a contemplative in Christian and Buddhist traditions, an Islamic Sufi, or a Sikh Saint;*

(d) *An examination of the concept of secularisation.*

(4) to understand some of the religious and non-religious principles involved in contemporary social, political and moral issues—so that they could for example:

(i) appreciate why differing views may be held, even by people whose basic convictions are similar, about certain moral issues;

(ii) intelligently appraise problems, and attempted solutions, relating to world resources, oppressed minorities, etc.;

(iii) reasonably evaluate issues raised by recent developments in medicine, science and technology;

(iv) apply such principles to situations which could arise, perhaps calling for decision and action, in their own experience.

Illustrative material:

(a) *A study of such issues as abortion, capital punishment, euthanasia, the use of sexuality, violence.*

(b) *Problems of over-population, poverty, distribution of resources, international aid, war and peace, etc.*

(c) *Ethical considerations raised by such practices as artificial insemination, genetic engineering and organ transplantation, by the availability of nuclear power, and by techniques of automation.*

(d) *Biographical and autobiographical examples of people applying principles to life-experiences.*

Visitors as Contributors to R.E. and Assembly

INTRODUCTION

Visitors welcomed into a school offer both a social opportunity and a useful variation in curriculum activity. They can form part of a planned programme, and will enrich pupils' experience by:

extending the range of points of view available to the pupils;

tapping areas of expertise and talent not otherwise readily available;

providing direct contact with people involved in local and national issues;

building bridges between the school and the many, and often conflicting, interests of the surrounding community.

However, headteachers sometimes find themselves faced with decisions in response to individuals who represent particular causes or religious organisations and who wish to present their case to pupils. It would be unwise to lay down hard and fast criteria, but it may be helpful to draw out some principles by giving answers to five key questions.

What is the purpose of having visitors in the school?

Hampshire's statement of policy on the school curriculum declares that pupils should be helped to acquire "a reasoned set of attitudes, beliefs and values". An important contribution to this end can be made by pupils encountering people who hold decisive commitments—not least, religious commitments. In the course of, or subsequent to, such encounters, discussion and debate will be essential; only so can pupils increase their ability to distinguish between opinion and fact, and be protected from the influence of mere bias and bigotry. In the limited group of the classroom, there is plenty of opportunity to question, to probe, to disagree, to weigh the visitor's words against previously held ideas and against ideas expressed by others in discussion. In the school Assembly, the wide age-range poses extra problems to the visitor, and dialogue is almost precluded; in addition—and it may be an unfortunate addition—the visitor is sometimes invested with an authority which may appear to pupils as beyond challenge. Nevertheless, within the constraints present in particular schools, some careful planning may increase the value of Assembly:

by ensuring that the number and age-range of the pupils is appropriate to the speaker and his or her subject;

by arranging seating and the physical setting whenever possible to promote involvement and discussion;

by giving due attention to preparation and to follow-up activities.

What is the context into which the contribution of the visitor will fit?

Sometimes a single visit, if of a sufficiently stimulating nature, can act as a spur to subsequent activity. More often visitors are best organised in sequences which ensure breadth of coverage. There should be preparation for the visit, a plan for the actual meeting, and appropriate follow-up activities and discussion. The teacher will need to give a clear brief to the visitor about the educational purpose of the visit and about the context into which the contribution fits. He or she will also need to give information about the physical setting and the facilities available, the nature and size of the group, and the ways in which it is proposed to involve the pupils. Planning should also take account of the range of contributions which can be made by visitors. These may include an aesthetic performance, an illustrated talk, a discussion, a dialogue deliberately presenting different points of view, or a demonstration of skill.

Who should be invited?

The teacher's aim is to promote worthwhile learning experiences. It is, therefore, a normal part of his or her professional task to exercise discrimination in deciding who should, and who should not, be invited to address and to enter into dialogue with pupils. No person should be regarded as unacceptable solely on the grounds that he or she holds strong convictions or opinions—pupils ought not to be insulated from these; but a person might properly be excluded on other grounds, e.g. that he or she cannot communicate successfully with young people, or refuses to allow him or herself to be questioned or contradicted. It would be irresponsible to arrange a "blind date"; the teacher should take pains to be well informed about the proposed visitor, if possible consulting a colleague who knows the person and whose professional judgement is respected. Teachers' Centres may play a part in maintaining lists of people and organ-

isations available to schools and in providing facilities for groups of teachers to preview material offered by commercial and charitable institutions. Some distinction also needs to be drawn between organisations whose aims are predominantly educational and others whose concern is predominantly fund-raising or proselytising.

What is the relationship between the visitor and the teacher?

One thing that the visitor is *not* is a substitute for the teacher! Rather, as suggested above, the visitor is a resource at the teacher's disposal. It is the teacher who knows the class, the pupils' abilities and needs, and the place which the visitor has in the scheme of things. The teacher should therefore be present throughout, as the indispensable chair of the proceedings, in control of them; he/she thus has the right (just as the pupils have the right) to express disagreement with the visitor, and if necessary to intervene and to give direction to the talk or discussion. The teacher's task will be to create a spirit of open enquiry so that opinions can be exchanged and personal integrity respected, and to set an example of courtesy and fair-mindedness.

Afterword: What about parents' reactions?

Sometimes information, more or less accurate, more or less garbled, about what happens in school filters through to parents: what if some parents protest about the contribution of a visitor in a R.E. lesson or an Assembly? The best remedy for this is to anticipate the questions of parents and other interested parties and, if considered appropriate, to inform them in advance of the purpose and details of any particular departure from routine activity. Thereafter the principal lines of reply are surely to explain the curriculum context within which the visit was made, and to reassure parents that the occasion when the visitor presented his or her material was adequately controlled by the teacher responsible. If the guidance given here is followed, any misunderstanding should be fairly easy to dispel.

Useful Addresses

When writing for information or catalogue, remember to enclose a stamped addressed envelope of appropriate size.

Ann & Bury Peerless 22 King's Avenue Minnis Bay Birchington Kent CT7 9QL	Sets of slides on various religions
Argus Communications DLM House Edinburgh Way Harlow Essex CM20 2HL	Posters, especially the "Inspirational" series (photographs with quotations etc.)
Articles of Faith (Mrs. C. M. Winstanley) 123 Nevile Road Salford M7 0PP	Artefacts relating to various religions
BBC Publications 35 Marylebone High Street London W1M 4AA	Orders for materials should be sent to: BBC Publications, School Orders Section, 144 Bermondsey Street, London SE1 3TH
Bhaktivedanta Book Trust Croome House Sandown Road Watford WD2 4XA	Audio-visual materials (posters, videos, etc.) and literature on Hinduism
British Humanist Association 13 Prince of Wales Terrace London W8 5PG	Information and materials on Humanism
The British Mahabodhi Society London Buddhist Vihara 5 Heathfield Gardens London W4 4JU	Information and materials on Hinduism
Buddhist Society 58 Eccleston Square London SW1V 1PH	Information and materials on Buddhism, including a useful *Guide to Resources for Teachers*
Catholic Fund for Overseas Development (C.A.F.O.D.) 2 Garden Close Stockwell Road London SW9 9TY	Posters and Information, mainly on Third World needs
Centre for World Development Education Regents College Inner Circle Regents Park London NW1 4NS	Literature and audio-visual materials relating to Third World countries

Christian Aid
P.O. Box No. 1
London SW9 8BH

Posters on areas of need worldwide, often with notes and suggested
  activities
Information leaflets
Simulation game on world food

Christian Education Movement
Lancaster House,
Borough Road,
Isleworth,
Middlesex,
TW7 5DU

Termly magazine "R.E. Today"
Termly mailings of resource materials for Primary and Secondary
  R.E.
Posters on various religions
Literature about, and for use in, R.E.
Termly "British Journal of Religious Education".

Concord Films Council Ltd.
201 Felixstowe Road
Ipswich
Suffolk IP3 9BJ

Comprehensive collection of films and video resources

C.T.V.C. (Churches'
  Television Centre)
Video and Film Library
Beeson's Yard
Burry Lane
Rickmansworth
Herts WD3 1DS

Visual materials on social and moral issues

Education Department
Board of Deputies of
  British Jews
4th Floor
Woburn House
Woburn Place
London WC1H 0EP

Information and materials on Judaism

Gohil Emporium
331 & 366 Stratford Road
Sparkhill
Birmingham 11 4JZ

Suppliers (to callers only) of Hindu posters and artefacts

Hindu Centre
39 Grafton Terrace
London NW5

Information and materials on Hinduism

Independent T.V.

(See the note at the end of this list)

The Islamic Foundation
  Publications Unit
Unit 9
The Old Dunlop Factory
62 Evington Valley Road
Leicester

Audio-visual materials (posters, maps, etc.) and literature on Islam

Jewish Education Bureau
8 Westcombe Avenue
Leeds LS8 2BS

Supplier of artefacts, visual materials and literature relating to
  Jusaism

Mary Glasgow Publications
  Ltd.
FREEPOST
Brookhampton Lane
Kineton
Warwick CV35 0BR

Audio-visual materials (video, filmstrips, slides, cassettes) on various
  religions, festivals, etc., with accompanying books for the teacher

Moral Education Centre
St. Martin's College
Lancaster LA1 3JD

Literature and materials on Moral Education

Muslim Educational Trust 130 Stroud Green Road London N4 3RZ	Information and materials on Islam
The National Baha'i Centre 27 Rutland Gate London SW7 1PD	Information and materials on the Baha'is
Pictorial Charts Educational Trust 27 Kirchen Road London W13 0UD	Wall-charts full of pictures and informative text, with accompanying notes
Ramakrishna Vedanta Centre 54 Holland Park London W11 3RS	Information and materials on Hinduism
St. Paul Book Centre 199 Kensington High Street London W8 6BA	Supplier of filmstrips, photo sets, etc.
Sikh Cultural Society 88 Mollison Way Edgware Middlesex HA8 5QW	Information and materials on Sikhism
Sikh Missionary Society 27 Pier Road Gravesend Kent DA11 9NB	Information and materials on Sikhism
The Slide Centre Ltd. 143 Chatham Road London SW11 6SR	Comprehensive range of slides
T.V. Recording Licence Department Guid Sound and Vision Ltd. 6 Royce Road Peterborough PE1 5YB	For information about recording of Channel 4 T.V. programmes

Note on Independent T.V. For information and publications relating to schools programmes on I.T.V., contact the Educational Department of the regional T.V. company (e.g. in the South, Community Unit, T.V.S., T.V. Centre, Southampton SO9 5HZ).

See also the list included in An Approach to India, p. 26.
The lists in *Paths to Understanding* pp. 133–135 are more extensive, but addresses should be checked, as some have changed since publication.

Glossary

This Glossary contains only words which appear in the text of this book. For the meanings of a much wider range of words, but little guidance on their pronunciation, P. Bishop's *Words in World Religions* (SCM Press 1979) is useful.

In many instances, spellings are variable, depending on the language or dialect employed; English translations introduce further variation, a particular variant being perhaps favoured for only a limited period. Pronunciations also vary, and it is difficult, in any case, to be specific about them without using an array of phonetic signs; it is hoped that those used here are adequate, and helpful rather than confusing. The meaning of a word is liable to change over time, and the same word may be used in different senses in different religious traditions, or in different contexts: definition, especially if it is brief, is hazardous even though necessary. In all three respects (spelling, pronunciation and meaning) care has been taken to ensure that the reader can employ these words in the confidence that he/she is following a widespread usage. It would be a step forward if the use, by teachers and pupils, of the proper terms, rather than (often misleading) English "equivalents", were to become normal practice.

Pronunciation (based on standard English usage)
Stress
The mark ′ indicates that the preceding syllable is accented.
Vowels

ā	as in name	ī	as in side	$\overline{oo}$	as in boot
ä	as in grass	i	as in pit	ŏŏ	as in foot
a	as in hat	ō	as in bone	ū	as in tune
ē	as in been	ö	as in ball	u	as in but
e	as in bed	o	as in hot	û	as in bird

Neutral, unaccented vowels (e.g. the "e" in "butter") are indicated by ə (a sort of inverted e).
Consonants normally represent the *sound* of the letters in a word (e.g. "rough" would appear as "ruf", "knee" as "nē", "city" as "sit′i", "one" as "wun", "yacht" as "yot").

ch	as in much	ngg	as in longer	th	as in thin
hh	as in loch	sh	as in ship		

(h) following b, d or t indicates a gentle aspirant, which softens the consonantal sound.
A double consonant indicates a lengthening (almost a double-sounding) of the consonant.

BUDDHISM

The Theravada tradition retains the Pali words, and these are given here; if the Sanskrit form is more commonly used in the West, it is also given, marked (S).

The help of sisters of the Chithurst Forest Monastery (Theravadin), Sussex, was invaluable, as regards both the meaning and the pronunciation of terms.

WORD	PRONUNCIATION	MEANING
ANATTA	a-nat′tä	"Not-self": the doctrine that a human being has no permanent "soul" or "self", no finite "individuality". A "human being" is an ever-changing configuration of matter and mind (the latter comprising feelings, perceptions, volitions and consciousness). Failure to understand this is the basic cause of dukkha.
ANICCA	a-nich′ə	"Impermanence": the doctrine that all things, including people, are constantly changing state.

WORD	PRONUNCIATION	MEANING
BHIKKU	b(h)ik′o͞o	A member of the highest order of monks: he undertakes to observe 227 precepts; is ordained with special ceremonies; depends on alms; may be itinerant or (more commonly in the West) live in community.
BODHI	bō′di	The name given to the tree beneath which Siddhartha attained enlightenment.
BUDDHA	bo͞o′d(h)ə	"The enlightened one": applicable to any "enlightened" person, this title usually refers to Siddhartha, the founder of Buddhism.
DHAMMA DHARMA (S)	d(h)um′mə dûr′mä	The whole body of the Buddha's teaching; "the Truth", including natural laws and universal principles. (See p. 108ff.)
DUKKHA	do͞o′kä	Unsatisfactoriness: the doctrine that life inevitably involves distress, sadness, loss, dissatisfaction, dis-ease—all of which sufferings are only to be relieved by enlightenment.
GOTAMA GAUTAMA (S)	gōtə-mə	The family name of the founder of Buddhism.
HINAYANA	hi′nə-yä′nə	The "Lesser Vehicle": orthodox Buddhism. (See THERAVADA)
JATAKA	jä′tə-kə	A collection of folk tales concerning previous lives of the Buddha, during which he developed various qualities.
KAMMA KARMA (S)	kum′mə kär′mə	"Action": the doctrine that, for all sentient beings, the quality of their actions has a cumulative effect in determining their destiny. (See p. 110)
LUMBINI	lo͞om-bi-nē′	The birthplace of Siddhartha.
MAHAYANA	ma′hə-yä′nə	The "Great Vehicle": developed (possibly syncretistic) Buddhism. (See THERAVADA)
METTA	met′tä	(Loving-)kindness, unlimited in its scope: one of the four spiritual qualities commended by the Buddha.
NIBBANA NIRVANA (S)	nib-bä′nə nŭr-vä′nə	The state of "coolness", untroubledness, which is attained when a person lets go of all self-interested attachments and desires. (See p. 110)
PALI	pä′li	The original language of Buddhist scriptures and discourse.
PARI-NIBBANA PARI-NIRVANA (S)	pa′ri-nib-bä′nə pa′ri-nŭr-vä′nə	The physical death of the Buddha; the final release from samsara.
SAMATHA	sa′mə-t(h)ə	"Focussing meditation": the intention is to calm the mind, by concentrating on a specific object (e.g. the breath, as the Buddha recommended).
SAMSARA	sung-sä′rə	The cycle of existence, in which a person is bound until enlightenment is attained. (See p. 110)
SANGHA	sang′g(h)ə	The community of monks (and nuns). Membership implies the taking of vows (perhaps for life), the acceptance of moral discipline, and the wearing of a (saffron) robe. (See p. 111f.)
SIDDHATTA SIDDHARTHA (S)	sid-ä′tə sid-är′t(h)ə	The personal name of the founder of Buddhism.
STUPA	sto͞o′pə	A structure shaped like a bell or dome (the centre of which may rise to a point), serving as a memorial shrine or as a focus for religious ceremonies.

WORD	PRONUNCIATION	MEANING
THERAVADA	t(h)er'a-vä'də	The tradition of Buddhism which preserves the teaching in its original form: it developed within the Hinayana (orthodox) school, and contrasts with the later-developed and more culturally influenced Mahayana school, with its more popular modes of expression.
VIHARA	vi-hä'rə	Primarily, a place of residence for monks. (See p. 112)
VIPASSANA	vi-pas'ə-nə	Insight meditation: the intention is to become aware of what is happening in one's consciousness, and to "see" more clearly the total reality of which it is a part.
WESAK	we'sak	The festival commemorating the birth, enlightenment and passing away of the Buddha. (See p. 112)

CHRISTIANITY

WORD	PRONUNCIATION	MEANING
EUCHARIST	ū'kə-rist	The Greek word for "thanksgiving": one of the terms used to denote the sacrament of the Lord's Supper. (See p. 33ff, 83)
ICHTHUS (IXΘYS)	ik'tho͞os	The Greek word for "fish", an important symbol in the Early Church. (See p. 71f.)
LITURGY	lit'ər-ji	The Greek word for "(public) service": the form of worship or ritual regularly employed (especially for the celebration of the Eucharist) by a Christian community or church. (See p. 34)

ISLAM

WORD	PRONUNCIATION	MEANING
MUHAMMAD	mo͞o-ham'əd	The founder of Islam. This is now the preferred spelling of the name.
MUSLIM	mo͝oz'lim	An adherent of Islam. This is the preferred term: the term "Muhammadan", or its equivalent, should not be used.
RAMADAN	ram-ə-dan'	The month of fasting during the hours of daylight (in 1986, observed in May–June).
SUFI	so͞o'fē	A mystic, seeking, through personal purity and spiritual discipline, direct knowledge and experience of the Transcendent.

HINDUISM AND INDIAN LIFE

The classical language of India and Hinduism is Sanskrit; the pronunciations given here are, however, those of the more widespread and officially promoted Hindi.

Word-endings are particularly variable. (ä), (ə) or (n) at the end of a word indicates that the letter is sometimes sounded, sometimes not.

Dr. G. K. B. Banerjee and Mr. B. K. Sen-Gupta, of Portsmouth, helped greatly with the definitions, and Dr. K. Venkatraman, also of Portsmouth, with the pronunciations.

WORD	PRONUNCIATION	MEANING
AHIMSA	ə-hin′sä	Non-violence, in respect of all living creatures.
ARTI	är′ti	Offerings and oblations to the deity.
ASHRAMA	äsh′rə-mə	Any one of the four life-stages. (See p. 105)
ATMAN	ät′mä(n)	The soul: the eternal element in all living beings. The word came to mean also "the self", which is, in reality, one with Brahman: realisation of this oneness liberates a person from the cycle of existence.
AVATAR	av′tär(ə)	An incarnation of the Supreme Being (especially of Vishnu), as a saviour of mankind whenever crisis theatens. (See p. 102)
BHAGAVAD GITA	b(h)äg′a-vəd gē′tä	A section of the epic Mahabharata (mə-hä′-b(h)är′ə-tə) in which Krishna (in the role of God) counsels and inspires the warrior Arjuna.
BHAJAN	b(h)u′jən	A religious chant, song or hymn.
BHAKTI	b(h)uk′ti	"Devotion": personal faith and worship, centred on a personal saviour-god (often Vishnu, especially in the form of his avatars Rama and Krishna, or Shiva); the most popular, and non-philosophical, form of Hinduism. (See p. 103)
BRAHMACHARI	brä′məchä′ri(n)	"Celibate": the first of the four life-stages (sometimes prolonged for a person's whole life), a period of apprenticeship to a guru. (See p. 105)
BRAHMA	bra-mä′	The Creator-God: one of the Trinity (with Vishnu and Shiva) of the Supreme Being.
BRAHMAN	brä′-män′	The Universal Spirit, the Ground of Being: impersonal, omnipresent and omnipotent.
BRAHMIN	brä′man	A member of the highest, i.e. the priestly, class.
CHAPATTI	chə-pä′ti	A flat, round "pancake" of flour and water.
CHATTI	chu′ti	A water-pot.
DEVA	dā′və	"Shining one": a divine spirit.
DHAL	däl	Peas, beans or lentils, perhaps mixed, puréed or curried.
DHARMA	d(h)är′mə	"Religion": the way of life appropriate to an individual; one's particular duty, to be discovered and done. (See p. 103)
DHOTI	d(h)ō′ti	A loin-cloth.
DIVALI or DIWALI	di-vä′li	The autumn festival of lights. (See p. 104)
DURGA	door′gä	The ten-armed consort of Shiva, in her terrible aspect as destroyer of evil.
GANDHI	gän′d(h)i	A lawyer, prominent in India's gaining independence, in raising the status of low- and no-caste people, and in developing local industries. (See p. 105)
GANESHA	gan-ā′sh(ə)	The elephant-headed god. (See p. 101)
GARUDA	gar-ood′(ə)	The eagle-headed, human-bodied steed of Vishnu.
GRIHASTHA	gri-has′th(ə)	"Family-man", "Householder": the second of the four life-stages. (See p. 105)
GULI DANDA	goo′li dan′də	A sort of rounders game. (See p. 23f.)
HANUMAN	han′oo-män	The immortal monkey-god, notable for mobility and cunning.

WORD	PRONUNCIATION	MEANING
HOLI	hō′li	The spring festival of colour, jollity and general revelry, which celebrates Krishna.
KARMA	kär′m(ə)	"Action": the divinely governed working of cause and effect in the ethical realm; the consequences of one's conduct operate through successive lives. (See p. 103)
KOTLA CHHAPAI	kōt′la chŏo′pī	A running game. (See p. 24)
KRISHNA	krish′n(ə)	As an avatar, and possessor of all-too-human qualities, a focus of popular devotion. Stories about him may have some historical basis.
LAKSHMI	luksh′mi	The consort of Vishnu, and goddess of material wealth.
MAHATMA	mə-hät′mä	"Great soul": a title indicating a wise and holy leader.
MANDIR	mun′dēr	A temple.
MANTRA	man′trə	A verse, or group of verses, from the Vedic scriptures, recited or chanted as a form of meditation or worship.
MEHENDI	me′hen-dē′	Henna, for decorating hands and feet on festive occasions.
MOKSHA	mōk′sh(ə)	Release from the cycle of birth, living, dying and rebirth; attainable by means of knowledge, or right actions, or personal devotion. (See p. 103)
NATARAJAN	na-ta-rä′jən	Shiva in his character as Lord of the Dance, representing both joy and destruction (which makes new creation possible). (See p. 22, 101f.)
NAVARATRI	na-və-rä′tri	An autumn festival celebrating female deities.
PRASADA	pra-säd′(ə)	Any food which has been dedicated to a deity, and blessed.
PUJA	poo′jä	"Worship": observance in home or temple, or celebration in public festival. (See p. 22, 103f.)
PURANA	poo′rä′nə	"Ancient (times)": one of several inspirational texts (including miracle stories and stories about Krishna) used in the practice of bhakti.
RADHA	rä′dä	The consort of Krishna: many stories tell of their love.
RAMA	rä′m(ä)	The prince who is the virtuous and victorious subject of the epic Ramayana; regarded as an avatar of Vishnu.
RAMAYANA	rä′mə-yä′nə	The popular epic in seven books, relating to the story of Rama, and dating from the first century C.E. or earlier. Accepted by many as historically authoritative.
RANGOLI	ranggō′li	Patterns made on the ground with coloured powders, as part of the celebration of Divali (principally) and Holi.
RAVANA	rä′vən(ə)	The great enemy of Rama in the Ramayana, representing the principle of evil.
SADHU	sä′d(h)oo	A "holy man", ascetic and mendicant.
SAMSARA	san-sä′r(ə)	The cycle of existence (birth, life, death, rebirth) in which a person is bound until moksha is attained. (See p. 103)
SANNYASI	san-yä′si(n)	The last of the four life-stages: renunciation of all life's goods and pleasures, in the search for moksha. (See p. 105)
SARI	sä′rē	A dress, consisting of a length of material draped round the body.
SHIVA	shi′v(ä)	The Destroyer-God, primarily, but also venerated for other attributes. Popularly symbolised by the linga, a phallic object which suggests his re-creative power.

WORD	PRONUNCIATION	MEANING
SITA	sē′tä	The princess who became Rama's wife, and who figures largely in the Ramayana; her virtues make her a model of womanhood.
UPASANA	o͞o-pä′sə-nä	A mode of worship appropriate to a particular deity.
VANAPRASTHA	vän′(ə)-präs′th(ə)	The third of the four life-stages; withdrawal into the forest, to pursue the quest for moksha either in solitude or in community. (See p. 105)
VARNA	vär′n(ä)	The division of Indian society into four classes, viz. priests, warriors/rulers, traders and labourers. Sub-divisions into numerous castes developed later.
VISHNU	vish′no͞o	The Preserver-God. A focus, often in the form of one of his avatars, of bhakti.
YOGA	yō′g(ə)	Both a philosophy and a system (based on the philosophy) of personal discipline and development, with the ultimate goal of spiritual liberation. (See p. 103)

JUDAISM

Compiled with the help of the Minister of Southsea Synagogue, Rev. Anthony Dee.

WORD	PRONUNCIATION	MEANING
AFIKOMEN	a-fē′-kō′mən	"Dessert": a piece of unleavened bread eaten at the end of the Passover meal.
ARBA'AH MINIM	är′bä mi-nim′	The "four species" (palm-branch, myrtle, willow and etrog) used in the festival of Succoth.
CHALLAH	hha′lə	A plaited loaf of bread, eaten on Shabbat.
CHAROSET	hha-rō′set	A mixture of apple, cinnamon and wine, eaten during the Passover meal; reddish-brown in colour, it symbolises the material used for brick-making by the Israelite slaves in Egypt.
ETROG	e′trog	Citrus fruit, used in the festival of Succoth.
HAMETZ	hho′mets	"Leavened" (bread).
KIPA	ki′pə	The skull-cap worn by male Jews.
MATZAH	mat′sə	(A piece of) unleavened bread.
MENORAH	men-ō′rə	A candelabrum (of 7 or 9 branches) used in synagogue services.
SEDER	sä′dər	The set ritual order of the Passover meal.
SHABBAT	sha-bat′	The day of rest (from sunset on Friday to sunset on Saturday), for celebration and worship at home and for services in the synagogue. (See p. 43f.)
SHALOM CHAVERIM	shə-lōm′ hhav-ər-ēm′	"Welcome, Friends!" A popular song.
SHEMA	shə-mä′	One of the main prayers in Judaism, quoting Deut.6.4f.
SUCCAH (pl. SUCCOTH)	so͝o′kä (so͝o′kot)	A temporary structure, central to the eight-day festival (Succoth) of thanksgiving for harvest, and recalling the forty wilderness years. (See p. 52f.)

WORD	PRONUNCIATION	MEANING
TALLITH	tal-it′	The fringed scarf or shawl worn by men for prayers, at home or in the synagogue.
USHPIZIM	o͝osh-pē′zəm	"Guests": people invited to participate in one's succah.
YAD	yud	"Hand": the pointer used by a reader in following the text of a scroll.

Index

N.B. the entries in *italics* relate to the companion
volume *Paths to Understanding.*

SUBJECTS	DETAILS AND REFERENCES
ARTEFACTS	Christian symbols for investigation 70f. Typifying people and life-styles 22f. Use in classroom 44n., 45, 63f., 106ff.
ASSEMBLY	As a celebration 35, 40, 56 Based on story used in classwork 46, 56 Series on aspects of Difference 56 Using children's contributions 46, 57 Using children's classwork 9, 38, 57 Using dialogue and discussion 57 Visitors 120f. *In First school 4* *In Middle school 35* *General 117ff.*
AUDIO-VISUAL MEDIA (see also ARTEFACTS)	Engaging the pupils 63 Images in Hinduism 102 Lists of materials used 16, 38 Strip-cartoon story of the Buddha 108f. *Use of Works of Art at Secondary level 81f.*
BAPTISM	Artefacts and memories 45 Children's investigation 41 Pupil's account 72
BIOGRAPHY (see MARTYRS And WITNESSES)	
CELEBRATION (see also EUCHARIST and FESTIVALS)	Birthdays 32 Classroom meal 12 Planning for a class celebration 35 *In First school 24f.*
COMMUNITIES	Christian examples 81f. Classroom treatment: Taizé community 82f. Early Christians 88, 89f. Need for guide-lines 111 *Exploration of "Community":* *in Middle school 46f.* *in Secondary school 86ff.*
CONSTRUCTION	Instructions for building a Succah 33 Making hide-outs 55 Making models, as a group-work experiment 45f.

SUBJECTS	DETAILS AND REFERENCES
ROLE-PLAY (see DRAMA)	

SELF-EXPLORATION	Groups:
	   Belonging 39f.
	   Isolation 41ff., 58f., 59f.
	Individual characteristics 39f.
	Memory:
	   Experiences 27, 29
	   Ability to remember 30f.
	   Mental disciplines 112n.
	Need for personal involvement and responses when studying issues 114f.
	Search for meaning and identity 67, 68f., 118
	Speech 52ff.
	Stages and goals of life 65f., 102f., 105, 107n.
	
	At First school level 6ff., 19
	At Middle school level 41f.
	At Secondary level 75

SIMULATION	An Indian Day 23 Baptism 41 Buddhist worship 108 Communion 35 Hindu shrine and Puja 22, 103f. Jewish . . . Passover 96, . . . Sabbath Eve meal 44

STORIES AND
  STORY-TELLING
	Effective use of stories 8n., 39, 64, 66f., 94ff.
	Significance of stories 21, 66f., 94
	Stories in the Gospels 91f.
	Useful stories for young children 6
	Value of stories with older Secondary pupils 115
	Particular stories:
	   The Blind Men and the Elephant 21
	   The Bronze Bow 38–46 passim
	   The Diary of Anne Frank 55
	   I am David 38–46 passim
	   Let the Balloon Go 66f.
	   Miracle on the River Kwai 79ff.
	   My Mate Shofiq 55
	   Perpetua and Felicitas 77f.
	   Two Knights, one statue 59
	
	Books recommended for use in First school 30ff.
	Books recommended for use in Middle school 58f.

SYMBOLS	Association with words 94, 95n.
	Church structure and furnishings 72ff.
	Classroom treatment:
	   Buddhist Wheel 107n.
	   Buddhist worship 108
	   Christian Fish symbol 71f.
	   Coventry Cathedral 75f.
	   Hindu Puja 103f.
	   The Last Supper 86
	Distinguishing between "signs" and "symbols" 7n., 41
	Importance in religion 67, 70f.

VISITORS	Main article 120f. Preparation and follow-up 18, 30, 34f. 63